# HANDBOOK OF
# COUNSELING IN
# HIGHER EDUCATION

# HANDBOOK OF COUNSELING IN HIGHER EDUCATION

Phillip J. Gallagher
George D. Demos

PRAEGER

PRAEGER SPECIAL STUDIES • PRAEGER SCIENTIFIC

**Library of Congress Cataloging in Publication Data**

Main entry under title:

Handbook of counseling in higher education

  Bibliography: p.
  Includes index.
  1. Personnel service in higher education—
Handbooks, manuals, etc.     I. Gallagher, Phillip J.
II. Demos, George D.
LB2343.H273   1983        378'.194                    82-14484
ISBN 0-03-063216-1

Published in 1983 by Praeger Publishers
CBS Educational and Professional Publishing
a Division of CBS, Inc.
521 Fifth Avenue, New York, New York 10175 U.S.A.

3456789 052987654321
Printed in the United States of America

# PREFACE

Major changes have occurred since the Counseling Center in Higher Education was published in 1970. Many were in the expected direction: further professionalism in college and university counseling centers, a diminishing of the fad aspects of sensitivity groups, and a return to calmer campuses, to cite a few. Many changes were unexpected. It was believed that greater financial support would be given to counseling centers in higher education, especially those programs providing more support for minorities. "Taxpayer revolt" legislation was not expected, although we anticipated shrinking enrollment in colleges and universities. We did not expect inflation as it has occurred, or the return of an almost "cold war" atmosphere, or the recession and recent increase in enrollment. Some counseling centers have been diffused into various divisions within colleges and universities, most have felt an unexpected budget crunch, and many are seeing their future as a shrinking one rather than an expanding one. It is clearly a difficult task to improve quality with so much less financial support, but that appears to be our present challenge.

Although there are some advantages to decentralization by placing counselors in schools, colleges, or divisions within a university, our position is that the disadvantages outweigh the advantages, and therefore the center concept and practice is still adhered to.

We quote from the preface of Counseling Center in Higher Education:

> The primary purpose of this book is to provide, by means of a compilation, a ready access to information that has been heretofore scattered in various textbooks, brochures, memorandums and, in many cases, not formulated in print. A second major purpose is to make the college and university counseling center more visible to the academic world as well as to the general public. In addition to its use as a textbook for counselors (counseling psychologists) in training, the book is seen as valuable to those entering any area of student personnel services, or college or university administration. Those in junior college and high school counseling and administration should obtain a

v

clearer understanding of what services are available to their students on transfer to a four-year institution.

The book is not a technical manual or an abstract treatise but rather is an informative work. We would even hope that parents and others concerned with higher education would be acquainted with its contents. We are of the opinion that the counseling centers in higher education are doing an excellent job—contributing significantly to humanity and the betterment of mankind, and we would like as many people as possible to know about the contributions being made in these settings. The more people know, the more support we can receive, and the more and better services we can provide for students.

Nevertheless, the book is most germane to those establishing, enlarging, or modifying a college or university counseling center. However, we also see the book as essential to those in training as student personnel specialists, counseling psychologists, admissions officers, financial aid officers, housing personnel, placement counselors, health services personnel, student activities specialists, deans in student personnel services, and administrators in higher education.

Although most of the contributing authors are now on the west coast, and their affiliations are with the California state college or university systems, we do not feel this necessarily makes the text provincial. In terms of education and training, the authors represent a good cross section of higher education—private and state universities as well as sectional.

The influences of Carl Rogers (Western Behavioral Sciences Institute), H. B. McDaniels (Stanford), Leona Tyler (Oregon), Merle Turner (San Diego State), Dan Feder (San Francisco State), to name only a few, are present and lead to the second major reason we believe the authors can speak for counseling centers in higher education in general: There is excellent intercommunication between counseling psychologists (APA, APGA journals and meetings), directors of counseling and testing (annual meetings), and deans of students.

The above statements hold true; however, we need to add what follows:

The appeal for a consideration of the spiritual, emotional/ personal, and physical as well as intellectual development of students deems finally to have been heard. It is becoming increasingly difficult to imagine a college or university without an opportunity for students to talk about their concerns—past, present, and future—in a one-to-one relationship with a professional counselor. Although workshops, research, special programs, and group work are unquestionably valuable, the core of our efforts is the individual sessions.

The <u>Standards for Providers of Psychological Services</u> and the <u>APA Code of Ethics</u> are a convenient and essential part of this volume, as are "Specialty Guidelines for the Delivery of Services by Clinical Psychologists" and "Specialty Guidelines for the Delivery of Services by Counseling Psychologists." Exact reproduction was considered necessary despite some redundancy in the "Standards" and "Delivery" documents.

It is believed that the present work will provide counseling centers with a comprehensive reference work as well as guidelines for changes and day-to-day operations. It is hoped that this book will also provide needed information to those not directly in centers—for example, high school counselors, other student personnel workers, teaching faculty, administrators, parents, and students.

We feel very fortunate in having the contributions of the various authors, and wish to express in print our appreciation for their time taken from heavy schedules, and for their patience with us during delays.

The reader will note different opinions and approaches to assisting the college or university in meeting its responsibilities and goals. Each author has taken responsibility for his or her particular chapter. If there is a general book bias, its base is in the selection of authors, although we are convinced that other members of our profession would use similar criteria in the selection.

We would especially like to express our appreciation to the American Psychological Association for its prompt and efficient response to our request to reproduce its documents, and to thank Sally Graetz and Anita Kramer for their assistance with the early phases of this project. We would also like to acknowledge the assistance provided by George Zimmar, senior editor at Praeger.

# CONTENTS

# HANDBOOK OF
# COUNSELING IN
# HIGHER EDUCATION

# 1

# THE PSYCHOLOGICAL COUNSELING CENTER: MODELS AND FUNCTIONS

## George D. Demos
## Travis M. Mead

POSITION STATEMENT

This book is predicated on one major philosophical/theoretical assumption: that the psychological counseling center is still a viable modality for delivery of counseling services to students. It is not being suggested that the psychological counseling center is the only viable means for delivery of counseling services. Counseling, in one form or another, is provided by student personnel workers in a variety of areas, such as career planning and placement, financial aid, veterans' affairs, international students, housing, health services, and student activities. What is being asserted here is that the psychological counseling center has the unique potential for providing counseling services on a holistic, global level. The student can be dealt with as a whole person having multiple and complex needs. Since the psychological counseling center is not limited to just one or two areas of counseling, as other student personnel areas are, the opportunity to counsel on all areas of life experiences is present. These areas include behavior, cognition, affect, and sensation, in general terms, and every specific situation in the student's life where these four areas of life experience become matters of concern.

It is further asserted that dealing with students as whole persons facilitates students' experiencing themselves in a more integrated manner. If counseling is totally decentralized, students must obtain assistance for one aspect of life here and assistance for another aspect over there. But what about the concerns of students that involve a complex interaction among multiple aspects of their lives? To serve this need of the students, a psychological counseling center is needed. This need becomes especially relevant when one considers the willingness of students who are experiencing difficulties in their life to come into a counseling center for an educational/vocational problem versus a personal/social problem.

Tryon (1980) conducted an extensive review of the literature on preferences and perceptions of counseling center services. One of her major conclusions was that some of the studies reviewed suggested that students are more likely to use counseling center services now, compared with the early 1960s, but are still more willing to come in for help with an educational/vocational problem than with a personal/social problem. This corresponds to the casual observations of the authors and other experienced counselors. Coming in for an educational/vocational concern is less threatening for students than directly stating a personal concern. It has also been the authors' observation that the educational/vocational concern frequently provides an entry for the student into personal matters. It allows the student to "feel out" the counselor and their relationship. If educational/vocational counseling and personal/social counseling are parceled out to different offices, this type of exploration by the client is prevented. This entails a loss to the student and reduces the efficacy of educational/vocational counseling, because there are frequently personal concerns concomitant with lack of information when students experience difficulty in deciding on a major and/or career.

Decentralization appears to be a promising organizing strategy for academic advising and programming. However, what works well for advising is not the optimal solution for counseling. In advising, the primary concern is the accurate communication of relevant information to the student, whereas in counseling, the main focus is on human interaction with a complex person who frequently is dealing with some highly involved issues. The simplicity of advising lends itself to decentralized programming. The complexities of counseling invalidate the viability of a decentralized, programmed approach.

It has been the authors' experience that many students are fragmented and scattered because of an inability to integrate the various dimensions of their lives: home, school, work, peers. It is not in their best interest to provide further fragmentation through massive decentralization of services. It was asserted previously that treating students as whole persons facilitates their experiencing themselves as more integrated. The converse is also a sound assumption. If students are treated in a fragmented, decentralized manner, their experience of themselves as being fragmented and scattered will be compounded. One clear and consistent fact that has emerged from behaviorism and learning theory is that people

respond to and interact with their environments. Human beings do
not live in intrapsychic vacuums, and students are no exceptions.
The structure and organization of the college environment do make
a difference in terms of its influences on students. If it is desired
to facilitate integration among students who utilize counseling services, then the counseling services themselves must be integrated.
Therein lies the unique importance of the psychological counseling
center.

MODELS OF COUNSELING CENTERS

In the preceding section the importance of an integrated counseling center was emphasized. It was further proposed that such a
center has the potential to deal with multiple aspects of the student's
total life situation. This is a potential unique to the psychological
counseling center, but it is not always a reality. Budget cuts, administrative decisions, and the sociocultural composition of the
community are factors that may affect the degree to which this
unique potential is actualized. Even in centers that deal with the
student's total life situation, different emphases will be found. Some
centers emphasize therapy and personal counseling, while others
focus more on a developmental or coping skills approach. In con-
ceptualizing the psychological counseling center, it is of heuristic
value to think in terms of models of counseling centers, with each
model having a different emphasis. These are not purely homoge-
neous models that focus only on certain aspects of the student.
Rather, they are conceptual aids and suggest areas of emphasis,
not exclusive concerns.

The following discussion of models is based on the work of
Oetting, Ivey, and Weigel (1970). These researchers found several
basic counseling center models: the traditional model, the psychotherapy model, the vocational guidance model, and the training
model. Empirical support for these four models as valid constructs
comes from a study by Elton and Rose (1973). Their investigation
centered on a factor analysis of 19 variables taken from the College
and University Counseling Centers' 1971-72 Annual Data Bank Survey of 157 centers, made by Thomas Magoon of the University of
Maryland. Four factors were identified that corresponded descriptively with the four counseling center models proposed by Oetting
et al. (1970).

The following variables were found to have sizable, positive
associations with the traditional model (factor I): total professional
staff, total doctoral staff, total clients with educational/vocational
or emotional/social problems, number of groups, weekly interview

hours for educational/vocational or emotional/social problems, full-time-equivalent secretarial staff, salary of director, number of publications of staff.

The psychotherapy model (factor II) showed a positive association with the percentage of clients presenting emotional/social problems and negative associations with percentage of clients presenting educational skills problems, number of clients presenting reading and study skills problems, weekly hours devoted to reading and study skills problems.

Four variables were related to the vocational guidance model (factor III). Percentage of clients with vocational/educational problems and percentage of clients who were black were found to be positively associated, while numbers of encounter/growth/sensitivity groups and percentage of clients with emotional/social problems were negatively associated with the model.

The training model (factor IV) had positive associations with the following variables: percentage of females on professional staff, supervised time given to full-time interns, salary of director, percentage of black clients, number of publications of staff. A negative association was found between this model and full-time counselor caseload.

In another study of counseling center models, Gelso, Birk, Utz, and Silver (1976) had six groups (counselors, students, faculty, resident assistants, student personnel administrators, university administrators) rate the appropriateness of four models. Three of the four models were the same as used in the Elton and Rose (1973) study: the traditional model, the vocational guidance model, and the psychotherapy model. The training model was not used, and the consultation model was substituted for it. This model emphasized counselor contact with other personnel—faculty, resident assistants, deans, peer counselors—rather than direct contact with students. The objective of this model is to help others who have daily contact with students deal with them more effectively. In addition, the groups were asked to make their ratings only for campuses with student populations exceeding 10,000.

The results indicated that all of the groups but one rated the "jack-of-all-trades" traditional model as most appropriate; the exception was student personnel administrators, who rated the consultation model as most appropriate and the traditional model as a close second. All groups unanimously rated the psychotherapy model as least appropriate. The three nonstudent personnel groups (students, faculty, university administrators) rated the vocational guidance model as second in appropriateness. For counselors and resident assistants the pattern was reversed, the consultation model being rated second and the vocational guidance model third. It would appear that student personnel staff are considerably more impressed with the consultation model than is the rest of the university community, including the students being served. (This point will be further elaborated in the section "Consultation with Faculty, Administration, and Other Student Personnel Workers.")

It must be borne in mind that the above models are constructs, not necessarily realities. In actual practice, counseling centers may incorporate aspects of several models. Also, the model or combination of models that a counseling center may adopt in terms of its actual functioning tends to vary according to a number of other factors. Oetting et al. (1970) concluded that the attitude of the director is crucial in the adoption of a model and the functioning of the center. Anderson (1970) and Elton and Rose (1973) found that institutional size was highly important in accounting for differences among centers in terms of the model adopted and types of services offered. Wold and Dameron (1975) found significant differences beyond the $p \leq .01$ level between 20 two-year and 16 four-year college counseling centers. The two-year college centers spent significantly more time providing academic advice than personal/social/emotional counseling. The opposite was true for the four-year college centers. In terms of the models above, the two-year colleges tended to adopt more of a vocational guidance model. Thus, the two-year/four-year distinction is another important factor influencing choice of model and services offered.

Young and Harris (1977) propose that two-year community colleges are sufficiently different from four-year colleges in their institutional philosophies to warrant the development of a counseling center model that is especially suited to their needs. Further research will no doubt reveal other factors that influence the type of model adopted by centers. The next section of this chapter discusses in more specific terms what has been treated here in a more conceptual framework, the functions of the psychological counseling center.

## FUNCTIONS OF AND GENERAL PRINCIPLES FOR THE PSYCHOLOGICAL COUNSELING CENTER

Although the six functions discussed here cover all of the major ones for the psychological counseling center, all of them may not be present in each individual center. Which functions are present and the degree of emphasis placed on each vary according to which models the center tends to adopt. Before describing each function individually, some general principles for the maintenance and development of psychological counseling centers are offered.

The following principles have been modified from those set forth by Leventhal and Magoon (1979):

1. The core professional staff of the center should be composed of individuals who have completed the doctorate in clinical or counseling psychology or in counseling, with psychological licensing recommended; minimal qualifications include a master's degree in one of the above disciplines and expertise or skill in a specialty sufficient to be employed without a doctorate.

2. It is desirable, but not essential, that a significant number of counseling staff have part-time academic appointments or other forms of involvement in the academic community.

3. Efforts should be made to serve a broad range and large number of students, not just a select few.

4. Personal counseling and therapy should be based on a developmental and clinical foundation—that is, counselors should be well-versed in both developmental psychology and diagnosis and assessment procedures such as DSM III (see Chapter 5).

5. Confidentiality is essential, and special care must be taken to preserve it, including restricting access to other college personnel; any release of confidential information should be preceded by the signing of a consent/release form by the client, except in cases of danger to life.

6. Since a focus on any single theoretical background is too narrow, professional staff should be diverse in their training and background.

7. Consultation services are important, but they are supplementary to counseling services, which are the primary function of the center.

8. Direct observation, audiovisual taping, and audio taping are important for professional feedback and development, and should be implemented for professional staff, as well as for interns and trainees.

9. The services provided by a center will, and need to, vary according to the size, nature, and needs of the campus served.

10. Professional development for staff is essential, so that skills and knowledge may be updated; appropriate release time from duties must be given on a regular basis to facilitate this development.

11.  Accountability data are necessary for survival of centers; accordingly, systematic methods are needed for data collection and analysis of clients seen, demographic variables, and outcome measures.

12.  Alternative approaches to working with students—workshops, training modules—are needed as additions to, but not substitutes for, individual and group counseling.

13.  Counseling center staff should serve as consultants and trainers to students, faculty, administrative staff, and student personnel workers in developing peer counseling programs (academic advising, Educational Opportunity Programs [EOP], resident assistants, student activities), emphasizing basic, paraprofessional counseling and communication skills.

14.  In order for a counseling center to function efficiently and according to these principles, there must be understanding of and support for counseling services from both central university and student personnel administrators.


COUNSELING OF STUDENTS

The direct contact of students and counselors in counseling interactions, individual or group, is the major function of the psychological counseling center.  All other functions and activities must be considered supplementary to actual contact with students. In Gelso et al. (1976) the counseling function was broken down into ten subfunctions for evaluation:

1.  Individual personal counseling/therapy

2.  Short-term counseling/therapy (up to 12 sessions)

3.  Long-term counseling/therapy (one year or more)

4.  Group counseling/therapy

5.  Counseling students with severe psychological problems

6.  Counseling students with normal psychological problems

7.  Educational/vocational counseling

8.  Study skills counseling/training

9.  Reading instruction

10.  Tutoring for specific courses.

The last three subfunctions are coming to be more and more the domain of learning assistance centers rather than of counseling centers. Learning assistance centers, however, have frequently been the product of counseling outreach services.

As noted in the section "Models of Counseling Centers," Gelso et al. (1976) had six groups (counselors, students, faculty, resident assistants, student personnel administrators, university administrators) evaluate the appropriateness of counseling center functions. Although there were significant differences among the groups in terms of perceived appropriateness of the various subfunctions, certain consistencies were observed across all groups. Subfunctions that were viewed quite positively by all six groups were educational/vocational counseling, individual personal counseling, short-term counseling, and counseling students with normal psychological problems. Study skills counseling/training received favorable evaluations to a lesser degree across groups. Long-term counseling, counseling students with severe psychological problems, tutoring, and reading instruction received uniformly low evaluations across all groups.

These results support the authors' contention that counseling services should include both the personal/social and educational/vocational components, that they should be short-term so more students can be seen, and that more severely disturbed cases should be referred to community resources (for the same reason). The psychological counseling center is not a facility for the rehabilitation of severely disturbed students. Counseling center resources are needed to serve the greater student community with normal psychological and educational/vocational problems. Hence, when more severely disturbed students come in for counseling, an up-to-date and thorough referral system should be available.

There has been a considerable emphasis on group counseling since the 1970s. One interesting result of the study by Gelso et al. (1976) was that it was counselors, resident assistants, and student personnel administrators who favorably evaluated group counseling. Students, faculty, and university administrators perceived it as being "middle-of-the-road" in importance. Perhaps much of the enthusiasm for groups in the 1970s was generated by student personnel workers, rather than by those served by groups, in reaction to the "group explosion" in counseling psychology during the early 1970s.

In closing the discussion of Gelso et al. (1976), one important point emerges. All of the counseling subfunctions, except educational/vocational counseling, were consistently viewed as less appropriate by university administrators and faculty than by other groups, especially counselors and resident assistants. Given the decreasing budgets and funding likely to continue in the 1980s, the implication is clear. University administrators and faculty have traditionally had the greatest power and status. If and when budget cuts come, they are not as likely to come in those areas as in counseling and other student personnel areas. Counseling centers need to secure their position through accountability data and strong political involvement in the university/college system.

In a study by Carney and Savitz (1980), some interesting results were found on problem areas as perceived by students versus faculty. Students viewed substance abuse, career-choice or job-search frustration, sex-related difficulties, lack of knowledge of leisure and social activities, difficulties in negotiating the system, emotional problems, and adverse effects of stereotyping as more common problem areas than did faculty. On the other hand, faculty tended to perceive scholastic problems as more common. These results support the findings of Gelso et al. (1976) that faculty rated all counseling services, except educational/vocational counseling, as less appropriate. What these results suggest is that faculty, as a whole, do not have a clear understanding of the sorts of problems that students commonly experience. Naturally, they tend to view personal counseling as less appropriate. It is likely that the same holds for university administrators as well. This situation leads into one of the reasons for the next major function of the counseling center, consultation.


## CONSULTATION WITH FACULTY, ADMINISTRATION, AND OTHER STUDENT PERSONNEL WORKERS

Part of the reason for the consultation function is to educate faculty and administration about the variety of activities in which counselors engage. As was noted in the last section, faculty and administration may not have a clear understanding of the kinds of life problems that students bring into the counseling center. It is important that counselors publicize the types of problems with which they deal, and the number of students they see with various kinds of concerns. This is necessary to prevent mistaken beliefs on the part of faculty and administration that the counselors in the center just sit around and do academic counseling or psychotherapy with a few students. One way to accomplish this objective is accountability data, which are discussed later in this chapter (see subsection "Research"). Another method, and a complementary one, for accomplishing the same objective is personal contact with administration and faculty by counseling center staff. Consultation provides one avenue for such contact.

There are other reasons for implementing consultation. Consultation allows the counseling center to have a large indirect impact on students, as well as a direct one through actual counseling. Here counselors work with other university staff—faculty, peer counselors, and other student personnel workers—who have considerable direct student contact. A different rationale and focal point exist when consultation is with administration, which has very little direct contact with students. Here the objective is one of facilitating the administration's understanding of student needs. The rationale is that if administrators have better understanding of student needs, then important administrative decisions that affect students will be more geared toward meeting those needs, within the limits of budgetary and other considerations. This, of course, assumes an administration that is open, empathetic, and supportive of student needs. If this is not the case, the consultative impact of counselors will be limited. It may be necessary to convince administrators that meeting student needs better is in their best interest. For example, increased administrative concern for student needs may be developed into good public relations for the university, which in turn may increase enrollment, an increasing concern of many administrators.

Given that there is sufficient reason for doing consultation, one may ask what is the combination of skills that the psychological counselor brings to the consultative process. Rademacher, May, and Throckmorton (1980) cite good interpersonal skills, training in the behavioral sciences, an understanding of social and organizational systems, group dynamics skills, expertise in designing data-gathering methods, knowledge of how to plan interventions for initiating environmental changes, and the ability to show and gain trust. Not every individual counselor possesses all these skills. Rather, these reflect the skills of counselors as a group, which may be of help in the consultative process.

Although the consultative process is in reality a continuous one from beginning to end, breaking the process down into stages aids in its conceptualization. The following discussion is a condensation of the stages proposed by Rademacher et al. (1980) and Domke, Winkelpleck, and Westefeld (1980). The first stage may be called "entry" or "contact." In it the consultant is contacted by the consultee, or vice versa. The first pattern is more common, although the consultant may take the initiative if he/she thinks that there is good reason to do so. Next is the "negotiating" or "contracting" stage, in which the consultant attends to the consultee's needs, goals, objectives, and reasons for consultation. During this stage active listening skills are brought into play by the consultant. This stage merges into the "problem identification" or "diagnosis" stage, in which the consultant begins to take an even more active role and uses the information gleaned from the active listening to make a tentative diagnosis. At the end of this stage the consultant and consultee should have a clearer idea of the consultee's basic objectives.

The next stage may be called "goal setting and planning." This involves translating the basic objectives into specific goals. To a degree this may be considered operationalizing the theoretical objectives into concrete goals. After this has been achieved, the "planning" phase of this stage begins. Here brainstorming on alternative means of attaining the specified goals is undertaken, followed by critical evaluation of each alternative, and terminating with selection of the most realistic and appropriate plan or alternative. The consultation may end at this point, allowing the consultee to implement the plan. If it continues, the next stage of "implementation" is specifying the details of activities to be initiated and how these will be related to achieving the specified goals. Budgeting of time, resources, and personnel, and who is going to do what, where, when, and how all enter in at this stage. "Termination" is the final stage, with provisions (one hopes) being made for follow-up and reevaluation of the program after a trial period of operation.

The question arises as to the appropriateness of consultation as a function of the psychological counseling center. It was noted in the section "Models of Counseling Centers" that in Gelso et al. (1976) the student personnel groups rated the consultation model significantly more appropriate than did the nonstudent personnel groups. This pattern also holds when the same groups were asked to rate the appropriateness of consultation as a counseling center function. However, the rated appropriateness varied, depending on the focal point of consultation. The type of consultation in which counselors work with other staff who have direct student contact, in order to have an indirect impact, was rated as more appropriate by all three student personnel groups compared with nonstudent personnel groups. Consultation with administration to aid in understanding of student needs was rated more appropriate by counselors, resident assistants, and students compared with faculty, university administrators, and student personnel administrators. One upshot of this is that those being served—students—differed considerably from those who make decisions on student services—student personnel administrators—on the most appropriate type of consultation.

Another conclusion that may be drawn from the Gelso et al. data is that, overall, student personnel workers may be excessively enthusiastic about the importance of consultation. Gelso et al. assert, and the authors of this chapter agree, that counselors seem to be caught up in the zeitgeist of counseling psychology. Consultation is in style. It may be for the mid-1970s into the 1980s what the sensitivity/encounter groups were to the late 1960s into the early

1970s. It is interesting to note that by 1976, when Gelso et al. did their research, the appropriateness of groups was rated rather middle-of-the-road. It is not that groups were seen as inappropriate, but that they had fallen into perspective with time. The authors assert that the same will happen to consultation. With time, it will assume its proper place: as a supplementary function and service of the psychological counseling center, and in no way a substitute for direct counseling of students.

## OUTREACH ACTIVITIES

Outreach, as well as consultation, is part of the zeitgeist in counseling psychology, especially at university/college counseling centers. In fact, the two activities are frequently interrelated. Counseling center staff may serve as consultants in the organization of an outreach program, actually staff the program, or some combination of both. Even if center staff members do not participate in the outreach activities directly, the outreach staff positions are frequently allocated from the counseling center budget. In other words, the counseling center functions as the parent organization more often than not. Outreach programs and activities appear to have grown out of the impact of the community mental health model on the college campuses (Falk 1971). The emphasis is on preventive strategies and actions, rather than on remediation of existing problems. This model and movement may also be seen as a reaction to the psychotherapy model, in which the counselor sees a limited number of students for longer periods of time.

Common outreach programs include learning assistance/study skills, adult reentry, student orientation (both new and transfer students), international students/education, communication skills training, career development, stress management, test and speech anxiety management. Not all outreach activities may be organized into a formal program. In these cases the outreach may blend with consultation or training. Counseling center staff may give workshops for student organizations or residential (dormitory) students. Likewise, center staff may provide training for residence hall staff or peer academic advisers as a form of outreach.

Outreach programs and activities can be valuable supplements to counseling services through their preventive nature. The authors wish to assert here, however, that there is a danger in becoming too involved in the zeitgeist of outreach. In addition to losing perspective on the broader picture historically, there are more immediate hazards. As long as outreach is firmly linked to the counseling center as the organizational locus for services, integration and coordination of services can be maintained. The importance of this was argued at the beginning of this chapter in "Position Statement." Outreach programs can, and do, become alienated from the centers that spawned them. They become independently functioning centers in themselves. This results in massive decentralization and fragmentation of counseling and related services. It weakens both the counseling center and the outreach programs in terms of their ability to help the student in his/her total life situation. With this loss of consolidation, political power may also be lost, making the center more vulnerable to budget cuts.

Although outreach programs and activities are a viable and sound function of the psychological counseling center, integration of services is essential if the center and its programs are to survive to aid the student.

RESEARCH

Within the psychological counseling center several types of research may be specified:

1. Basic accountability data, such as number and types of students seen, and kinds of problems

2. Counseling research, which usually takes the form of outcome studies on the effectiveness of the therapeutic interventions

3. Student development/personnel research, which is more broad than the first two and may involve outreach and consultation to determine student characteristics, needs, and whether the university environment is meeting student needs.

The first two types of research are in-house, in that they deal only with data on students who utilize counseling services. The third type involves data collected on students in the university community at large. In Gelso et al. (1976) students rated the third type, student development research, as being the most appropriate for counseling centers. This would fit with their evaluations of consultation, because the results of student development research would be the most useful for consulting with administration on student needs. Counselors rated student development and counseling research as equally appropriate (basic accountability research was not rated). The other student personnel groups, particularly administrators, and faculty rated counseling research as more appropriate.

Basic accountability research is a political necessity if counseling centers are to survive. In times of shrinking budgets it is no longer enough for counselors just to do a good job; they must be able to show some data that they are doing a good job. Unfortunately, this often results in an emphasis on quantity (the number of students seen) rather than quality (whether the counseling intervention was effective). It is much easier to count heads than it is to determine the efficacy of counseling. (The complexities and intricacies, as related to the issue of accountability, are discussed in Chapters 2 and 4, respectively.)

In more sophisticated analyses of data, as opposed to basic recordkeeping, the authors agree with Williamson and Biggs (1975) that it is the importance and meaningfulness of the problem that should form the focus of the research. Too often inconsequential problems have been investigated with an elaborate statistical arsenal to give the research pseudo respectability. This is not to deny the importance of statistics in social science research. However, the analysis should follow from the nature of the problem being investigated and the questions being asked, not vice versa. At times simple $t$ tests and correlations may be sufficient to answer the relevant research questions. As the research questions become more complex and the number of variables increases, it becomes more likely that multivariate methods may be in order. One advantage of multiple correlations and multiple regression techniques is that they are more appropriate for applied research. This is different from experimental laboratory research, in which one has more control over the variables and can manipulate one variable while holding the others constant.

In a counseling center such control is not possible, so it is necessary to focus less on cause and effect and more on meaningful predictions and associations among the variables of interest. Meaningful research, however, need not have any statistical analysis; just descriptive, summary statistics can be valuable. For example, Thomas Magoon of the University of Maryland conducts a yearly survey of college and university counseling centers across the nation. He collects data on services offered, staff composition, number of clients seen, types of client problems, trends, and other valuable information. The results of the survey are available to other professionals, and have served as the basic data in other research studies, such as the one by Elton and Rose (1973). Rather than inhouse accountability data, this research may be termed interhouse accountability data, because of its national breadth.

## TRAINING OF INTERNS, PROFESSIONALS, AND PARAPROFESSIONALS

Training, in this section, refers to the teaching of and experience in various psychological and counseling-related skills provided by center staff for other professionals and paraprofessionals, including interns. (The training of students in various life skills, such as assertion and stress management, is considered in the next section, "Teaching.")

Counseling centers have traditionally been viewed as training sites for students in psychology and counseling graduate programs. Technically, doctoral-level students are referred to as interns, while masters-level students have been called trainees or fieldworkers. Many individuals who have completed their educational degree come to centers for postdoctoral or post-masters internships in order to accrue hours for licensure. Over time the distinctions among interns, trainees, and fieldworkers have become somewhat blurred. The term "intern" is now commonly used for all graduate students and postgraduates seeking hours of experience and training in the behavioral sciences. It is generally recommended that centers provide their interns with one hour of weekly face-to-face (individual) supervision, plus some supplementary form of group supervision.

The types of training provided for the interns will vary as a function of the variety of services offered by the center. Generally, it is expected that interns will receive training in individual personal counseling, individual educational/vocational counseling, group counseling, diagnosis and assessment, and test interpretation. Other centers may offer specialized training in biofeedback theory and practice, family and marital therapy, and how to give workshops on special topics. In Gelso et al. (1976) counselors and student personnel administrators rated the appropriateness of intern training considerably higher than did the nonstudent personnel groups. Of the six groups, students rated it least appropriate.

Interns are not the only group trained in counseling centers. Faculty members, particularly from psychology, educational psychology, or counselor education, may come to the center to brush up or develop their clinical/counseling skills. These faculty members may desire a more applied education in the behavioral sciences to complement their academic education, or they may wish to refine existing skills. Counseling or clinical professionals from other centers, agencies, clinics, or hospitals may come to a specific counseling center if it offers a very specialized training program, such as one for psychiatric residents or biofeedback certification. A counseling staff may work with paraprofessionals (resident assistants, peer advisers, student government officers) to train them in communication skills, group dynamics, basic crisis intervention, or other relevant skills. Here outreach and training may interface.

Consultation and training may also interface when counseling staff provides training for other student personnel professionals, such as student activities coordinators, and for faculty members who work closely with students. Finally, counseling centers need to provide in-house professional development and training for their own staff. The field of counseling psychology is a rapidly changing one in many regards, and counselors need to be aware of these changes, as well as of ones in related fields.

## TEACHING

It may be asserted that all counseling involves teaching. To a degree this is true. Counseling is an experiential learning process, and all counselors impart some information or teach certain skills in the course of the counseling process. As the term is used here, however, it denotes a more purely didactic process. Teaching need not occur only in the classroom, but may also be undertaken in the counseling center, dorms, or student union. Thus, it would include workshops given by center staff, as well as academic and nontraditional courses.

At some universities counseling center staff teach traditional academic courses, usually in the departments and/or schools of psychology and education. Center staff may be able to bring a more applied, hands-on flavor to basic courses in counseling theory, group counseling, or intruduction to clinical psychology from their actual counseling experiences. This also has the advantage of generating respect for counselors as academicians within the university community (Williamson and Biggs 1975). Some sort of exchange program is commonly arranged whereby faculty can come to the counseling center for training and experience, and counseling staff can bring their clinical experience into the classroom.

Counseling center staff are often instrumental in setting up nontraditional courses, either as part of the regular department offerings or through extension education. Their content areas are frequently the same as those of workshops: career development, time management, biofeedback training, human sexuality, communication skills, parent effectiveness training. These courses are highly variable, ranging from extended workshops to classes that meet for a semester on a regular basis. Usually an attempt is made to integrate some experiential learning with didactic lecturing.

Workshops cover the same basic content areas as the nontraditional courses but are shorter in duration, ranging from an hour or so to a maximum of one day. A series of workshops may be arranged over a longer period of time. Workshops also tend to be more casual than nontraditional courses. Whereas the courses may be open to anyone, workshops are often set up for specific target groups including dorm residents, student clubs and organizations, and EOP students. Workshops may also tend to blur with orientation activities for new, returning, or transfer students.

STAFFING AND STAFF COMPOSITION

The composition of the psychological counseling center staff needs to vary according to the characteristics and needs of the specific campus. The model that the center tends to emulate will also influence the staff composition. For example, a center based on the psychotherapy model would need trained clinicians and psychologists. In the vocational guidance model, doctoral training would not be nearly as important. Staff functioning in a consultation model would require expertise and background in program and organizational development, research, and training more than clinical skills.

Of the models examined, the traditional model is the most flexible and offers the greatest latitude for dealing with the student's total life situation. Staff members frequently serve as "jacks-of-all-trades," in that they may provide personal/social counseling, educational/vocational counseling, group counseling, some consultation, some training, plus various specialties. What is being suggested here is that staff members be enough of generalists to deal with all of the common concerns of students and develop one or two areas of specialization in which they concentrate on quality of expertise.

The authors agree with Leventhal and Magoon that doctoral-level counseling and clinical personnel should form the core of the staff. This is not to imply that doctoral level in the above disciplines in and of itself implies competence, or that qualified individuals without a doctorate should automatically be eliminated. Rather, the position is taken that a doctorate in counseling or clinical psychology represents the minimum requirement for being part of the core staff in the psychological counseling center. Work experience, additional training, and certification also need to be considered in determining competence.

In addition, there are many individuals who possess a rich background of experience and training, particularly in various specializations, who for one reason or another have not completed the doctorate. It would be rather narrow-minded to eliminate these individuals merely because they do not possess their "union card." Provisions should be made for masters-level staff in the psychological counseling center, based on demonstrated expertise. This is a particularly viable approach when staff members are needed in specialized areas such as career development, biofeedback, or communication skills training. These staff members should not be relegated to technician status, but should be considered and classified as auxiliary or ancillary professional staff.

For the staffing of the counseling center in terms of the number of counselors, a formula is typically used. It is usually based on a counselor-to-students ratio. For example, the chancellor's office for the California state universities and colleges recommends one counselor per 1,100 full-time-equivalent students. Full-time students carry 12 units of course work. It takes two half-time students (6 units each) or four quarter-time students (3 units each) to make one full-time-equivalent student. The problem with this approach for counseling services is that counselors do not see half or a quarter of a student; they see a whole person. A quarter-time student takes just as much time and attention in counseling as a full-time student. If counselors typically see a student for 10 sessions, does this mean that a half-time student is eligible for 5 sessions and a quarter-time student for 2.5 sessions? This hardly seems congruent with professional ethics, yet counseling center staff positions are allocated and budgeted on the basis of the number of full-time-equivalent students. With this in mind, the following formulas are given for minimal staffing at the psychological counseling center:

1 director of counseling

1 full-time counselor per 1,100 students (regardless of units carried)

1 psychometrist per 8 full-time counselors (or fractions thereof)

1 secretary (department secretary) per director

1 stenographer/typist per 3 full-time counselors.

A full-time counselor position is considered to be 40 hours per week. The equivalent of one full workday (eight hours per week) should be allowed for professional development, research, consultation, and outreach. This would leave 32 hours of actual contact time with students and interns, and for meetings. If counselors are assigned to work on additional or special duties, such as the development of a program, additional release time from the 32 hours of contact time may be required. Counselors should not be forced to give up their professional development time in order to work on some special project. This would very likely result in a decrease in the quality of counseling services provided. It seems fair, however, that if counselors are guaranteed their professional development time, they should be able to document how they have spent it for accountability purposes.

INNOVATIVE PROGRAMS

This section summarizes some of the more interesting and promising programs reported under "Innovative or Novel Functions Performed by Counseling Centers" (item 33) in Magoon (1981). The majority of functions/programs reported involved standard consultation, outreach, workshops, and nontraditional courses as discussed in the "Functions" section of this chapter. Hence, to avoid repetition, only those programs that are interesting because of their unusual nature, or promising programs for other centers to adapt, are included here.

The programs reported by Magoon (1981) included the following:

1. A number of workshops and groups on holistic health, dealing with nutrition (diet), exercise/running, psychological state of mind, yoga, and dental care, including a "Wellness Day"

2. Preparation and distribution of a pamphlet to all faculty and staff having direct contact with students on specific symptom patterns to look for in distressed students, how to make a referral, and a list of crisis phone numbers

3. A support and counseling service for students who have failed to pass graduate proficiency exams in English, mathematics, and reading

4. A Men's Collective Organization for the community and college that focuses on sexist behavior in men and the process men go through when relationships end

5. Outreach services to the high schools, including career search workshops and efforts to provide greater access to the college campus resources for high school administrators and teachers

6. Computer-assisted and self-instructional vocational guidance for students

7. A family systems orientation on counseling the college student

8. A Veterans Upward Bound program, including testing and educational/vocational counseling

9. Nontraditional therapy programs such as individual and group art, poetry, dance, and music therapy

10. January mini-term course for students going into the helping professions

11. Provision of mental health assistance following a disaster, involving the county civil defense plan and the local mental health center, and including predisaster training for staff of all agencies involved

12. Development and use of psycho-educational videotapes for workshops, goups, and classroom

13. A personal counseling group for students who are Vietnam combat veterans

14. A course in supervision for doctoral students, in which they supervise masters-level trainees in practicum and are in turn supervised by faculty

15. A mental health self-help phone line that provides coverage on a variety of topics (audio tapes)

16. Training workshops for athletes on the psychological aspects of sports

17. An exchange program in which a crisis team of graduate students and interns goes to a community mental health center on weekends and the mental health center staff comes to counseling at the center during the week, providing for a broader and more intensive training experience in crisis intervention

18. Automated relaxation training, in which a room is available 24 hours a day for students to check in and listen to any of a series of relaxation tapes, after an initial session with a counselor who determines the appropriateness of relaxation training as a primary intervention

19. Use of the counseling center as a training wing for marriage and family therapists after regular business hours

20. Correctional center seminars in which counselors and faculty help inmates, who are interested in college enrollment, assess their academic competency

21. Publication at cost of a series of monographs for counselors on special topics

22. In-service training sessions that are held weekly and open to all psychologists on the campus

23. Campus radio programs and columns in the student newspaper to which students can call or write in questions on mental health issues

24. Special programming and support services for single parents and displaced homemakers

25. A health and counseling liaison team that puts on joint workshops on topics in which psychological and physical health factors interface, such as a headache clinic or a weight-control clinic

26. Classes that are coinstructed by counseling center staff and academic faculty, such as a human sexuality course.

## REFERENCES

Anderson, W. 1970. Services offered by college counseling centers. Journal of Counseling Psychology, 17: 380-382.

Carney, C. G., and C. J. Savitz. 1980. Student and faculty perceptions of student needs and the services of a university counseling center: Differences that make a difference. Journal of Counseling Psychology, 27: 597-604.

Domke, J. A., J. M. Winkelpleck, and J. Westefeld. 1980. Consultation and outreach: Implementation at a university counseling center. Journal of College Student Personnel, 21: 211-214.

Elton, C. F., and H. A. Rose. 1973. The counseling center: A mirror of institutional size. Journal of Counseling Psychology, 20: 176-180.

Falk, R. B. 1971. Innovations in college mental health. Mental Hygiene, 55: 451-455.

Gelso, C. J., J. M. Birk, P. W. Utz, and A. E. Silver. 1976. A multi-group evaluation of models and functions of university counseling centers. Research report no. 8-76. College Park: University of Maryland.

Leventhal, A. M., and T. M. Magoon. 1979. Some general principles for university counseling centers. Professional Psychology, 10: 357-364.

Magoon, T. M. 1981. College and university counseling centers' 1980-81 annual data bank. College Park: University of Maryland. (Mimeographed.)

Oetting, E. R., A. E. Ivey, and R. G. Weigel. 1970. The college and university counseling center. American College Personnel

Association Monograph no. 11. Washington, D.C.: American Personnel and Guidance Association.

Rademacher, B. G., R. J. May, and R. Throckmorton. 1980. Consultation as a change strategy in student personnel divisions. NASPA Journal, 17: 46-51.

Tryon, G. S. 1980. A review of the literature concerning perceptions of and preferences for counseling center services. Journal of College Student Personnel, 21: 304-310.

Williamson, E. G., and D. A. Biggs. 1975. Student personnel work: A program of developmental relationships. New York: John Wiley and Sons.

Wolf, J. C., and J. D. Dameron. 1975. Counseling center function in two-year and four-year colleges. Journal of College Student Personnel, 16: 482-485.

Young, J. W., and K. A. Harris. 1977. A community college model of counseling. Journal of College Student Personnel, 18: 133-137.

# 2

# THE COUNSELING/CLINICAL PSYCHOLOGIST IN THE COLLEGE OR UNIVERSITY COUNSELING CENTER

## *Phillip J. Gallagher*

A review of the topics in professional journals, activities of professional organizations, and the advent of certification and licensure laws since the 1960s is, at least partially, a function and manifestation of the national concern for the delivery of medical and psychological services. Most people reject the proposition that we have one quality of services for upper- and middle-class Americans and another quality for the poor. Likewise, students should have access to the same quality of service whether they attend a rich university or a state college, whether they are members of a majority or a minority group. The nature of economics in higher education, of course, precludes extensive medical or psychological treatment; however, it is assumed that the student needs and should receive evaluations and short-term health services from adequately educated and trained medical and psychological personnel. (This will be discussed further, later in this chapter.) The first section of the chapter will treat briefly the counseling/clinical psychologist in the college or university setting, and especially the training deemed necessary to perform customary counseling/clinical functions. The second section will consider the services provided by the clinical/counseling psychologist. The final section will treat the evaluation of the services provided.

## THE COUNSELING/CLINICAL PSYCHOLOGIST

### Background

Although Garfield (1981), in an excellent 40-year appraisal of psychotherapy, saw the shift of clinical psychology from pri-

23

marily psychoanalytic and diagnostic to therapeutic in the early
1960s, our personal experience puts the shift somewhat later. In
the middle and late 1960s we found, in interviewing clinical psychologists for positions as counseling psychologists, that most of
them were not suited for this role. Generally they were peculiarly
not interested in mental hygiene and preventive efforts, talking to
students regarding career or academic matters, or evaluating their
own work. What seemed of interest to them were diagnostic efforts
coupled with a desire to discuss dynamics in a general way and an
opportunity to provide long-term psychotherapy with clients of their
choice. They felt an almost compelling need for psychiatric supervision and the services of a social worker.

With the advent of increased training in psychotherapy and
training directed toward competency in independent practice, the
clinical psychologist now fits much more smoothly into the work of
the psychologist in a college/university counseling center. It is believed that this is also true of those who received their education
and training prior to the 1960s, partly because of the professional
trend toward greater independence in practice.

Garfield does not cite Pepinsky and Pepinsky (1954) or Patterson (1966) in his account of the evolution toward greater emphasis
on psychotherapy in clinical psychology; however, many of us in
university/college counseling centers were strongly influenced by
the appeal by Pepinsky and Pepinsky that we anchor our inferences
in basic observational data and constantly to evaluate our inferences. In counseling centers the emphasis was on counseling or
therapy much earlier. The force of the reminder to remain fairly
close to scientific methodology in our professional practice contributed at least partially to the eclecticism in counseling centers.
Albert (1968) reported 72 percent of counselors considered themselves eclectic (the second largest proportion—22 percent—was
Rogerian). Another factor contributing to the eclecticism probably
is the variety of tasks and problems faced by counselors and centers (Clark 1968). In the early 1960s the bent in university and college counseling centers was clearly toward treatment rather than
diagnosis. (These activities will be discussed in greater detail
later in the chapter.)

Because of the rather mundane nature of many of the duties
within a center, a strong argument was made for the "good guy
theory" of staffing centers. Many centers were staffed by transfers
within the college or university of personnel were sought out by students with problems. Others had specific interests or specialties
suited to service provision, such as study methods, career information, and group discussions. This assortment of people with
varying backgrounds resulted in a hodgepodge of people trying to

assist students. It has been said that student personnel services is a varied group of people in search of a profession. Some counseling centers were not that different in the recent past (a more thorough "history" can be found in Chapter 3).

Recommendation and Projections

The quagmire resulting from the problems in measurement of both dependent and independent variables, and the methodological difficulties inherent in establishing reliable empirical relationships between counseling and its effects (see Chapter 4; also see Garfield 1981; Phillips and Bierman 1981), appears to demand the continuation of a combination of nomothetic and ideographic approaches, with heavy emphasis and reliance on the adequate scientific and professional education and training of practitioners (counselors).

The above is seen as both a recommendation and projection, and as quite consistent with the present zeitgeist in American psychology. The trend appears clearly to establish minimal qualifications for professional psychologists in both the private and public sectors; for example, the Veterans Administration has made licensure a requirement for their psychologists, and most states now require either a license or certification for private practice. This is the direction taken by the other professions, such as medicine and law, and seems a viable basis for the selection of counselors for college/university counseling centers.

Dorken and Webb (1981) report on increases in licensed psychologists: ". . . a 42% growth over this five year (1974-1979) period. Given an unduplicated count of 25,510 licensed psychologists nationally in 1976, these trends suggest a national projection, as of 1980, of 35,100 licensed psychologists . . . of whom 24,300 are clinically active doctoral level health service providers." They predict a further advance in the 1980s. Their data also suggest a proportion of about 21 percent for counseling psychologists (counseling/clinical and counseling).

In a survey study titled "Differentiating roles of clinical and counseling psychology interns," Prince and Randolph (1981) report that the clinical psychologist is being trained more in diagnosis, learning disabilities, brain damage, and projective testing, while the counseling psychologist is trained more in vocational-career guidance, public relations, and aptitude testing. These data appear consistent with previous training and functions. The counseling psychologist continues to work with clients having less severe problems. (For further definitions of clinical and counseling psychologists, see Appendixes C and D.)

Mills, Wellner, and Vanden Bos (1979) reported on a survey of 25,500 licensed psychologists. Out of 19,000 respondents, 1,600 identified themselves as both counseling psychologist and health service provider.

The position taken here is that either licensed clinical or counseling psychologists are qualified to do the work of the college/university counselor. Our bias is toward having centers staffed by a majority of counseling psychologists. It is believed that all should have a good background in research methodology.

It is doubtful that anyone knowledgeable regarding the services offered by counseling centers would argue that these centers do not provide psychological services. The American Psychological Association has established and published Standards for Providers of Psychological Services (reproduced in Appendix A).* It is recommended and projected that members of centers will follow these standards. It follows that those within a psychological unit should adhere to the APA Code of Ethics (this is reproduced in Appendix B).

A way of assuring equal psychological services to all students is through the procedures used by other professions. For our profession this currently entails adequate education: the doctorate in an appropriate field, postdoctoral training, and examinations for certification or licensure.

Another major trend in both medicine and psychology is the recognition of the desirability of continuing education. The notion that the professional person can acquire a degree and a license, then practice indefinitely, is generally rejected, and although most practitioners probably continue their professional growth, there appears to be a strong push toward requiring (by law) continuing education. At present the California State Psychological Association issues a three-year Continuing Education Certificate. There are bills pending to require evidence of continuing education for license renewal. This trend is seen as desirable and is particularly necessary for those practicing in a university/college counseling center because of the present lack of consistent qualification standards.

---

*In addition to the APA Standards for Providers of Psychological Services, "Specialty Guidelines for the Delivery of Services" have been reproduced in the American Psychologist. "Specialty Guidelines for the Delivery of Services by Clinical Psychologists" and "Specialty Guidelines for the Delivery of Services by Counseling Psychologists" are included in this book as appendices C and D.

Academic Rank

The American Psychological Association has defined psychology as a science, a profession, and an academic discipline. It follows that those working in the counseling center should be an integral part of the college/university community. The issue of academic rank for counselors (see Gallagher and Weisbrod 1970) is still not resolved. The bias of the present writer favors full academic rank. The alternative of clinical professor in counseling is a second choice. The designation "closely related academically" seems minimally acceptable. It is believed that a careful reading of the remainder of this chapter will probably result in the conclusion that academic rank is desirable for the counseling/clinical psychologist working in a university/college counseling center. Counselors have served, and do serve, on a variety of committees; have equivalent degrees; need professional development—including sabbaticals; "teach" in the cognitive and affective realms as well as the technical; serve on thesis and dissertation committees; need and have tenure; and teach (usually graduate courses).

It is maintained that with adequate provision, counselors can have academic rank without being in an evaluative posture with students.


COUNSELING SERVICES

The following services are considered the core duties and responsibilities of counselors.


Academic Counseling

Most universities and colleges have taken varying degrees of responsibility for students they have admitted. If students are having difficulty in acquiring a degree, they are assisted in various ways by various units of the college. The college counseling center is the major agency for helping students with problems.

Estimates of the number of college students in need of some form of counseling vary considerably; however, most counseling centers have developed from two assumptions important for this discussion. First, the counseling center was to have a unique role in the total educational process. It was to be a place where a student could discuss his/her problems in a nonjudgmental atmosphere. The center was not to be identified with the teaching faculty or the administration, and especially not as a disciplinary agency. Second, it was assumed that the students would be unaware of the services afforded, especially the rather subtle supportive role the center wished to establish; therefore, a major activity of many counseling centers has been to establish student-counseling center contact.

Counselor activities should be viewed in light of the above assumptions, particularly the "student-counseling center contact" function. Without belaboring the point, many students experiencing profound improvement in their lives originally came to the center about a relatively minor matter—probation or academic advice, for instance. When the student is met by a professional who seems to care and is there to assist him/her, the student not only sees and hears about the counseling center, but is more likely to feel its purpose.

As for information services, the clinical/counseling psychologist needs to be generally acquainted with the academic institution. In addition to being knowledgeable regarding its organization and the services available to the student, he/she must be able to assist the student in meeting general requirements for the degree. Because pupils and parents generalize from their own experience and are led to believe by counselors, from elementary school on, that if you need any kind of information, you should talk to a counselor, these people, upon arriving at a new university or college, seek a counselor if they wish information about the institution. The counselor needs to be prepared for this function. Although it is generally acknowledged that academic advising should be the responsibility of the teaching faculty, many students, because of their past experiences, do not know this; furthermore, many are intimidated by teaching faculty and prefer going to a counselor. Even where an academic advising center has been established, large numbers of students and parents still end up in the counseling center. This was a problem in the past. The clinical psychologist was unwilling to fulfill such a mundane and elementary function: to tell a student or his/her parents how many units a freshman should sign up for, the meaning of a unit, or where to get the class schedule. The counselor or teaching faculty member who sees this type of information-giving as beneath him/her is not an asset to the university or college.

It seems somewhat wasteful and cumbersome, however, to expect all counselors to be competent to provide academic counseling. One solution has been to shift or maintain the major responsibility of academic advice to/with the teaching faculty, with perhaps a single counselor or the director of counseling in a consultative role. Another solution is not to make academic counseling a necessary duty of all the counselors. Selected counselors can be given this responsibility, primarily seeing students requesting academic counseling, and being resource persons for other counselors and for other agencies of the college. (See Chapter 8.)

The meaning of the term "academic counseling" continues to be ambiguous. One counseling center arbitrarily defines the term as academic advice if it is interpretation of college major programs, regulations, admissions, probation, disqualification, planning class schedules, and so forth. It arbitrarily uses the term "educational counseling" when any of the above is of sufficient complexity to require more than one interview. If the center accepts responsibility for providing academic counseling, then effective lines of communication between the administration and faculty committees and counselors need to be established, reviewed, and maintained.

Academic advice for undeclared majors seems a logical function for the counseling center because the counselors can provide educational and vocational counseling as well as assist the student in selection of a major and of necessary courses, regardless of major.

Programs of Assistance for Students on Probation

This function was considered vital by all counselors, and was ranked high in importance by both faculty and students.* In terms of providing student-counseling center contact, this should be a major concern of the center.

One of the first signs of something gone wrong in the student's college career is his/her being placed on probation. Usually, because it is an early sign, much can be done in prevention as well as rehabilitation. Without attempting to be even close to comprehensive, here are a few reasons students find themselves on academic probation: carrying too many units; carrying too many units in combination with hours of work; working too many hours; too much social life; semiconscious or unconscious need to fail or "success phobia"; lack of vocational goal; excessive fear of failure; overanxiousness in taking examinations; poor study habits; poor study methods; illness

---

*In a questionnaire attitude study at California State College at Los Angeles, teaching faculty, students, administrators, and counselors were asked to indicate "duties counselors should perform." Teaching faculty and counselors ranked personal counseling first. Students ranked it third (after academic and vocational). Since this study was conducted in 1967, this chapter is less directly dependent on it. The study will be provided on request.

in the family; guilt or anxiety over acceptance of help from parents; reading deficiency; deficiency in mathematics or English; unresolved feelings regarding death of significant other person; serious mental disturbance; physical disorder; pregnancy; love affair; religious conflicts; excessive concern with social problems; poor living conditions; depression ranging from minor feelings of "what's the use?" to suicide; rebellion against "adult" values; lack of self-motivation; LSD, marijuana, other drugs; heavy drinking; too much interest in student government, music, sports; preoccupation with sexual activities; wrong major or vocational goal; side effects of medication.

The reason most counselors believe that the student should see a counselor in the privacy of his/her office is readily apparent from the above list. Usually a complex combination of factors leads to a low grade-point average, and several sessions may be necessary before the student is able to define problems clearly and formulate plans to alleviate them. For this reason the procedure of including a carefully written letter to the student (along with probation notification) inviting him/her to come to the counseling center has been quite effective.

Some other means of encouraging the student to come to the center are items in the college paper; counselor's talks to student and faculty groups and organizations (such as fraternities); distribution of counseling center brochure; and group counseling sessions for other, specific purposes.

It is the author's opinion that the group approaches are in many cases a pragmatic substitute for the individual session; they range from lecture series to group psychotherapy.

It cannot be overemphasized that the reputation of the counseling center is a major factor determining whether it can fulfill its responsibility to the student having academic difficulty. The term "image" might have been used but is somewhat less desirable because of past usage. "Reputation" does not quite hit the mark either; however, the center maintaining strict confidentiality, a professional posture in other ways, and completely honest and open procedures and policies should, other things being equal, gain the desired respect and confidence of faculty, students, and administration.

Exit Interviews for Disqualified Students

With parents, teachers, and other forces in our culture pressing children from a very early age to go to college, some students seem to conclude, on an emotional-feeling level as well as an intel-

lectual level, that not to complete college means being a total failure.  There are suicides as a result of failure in college, as well
as other forms of disaster ranging from lifetime feelings of poor
self-worth to demoralization manifested by alcoholism, drug addic-
tion, and prostitution.  Success in college becomes a matter of life
or death to too many students.

Disqualification is traumatic in almost all cases, even when
it is based on a semiconscious need to fail.  Students will occasionally express having a "wave of relief" on receiving the disqualification notice; however, this seems to result in a perpetuation of
avoidance patterns and a negative self-concept.  The nature of the
disqualification situation demands a qualified counselor and an individual interview.  (For an excellent summary of the counseling
interview, see Gruen 1968a.)

In addition to dealing with the feelings of the disqualified student, the counselor should provide necessary information relating
to the student's future.  Universities and colleges vary in requirements for readmission or reinstatement.  The student needs to know
as exactly as possible the reality of his/her present predicament.
At a relatively large college of 21,000 students, at the end of any
given semester more than 1,000 students were subject to disqualification.  Many disqualified students feel very much alone—that it
rarely happens to anyone.  Just knowing his/her situation is not
unique may be helpful to such a student.

A series of empirical studies has supported the trend toward
requiring the student to make significant changes before being readmitted.  The requirements most consistent with recent empirical
data include disqualification for a specified time—usually one semester or two quarters—and completion of college-level courses with at
least some B grades, and/or counseling, including review of study
methods.

The problem of the college attempting to maintain or improve
academic standards is essentially that it is futile and wasteful for
all concerned to allow the student to continue if there is very little
chance of graduation.  The student was originally admitted because
of a prediction that he/she would succeed (make a C average and
graduate).  After disqualification the student needs to make better
than a C average, and all previous information leads to the prediction that he/she will make less than that.  This information, as
well as what the college will consider good predictive evidence of
success, is necessary for the student to formulate realistic plans
for completion of his/her education.

The purpose of the college or university is not to destroy or
damage students—not all students, not 50 percent, not even 1 percent.  It is, I think, the consensus of counselors that it is not

necessary to damage a proportion of students in order to enhance another proportion. The student who receives a disqualification notice, for example, because of lack of aptitude and/or distaste for abstract reasoning may actually be helped to accept this as the reason, and gladly change his/her goal without damage to his/her self-concept and without hate for college, intellectuals, and society in general. It is maintained here that the college or university has some responsibility for students who fail in their efforts to obtain a degree.

This responsibility has been given added emphasis by special admission consideration for disadvantaged youths.

Readmission Interview with Disqualified Students

At the time of disqualification, many students are not ready (or able) to take advantage of services available to them. The readmission or reinstatement interview can provide an opportunity for the student to make significant changes in himself/herself relating to his/her college career. Because of the predictive predicament discussed above, it is vital to have an interview in order to gain information on the chances of success at this second or third attempt. The information from the interview is passed on to a committee for final acceptance or rejection of the application for readmittance. In the writer's experience, a frank discussion of reasons for disqualification at the time of readmission can lead to very realistic plans for change (such as vocational, personal, marriage, or educational counseling).

Academic Advising

Advice in this area is normally provided by the academic department. The counselors may provide this service for new students and undeclared "majors." Counseling centers frequently provide consultation and/or training sessions with teaching faculty in interview techniques and/or university- or collegewide procedure and policy.

Many colleges and universities are utilizing teaching faculty for academic counseling (in addition to academic advice). In some of these programs the faculty members actually enter a training program and provide the services within the counseling center. Berrick (1968) provides a summary and references for this type of program. (See Chapter 8 for another viable alternative.)

Exit Interview for Withdrawing Students

The degree of concern with the exit interview for voluntarily withdrawing students is generally proportional to the number of students living away from home while at college and is inversely proportional to the age level of the students. All of the emotional factors discussed in considering the probational and disqualified students may be present in the withdrawing student; in fact, a feeling of failure, for example, may be coupled with the feelings that the student has run away, given up, "chickened out."

Of course, the college needs to have data on the reason for withdrawal. The personal exit interview is the most efficient means of securing meaningful data. If the university or college requires an exit interview, care should be taken to ensure that it does not take on the characteristics of persuasion. The freedom of choice needs to be made explicit in the early stages of the session—the counselor is not there to convince the student of the value of remaining in school; rather, the counselor is available to assist in clarifying the student's feelings regarding the withdrawal and any other matters discussed. In some cases the student will change his/her decision as a result of counseling, but this is clearly not the goal of the interview.

Special Programs for the Disadvantaged

The counselor is in a particularly good position, as a result of his/her training and experience, to make significant and valuable contributions to programs set up for disadvantaged students. More specifically, his/her work entails confrontation with motivational, social interpersonal, emotional, intellectual, and achievement problems.

Here the writer would like to state his belief that changing or lowering academic standards is undesirable and unnecessary. Special admission status could be provided with a limited number of courses allowed, which could be increased progressively from quarter to quarter or semester to semester. The specially admitted students could be required to take courses in study methods and in deficient areas, could be provided with individual tutors (college students), and could be included in group counseling to increase adjustment to the college milieu. Finally, in the author's opinion, unless careful planning is done to increase the probability of success of the disadvantaged college student, colleges or universities may do more harm than good in admitting these students. The student needs to experience success, but without special provision, either standards drop or these students are predicted to fail.

## Counselor Training Function

If the counseling center accepts the responsibility of training counselors, it is suggested that a formally written document be established specifying the goals, the type of training, and the criteria for selection. It would seem unnecessary to mention the above, but in the writer's experience, many training programs have existed on an extremely informal basis—with questionable results.

## Career-Vocational Counseling

In order to provide vocational counseling, an adequate testing center is necessary. Administratively, the testing center is usually placed under a director or associate dean of counseling and testing. In addition, a vocational library is necessary. This may be provided by the librarian, the placement officer, a counselor, or all three.

Gruen (1968b, p. 216) provides an excellent summary of career and vocational counseling, and references. In addition, he presents clearly the rationale for college and university responsibility in this area:

> In recent times many colleges and universities have taken on the responsibility of helping young people develop personally as well as intellectually, vocationally as well as academically. It is important to note that whole persons can be developed without diluting the intellectual experience that college primarily needs to be. The intellectual life need not be compromises when self-discovery is another congruent imperative. It is not really possible to compartmentalize the individual. The implementation of ideas, the marriage of cognitive and affective processes, the holistic notion of the total personality, the relationship and cross-fertilization processes—this is higher education at its best.

A center is greatly enhanced by having at least one counselor who has expertise and is specialized in vocational counseling. This person—in addition to carrying a caseload of vocational clients—

can serve as a resource person for other counselors, the test office, and the vocational library.

## Test Interpretation

The vocational counseling movement was clearly stimulated and directed by two important propositions (actually assumptions). Thorndike's said, "If anything exists, it exists in some amount, and if it exists in some amount it can be measured." And Beers defined vocational guidance as finding out about the job, finding out about the individual, and matching the two.

In finding out about the individual, a variety of tests have been used. The GATB is one example of attempting to measure aptitudes. The Kuder and Strong scales have attempted to measure interests. It is generally agreed that personality is the single most important factor in vocational adjustment, and the most difficult to measure. The reliability and validity of the personality tests do not reach the level of interest, achievement, or aptitude tests.

This brief discussion leads to the issue of psychometric versus clinical prediction. What appears to be the simple task of career counseling and test interpretation is in fact exceedingly complex. At the present state of our knowledge, both the psychometric and the clinical method require a battery of tests. The common practice of using one or two tests (for example, a personality and an interest inventory) does not square with either good psychometric or good clinical approach. We can only hope that the counselor realizes the tenuous and ephemeral nature of the assessment data and passes this realization on to the client. It is the apparent simplicity of test interpretation that has enabled the unsophisticated to use and misuse tests. The author had occasion to talk to an instructor of a career guidance class who had been trying out various tests to "see which was the best." I asked him if he was using norm- or criterion-references tests. He did not know the difference. I asked if the scores were ipsative. He didn't know. I asked him the standard error of one of the tests. He didn't know what that was. He was "too busy guiding students to do any extra reading."

## Providing Career Information

It appears that in many cases we have a similar level of sophistication. Holland, Magoon, and Spokane (1981) state that their review of counseling psychology (career interventions, research, and theory) covers primarily the period 1978-79. They provide additional references for a review of the literature in the general area of careers, and go on to say (p. 283):

Haase et al. (1979) show experimentally that the presentation of both positive and negative occupational information increases the cognitive complexity of a person's occupational perceptions. In contrast, the presentation of only positive information increases the simplicity of perceptions. These beginnings may make it possible to dispense occupational information in more compatible and beneficial ways. This work may also provide one of the keys to the understanding of treatment effects.

This quotation reveals much about the general tone and methodological shortcomings in career counseling, particularly in occupational information. The idea of having positive and negative occupational information is so out of touch with the basic scientific approach that it is discouraging. Information should be accurate, not upbeat or downbeat. The only place for negative and positive evaluations should be whether the information is up-to-date, secured in an unbiased manner, and described accurately. The place for opinions is in discussion of variations and trends.

Because of the apparent shortcomings in "finding out about the person and the occupation," the answer to the problem probably lies in the education of those who provide career information and test interpretation. It would seem best to require more courses in experimental psychology and to provide better inducements to enter the vocational-career specialty within counseling psychology.

It seems that early in the careers of counseling psychologists there is a shift from vocational counseling (test use and interpretation, and providing vocational information) to providing individual or group personal counseling. Career counseling is then left to those who believe what is written in the test manuals and the descriptions of packaged career information. If the counseling/clinical psychologist would accept more responsibility for those working in his/her unit in the area of career counseling (see APA 1977), perhaps greater hope could be held for the future.

At present each psychologist takes the responsibility for his/her own case and is probably doing a good job; however, it is very time-consuming and impossible to meet the demand. An immediate solution to the problem might be to have in-service training presentations and/or periodic peer review of career-vocational cases, which in the writer's experience is rare because of the apparently greater challenge of and interest in clinical cases.

Developmental Counseling

The majority of clients seen in college and university counseling centers probably are best classified as students who have problems that are age-related. Although the problem may be presented as "I think I'm going crazy," "I can't get a date," "I'm afraid I'm going to kill myself if she doesn't come back," it likely will turn out to be one of learning to cope with new sources of stress. The need for doctorate-level training and years of experience seems readily apparent here. Also, psychodiagnostic skill is imperative.

It is doubtful that very many counselors do not see their clients as future parents, and therefore almost all the work of the counselor can be viewed as having a major mental hygiene aspect.

Other means of providing mental hygiene influence to the academic community are committee work, workshops, developmental groups, articles in the university/college newspaper, and consultations.

Many, if not most, counseling centers have made major contributions to holistic medicine and psychology in their individual and group counseling, workshops, combined services and research efforts with medical centers, and articles on mental hygiene in university/college and local newspapers.


Crisis Intervention

The university or college is on safer legal ground if the responsibility for crisis intervention lies with a licensed psychologist or psychiatrist. It is advisable that one member of the center keep others informed of changes in resources and procedures. This person can also maintain records for the center for these vital services, and inform the university/college community of the referral procedures. Follow-up studies should be done by the center.

Each counselor must deal with crisis cases periodically. Consultation is absolutely essential, and the means and procedure for this vital function must be explicit and viable.


Personal Counseling

"Personal counseling," as used here, includes all the various approaches employed by counseling/clinical psychologists to assist students, whatever their personal problems may be. With some exceptions the therapist cannot provide long-term therapy. At one point in our center there was a "5 & 10 approach." After five sessions the counselor was required to consult with a colleague before going on. After ten sessions the case was again reviewed with a different colleague. In practice it was difficult to find time to accomplish the reviews, and the "5 & 10" was ignored, modified, or circumvented in numerous and ingenious ways. The attitude toward it was basically "a bureaucratic interference with our professional prerogatives" or "an insult to our profession." Certainly the psychologist should be given credit for being a responsible citizen, a responsible member of his/her profession. Nevertheless, some sort of review process seems necessary, and there is no doubt that with the limited resources of most counseling centers, extended psychotherapy cannot be provided.

The American Psychological Association's Project CHAMPUS (1981) established levels of (retrospective) psychological review. Level I is a technical one. Level II is mandatory: "after 8, 24, 40, and 60 sessions, and at every 24th session after the 60th [and] if the claim is for testing or assessment. . . ."*

The APA/CHAMPUS Outpatient Psychological Provider Manual (1981) has other valuable material for those working in counseling centers. For example, ". . . the provider is asked to rate the progress to date and the severity of the patient's current dysfunction in six general problem areas": home/family, job/school, interpersonal relations, bodily function, protection of self and others, and personal comfort. Each area is rated on a four-point scale for severity and progress.

It is assumed that in developing and reviewing the treatment plan with the patient, the provider will

---

*The nature of the 475 peer reviewers may be of interest to the reader: 82 percent were male and 18 percent female. Most possessed a Ph.D. (93.5 percent), and 35.8 percent reported postdoctoral training as well. Clinical psychology and counseling psychology were the most frequently indicated areas of concentration (77 percent and 7 percent, respectively). All reviewers were licensed or certified to practice in their state of residence, 82.5 percent were listed in the National Register of Health Service Providers in Psychology, 27.2 percent were diplomates of the American Board of Professional Psychology, and 97.3 percent were members of the American Psychological Association. The most common primary treatment orientation for psychological services was psychodynamic (45.7 percent) followed by behavioral (18 percent) and eclectic (16.6 percent)

> explain the expected course and outcome of treatment,
> and both patient and provider responsibilities. This
> discussion, along with an explanation of the provision
> for protection of confidentiality, will enable the patient
> (or guardian) to give his or her informed consent to the
> course of treatment and the required review proce-
> dures. (p. 3-2)

It is probably too soon to use the CHAMPUS Outpatient Psychological Providers Manual as a basic model, although it is understood
that several insurance providers are considering it that way. Of
special value are appendixes 4-B (peer review guidelines), 4-D
(APA/CHAMPUS second-level criteria), and 4-E (statements that
do and do not satisfy selected criteria for describing outpatient
mental health care).

It should be noted that developmental approaches, such as
Gestalt therapy, are not reimbursable from CHAMPUS at this time;
however, even though developmental counseling is a major part of
the counselor's work, the CHAMPUS Provider Manual seems of
great value, and with appropriate modifications can serve as an excellent skeleton on which to base a counseling center review document if adapted to fit particular needs of individual centers.

Phillips and Bierman (1981), both at the University of Denver,
provide an excellent review of the literature of individual methods
in clinical psychology from 1976 to early 1980. They note Frank's
(1979) summary of outcome studies thus: "He labels the amount of
well-established, clinically relevant knowledge as disappointingly
meager and intuitively obvious." On the other hand, they note that
the "methodological critiques are having a cumulative positive effect," and cite several references to substantiate their conclusion.
They also list the criteria of Luborsky et al. (1975) for evaluating
outcome studies. Among them is the criterion of adequate diagnosis.

Garfield and Gergin (1978) and Tyler (1969) are excellent references for the various approaches to counseling and therapy used in
counseling centers. (For further discussion on providing personal
counseling, see Chapters 1 and 9.)

Diagnosis

Although the DSM-II was of some value, there was considerable dissatisfaction with it among psychologists in general and especially among those in college and university counseling centers.
DSM-III is considered to be a vast improvement and is recommended
for use in counseling. It has been argued that any time a counselor
embarks on a treatment plan or counseling strategy, he/she has

made a diagnosis, whether it is explicit or not. It is suggested that the more formal approach offered by the DSM-III will enable the counselor to improve his/her counseling as well as communications with colleagues. (Chapter 5 covers this important topic.)

In order for center personnel to adequately use the DSM-III, study groups combined with case review are probably necessary. Again, this document is a good basis for a more refined diagnostic system. The multiaxial structure is conducive to further refinement. Already an additional axis for "motivation for change or therapy" appears desirable, as does a rating on social acceptance of an individual (appearance, social acuity, friendliness).

At any rate, the need for diagnosis seems as clear today as it was in the past, and ignoring the need because there are only relatively crude instruments and systems seems nihilistic at best.


Research

Theoretical-Experimental

The theoretical-experimental psychologist may formulate hypotheses that can be tested in the relatively controlled facilities of the counseling center. Of course, the counseling psychologist may note feasible empirical propositions logically derived from a particular counseling, psychotherapeutic, or personality theory. Further, he/she may observe empirical data that are not included in any present theory, and may take steps to establish them as reliable phenomena (see Underwood 1957) in need of explanation. Obviously the counselor is in a position to check empirically certain psychological treatments as opposed to others (Chassan 1967). In conjunction with the medical center or school, the counselor may also be involved in experimental evaluation of the effects of particular medication on concentration, relief of anxiety, increased motivation, and so forth.

Major contributions can be expected in the years to come in the form of methodological clarification and refinement. As the counseling centers move toward the mainstream of psychological research, methodological suggestions (Turner 1967; Schontz 1965; Rychlak 1968) can be attempted with feedback to the more scientific members of the profession, academic discipline, and science of psychology. At present there is precious little research of this nature in counseling centers, which is rather surprising in view of the physical proximity of psychology departments.

## Applied

The trend toward admission of more disadvantaged students should result in a flurry of studies related to remedial programs, study methods, motivation for success in college, and assimilation of these students into the college community. Tyler (1969) provides an excellent summary of applied research in counseling, as does The Annual Review of Psychology. Applied research is seen as a major responsibility of counseling centers.

## Institutional

The college or university needs to know why students are withdrawing, as well as the number of probationary and readmitted disqualified students who eventually graduate. There are a number of demographic factors that need to be determined, such as age, marital status, hours of work, and study load. The counseling center may be involved in the collection of these data, but the larger institutions are providing a director of institutional research for this purpose. The counseling center, of course, needs this information whether it helps in the data collection or not.

## General

Although the faculty, students, and counselors in the attitude study at California State College, Los Angeles, ranked assistance in educational research low on the counselor responsibility continuum, the counselors believed that some research activity is vital. There appear to be some strongly negative feelings/opinions as to research by counselors—an ironic state of affairs, coming from teaching faculty. It seems reasonable to expect increasing support for research within the counseling center as a result of the rising concern for the disadvantaged and for the "total" education of the college student. It appears that practically all concerned with higher education are becoming increasingly disenchanted, disappointed, and angered by conditions that result in the "emotional moron" with a college degree.

The developments and interests in the area of motivation, combined with concern for the culturally disadvantaged, will, it is hoped, result in closer cooperative research in this area. In order to point out the numerous research tasks in one basic area, I would like to turn to a brief consideration of treatment possibilities for the student coming to the counseling center. *

---

*There have been references to the passive nature of counseling centers and of the therapist in recent considerations of this

What kinds of treatments are possible for the student? First, the term "treatment," as used here, includes all possible dispositions or efforts open to the counselor and counselee.* Second, it is held that any diagnostic system must be anchored firmly in treatment possibilities. Finally, in reading the list of some of the possible treatments, it is suggested that one consider or imagine the amount of research necessary to be able to specify the characteristics and conditions that will indicate (or contraindicate) the most parsimonious treatment.

Some possible treatments include group therapy, group interaction (sensitivity or encounter), crisis intervention, referral to a psychiatrist for medication, intellective therapy, long-term treatment, hospitalization, marathon group therapy, partnership therapy, hypnotherapy, relaxation training, assertion training, biofeedback, learning assistance, academic advising, Educational Opportunity Programs, foreign student advising, life skills training, adult re-entry, conditioning or reinforcement therapy, Rogerian therapy, bibliotherapy, testing, career counseling, educational counseling, reading improvement, marriage counseling, supportive counseling, minimal-change counseling with more seriously disturbed students, extended group or individual (four- to ten-hour) sessions, referral to medical center/speech therapist/attorney/financial aid counselor/ placement counselor, stress management, paradoxical or social counseling.

## EVALUATION

Bourne provides a more thorough discussion of program evaluation as well as of outcome studies in Chapter 4. One could easily take the position that each activity and program should have evaluation built in as an essential part. Each activity or program would naturally have to have its own methods and criteria—for instance,

---

field. This seems to be a misperception or misconception. This reasoning would lead one to consider hospitals, as well as medical, law, and financial offices, as passive agencies. As to the functioning of the counselor, again, this reasoning suggests that listening is a passive activity, that observation (the major component of scientific method) is passive. In the opinion of the author, we are still (in counseling and psychotherapy) in the data-gathering (observational) stage of development.

*Including, for example, developmental and career counseling, which are not considered to be treatment for deficit conditions.

career counseling, brief psychotherapy, biofeedback, educational counseling.

Client evaluation of services is recommended; however, reasonable sampling procedures should be utilized rather than blanket evaluations for all clients. In our center several counselors used a rather thorough anonymous client evaluation of counselor and services. The results were clearly of the "thanks a lot" nature, and the "halo" effect was evident. This procedure is still considered of value when applied periodically to a sample of clients. Within the state university system student evaluation of teaching faculty is mandatory, and the client evaluations are consistent with this. Further, the results occasionally are very helpful to the counselor in reviewing his/her work.

The position has been taken in this chapter that education, licensure, continuing education, peer review, and client evaluation of services combine to form the best means of assuring quality services to students.

Education

Most people working in higher education have a profound and firm belief in the value of education. Through personal experience, teaching and counseling faculty are keenly aware of the intensification and acceleration of education between the master's degree and the doctorate. It is not surprising that the profession and institutions of higher education are demanding the doctorate. Included under education is the structured training of the predoctoral internship.

Licensure or Certification

Most states require, in addition to the doctorate and specific course work, internships and a large number of hours of clinical experience before the applicant is allowed to take the written and oral examinations. The formal peer evaluations of the applicant are of great value to both the profession as a whole and the individual professional exposed to all that the examination entails. The resources for this type of evaluation are clearly beyond the capability of individual counseling centers.

Continuing Education

Courses and workshops that are APA-approved are increasingly being offered, often to supply new knowledge required to update clinical/counseling practice, such as DSM-III, forensic psychology, developments in psychophysiology, and medications. It appears that in the not-too-distant future, continuing education will be required for renewal of the license or certificate to practice.

Peer Review

It is believed that the peer review documents and procedures used by third-party reimbursers can, and will, be modified to provide a more formal structure for peer review in counseling centers.

Student Evaluations

Client evaluations of counseling services are seen as at the infancy stage at best. There are numerous problems involved in this rather simple-looking notion. Many of these problems are considered elsewhere in this book and there are provided references. In the opinion of the author, continued efforts are desirable in order to refine the procedures, the methodology, and the collection of basic data.

Outcome Studies

Telch (1981) and Frank (1981) have attempted to clarify and provide direction for more parsimonious and efficient outcome studies. Telch summarizes Frank's (1979) generalizations thus:

> (a) All forms of psychotherapy are somewhat more effective than informal or unplanned help; (b) one form of therapy has rarely been shown to be significantly more effective than any other; (c) most clients who show initial improvement maintain it; and (d) therapeutic success lies more in the qualities of the client, therapist, and their interaction than in the therapeutic method. Frank argues that since therapeutic success depends primarily on client and therapist characteristics, clinical researchers should direct their attention to the identification of relevant attributes of clients and therapists. He suggests that future research explore the relationship between client characteristics (e.g., locus of control), therapist characteristics (e.g., degree of therapist participation), and therapy outcome. (p. 472)

Part of Telch's position is as follows:

> Though not denying that client and therapist character-
> istics can influence therapy outcome, I propose that
> the degree of influence exerted by client and therapist
> characteristics is inversely related to the potency of
> the therapeutic intervention. Potency is defined here
> as the degree to which a psychological procedure pro-
> duces significant improvement over a wide range of
> facets (i.e., measurement modality, client charac-
> teristics, therapist characteristics, etc.). (p. 474)

Telch recommends that researchers strive to develop more potent psychological procedures.

The articles by Telch (1981) and Frank (1981) are recommended reading. Both positions seem reasonable; however, one of the "clinchers" on Frank's side is that empirical data should confirm clinical impressions. The dimensions of therapy with which Frank is mainly concerned are at the very core. Without at least some relationship conducive to growth, learning, and change, therapy does not occur (the attrition rates in some incomplete, unpublished, unwritten studies are truly remarkable). Telch, of course, has not taken the position that therapist and client characteristics are not important; however, some of the difficulties in establishing these factors as the essence of therapy may be explained by the truncated distribution of characteristics. For example, in our center there are undoubtedly differences in our caring and concern for our clients, our empathetic ability, our motivation to help clients. However, our people were selected for these characteristics. Even our master's-level interns were selected on the basis of characteristics such as personal warmth.

If we are dealing with the upper 5 percent of the population on these various traits, it is not surprising to find very weak empirical support for hypotheses in this area. The relationship between caring and understanding and therapeutic success may be very great, but it is obscured by our truncated distribution. There is intuitive clinical and empirical support for the proposition that the client needs to be in a relationship of some kind in order for positive therapeutic change to occur: every outcome study should provide attrition frequency data. This does not seem an unreasonable request. In the writer's opinion, editors should refuse publication unless attrition frequency data are provided. If this information becomes a standard inclusion in reporting of empirical studies, long-term benefits should be considerable.

Psychotherapy outcome studies are clearly relevant to the work of the counselor, although the nature of counselor's efforts makes it difficult even to ask the question Is my work of real value? Much of the counselor activity described in this chapter provides immediate feedback on the value of the help provided. Nevertheless, the short-term psychotherapy effects are difficult to evaluate, and the meta-analysis study reported by Smith and Glass (1977) and the follow-up study reported by Landman and Dawes (1982) lend support to the clinical-intuitive position of most clinical/counseling psychologists in college and university counseling centers—that is, that their work is of immense value to students, the academic community, and the public. The New York Times headline "Consensus Is Reached: Psychotherapy Works" is probably overstating the case presented by Smith and Glass; however, further meta-analysis studies are seen as providing a less defensive position and as methodology for further identification and refinement of the variables operating in therapeutic effectiveness.

## REFERENCES

Albert, G. 1968. Survey of college counseling facilities. Personal Guidance Journal, 46: 540-543.

American Psychiatric Association. 1980. Diagnostic and statistical manual of mental disorders. 3rd ed. Washington, D.C.: APA.

American Psychological Association. 1977. Standards for providers of psychological services. Rev. ed. Washington, D.C.: APA.

American Psychological Association, Committee on Standards for Providers of Psychological Services. 1981a. Specialty guidelines for the delivery of services by clinical psychologists. American Psychologist, 36: 639-651.

_____. 1981b. Specialty guidelines for the delivery of services by counseling psychologists. American Psychologist, 36: 652-663.

APA/CHAMPUS. 1981. Outpatient psychological providers manual. Washington, D.C.: APA.

Berrick, M. E. 1968. General, academic, and preprofessional counseling. In M. Siegel, ed., The counseling of college students: Function, practice, and technique. pp. 137-152. New York: Free Press.

Chassan, J. B. 1967. Research design in clinical psychology and psychiatry. New York: Appleton.

Clark, David D. 1970. Current emphasis and characteristics of counseling centers in universities of over 10,000 enrollment. In P. J. Gallagher and G. D. Demos, eds., The counseling center in higher education, pp. 32-44. Springfield, Ill.: Charles C. Thomas.

Dorken, H., and J. T. Webb. 1981. Licensed psychologists on the increase, 1974-1979. American Psychologist, 36: 1419-1426.

Frank, J. D. 1981. Reply to Telch. Journal of Consulting and Clinical Psychology, 49: 476-477.

_____. 1979. The present status of outcome studies. Journal of Consulting and Clinical Psychology, 47: 310-316.

Gallagher, P. J., and K. D. Weisbrod. 1970. The counseling psychologist. In P. J. Gallagher and G. D. Demos, eds., The counseling center in higher education. pp. 45-61. Springfield, Ill.: Charles C. Thomas.

Garfield, S. L. 1981. Psychotherapy: A 40-year appraisal. American Psychologist, 36, no. 2: 174-183.

Garfield, S. L., and A. E. Gergin, eds. 1978. Handbook of psychotherapy and behavior change: An empirical analysis. 2nd ed. New York: Wiley.

Gruen, R. E. 1968a. The counseling interview. In M. Siegal, ed., The counseling of college students: Function, practice, and technique. pp. 45-76. New York: Free Press.

_____. 1968b. Vocational and career counseling. In M. Siegel, ed., The counseling of college students: Function, practice, and technique. pp. 215-239. New York: Free Press.

Haase, R. F., et al. 1979. Effects of positive, negative and mixed occupational information on cognitive and affective complexity. Journal of Vocational Behavior, 15: 294-302.

Holland, J. L., T. M. Magoon, and A. R. Spokane. 1981. Counseling psychology: Career interventions, research, and theory. In M. R. Rosenzweig and L. W. Porter, eds., Annual Review of Psychology. XXXII, pp. 279–305. Palo Alto, Calif.: Annual Reviews.

Landman, J. T., and R. M. Dawes. 1982. Psychotherapy outcome, Smith and Glass' conclusions stand up under scrutiny. American Psychologist, 37, no. 5: 504–516.

Luborsky, L., B. Singer, and Lisa Luborsky. 1975. Comparative studies of psychotherapies: Is it true that "everybody has won and all must have prizes?" Archives of General Psychiatry, 32: 995–1008.

Mills, D. H., A. M. Wellner, and G. R. Vanden Bos. 1979. The national registry survey: The first comprehensive study of all licensed/certified psychologists. In C. A. Kiesler, N. A. Cummings, and G. R. Vanden Bos, eds., Psychology and national health insurance: A sourcebook. Washington, D.C.: American Psychological Association.

Patterson, C. H. 1966. Theories of counseling and psychotherapy. New York: Harper.

Pepinsky, H. B., and Pauline N. Pepinsky. 1954. Counseling theory and practice. New York: Ronald.

Phillips, J. S., and K. L. Bierman. 1981. Clinical psychology: Individual methods. In M. R. Rosenzweig and L. W. Porter, eds., Annual Review of Psychology. XXXII, pp. 405–438. Palo Alto, Calif.: Annual Reviews.

Prince, M. T., and D. L. Randolph. 1981. Differentiating roles of clinical and counseling psychology intern. Journal of Clinical Psychology, 37, no. 4: 892–896.

Rosenzweig, M. R., and L. W. Porter, eds. 1981. Annual Review of Psychology. XXXII. Palo Alto, Calif.: Annual Reviews.

Rychlak, J. F. 1968. A philosophy of science for personality theory. Boston: Houghton Mifflin.

Schontz, F. C. 1965. Research methods in personality. New York: Appleton.

Smith, M. L., and G. V. Glass. 1977. Meta-analysis of psychotherapy outcome studies. American Psychologist, 32: 752–760.

Telch, Michael J. 1981. The present status of outcome studies, a reply to Frank. Journal of Consulting and Clinical Psychology, 49: 472-475.

Turner, M. B. 1967. Philosophy and the science of behavior. New York: Appleton.

Tyler, L. E. 1969. The work of the counselor. 3rd ed. Englewood Cliffs, N.J.: Prentice-Hall.

Underwood, B. J. 1959. Psychological research. New York: Appleton.

# 3

# ORIGINS AND HISTORICAL DEVELOPMENT OF UNIVERSITY AND COLLEGE COUNSELING

## Stephen E. Berk

According to Persons (1973), in early America and during most of the nineteenth century, higher education served as a means to equip a genteel elite with a coherent body of humane knowledge based on the Judeo-Christian and classical traditions. The colleges were denominationally affiliated and run by clergymen. All students studied the same subjects, ranging from rhetoric, classical literature, history, and philosophy to mathematics and general science (natural philosophy). Theology, the "queen of the sciences," molded knowledge from each of these areas into a unified whole, giving meaning and coherence to all phenomena. While applied science was revolutionizing knowledge, the structure and purpose of the liberal arts curriculum remained closer in many respects to that of the Middle Ages than to university instruction as we know it today. Persons describes the rationale for the traditional curriculum thus: "All students should study the same subjects since the object was to train an educated gentry, not to prepare students for a vocation."

In paternalistically nurturing a gentry elite, the colleges were providing the leaders of a society assumed to have common values, stable institutions, and overall cultural continuity. The academic clergy were among the leading opinion makers, for Americans at large drew their values from middle-class Protestantism. However, as the technological revolution proceeded, it displaced this older America with a more urban, centralized, and secular society. Rapid change gradually loosened the bonds of continuity, and people became less sure of their values and beliefs.

Secularization and technological change also worked to revolutionize the socialization of knowledge. During the later nineteenth century the stabilizing, familial atmosphere of liberal arts colleges began to give way to the impersonal atmosphere of the modern university, just as genteel America gave way to the mass society. In 1862 the Morrill Act created 69 public land-grant colleges. By 1900 many had grown into prominent state universities. Unlike the private colleges of the Ivy League, which began denominational and became secular, these schools were secular from the outset. They immediately began to stress fields of applied science, which drew heavily on a rapidly advancing technology. Scientific agriculture, engineering, and the new social sciences had attained prominence in schools like the University of Wisconsin by the end of the century. The more technical approach to education entailed a heavy emphasis on research. New state universities, together with transformed Ivy League colleges, added graduate schools staffed by Ph.D.s, many of whom were trained in the scientific rigor of the German universities. Leading university presidents of the time, such as William Rainey Harper of Chicago and Daniel Coit Gilman of Johns Hopkins, began to build great scholarly "think tanks."

These developments ushered in an "intellectualistic impersonalism" (Cowley 1949). Concern for the whole person atrophied as professional specialization and the elective system gradually supplanted genteel character building. According to Cowley, students were initially jubilant at their liberation from overbearing supervision. Instructors ceased to be surrogate parents as regulation of students' activities and personal morals outside the classroom receded in priority. Student social clubs proliferated, as did athletic events and other extracurricular diversions.

But while loosening the bonds of in loco parentis, the public universities had greatly broadened their student populations. If the collegiate experience was not to degenerate into shallow technical training for the populace combined with a hedonistic student life and instructors preoccupied with research, it was necessary to reconsider the issue of student development. Men like Harper and Gilman were farsighted enough to recognize students' need for competent guidance and an environment conducive to maturation. By the turn of the century, most universities had reintroduced residential living and the concept of the faculty adviser or mentor.

These developments set the stage for the reformers of the Progressive Era (1900-17) to lay the groundwork of modern university counseling. The main aim of that period was to adapt society's institutions to the great changes wrought by technology. Progressive reformism pursued two ideals: a scientifically based reorganization of society in order to bring rational efficiency out of blind chaos, and a humanitarian crusade for social reform, reflected in the muckraking, Social Gospel, and settlement house movements

(Noble 1981). These twin purposes often interacted, and one can find evidence of both scientism and the humanitarian spirit in the early counseling movement.

In 1899 Harper was calling for "the scientific study of the student" (Cowley 1949). In an address at Brown University he called for appointment of a social scientist "to study in detail the man or woman to whom instruction is offered." He further recommended "a general diagnosis of each student" pertaining to intellect, personal character, "special capacities and tastes," and social attributes. Here was the basis of what would become the trait/factor approach to vocational counseling as developed at the University of Minnesota in the 1920s and 1930s.

The Progressive reformers had to grapple with the explosion of new careers and the entrance of hundreds of thousands of high school and college graduates into an expanding urban employment market. White-collar jobs grew exponentially, and a number of fields, such as medicine, law, and economics, became professionalized, with specific academic requirements taught in graduate and professional schools associated with the universities. The growth of new occupations, together with greater specialization and increased need for technical training, became a cause for confusion in career planning. The counseling movement, which moved onto the campuses by the 1920s, evolved initially out of efforts to develop a scientific approach to vocational guidance.

The prime mover of the early vocational guidance movement was Progressive reformer Frank Parsons, in whom the scientific and humanitarian approaches of the Progressive movement were well developed. A strong advocate of social justice, he became a leader in Boston's settlement house movement. Civic Service House was a pioneer effort at social work established to provide support services for the immigrant poor as they adapted to life in a new culture. As part of this effort Parsons ran an adult education program. Out of this program, called the Breadwinner's Institute, grew his idea of helping such workers to become upwardly mobile by providing them with vocational guidance (Davis 1969). He established the highly successful Boston Vocational Guidance Bureau and wrote a classic work, Choosing a Vocation. Published posthumously, this little book exerted formative influence on the counseling movement.

Like the Puritan Cotton Mather or the Yankee Ben Franklin, earlier American self-help apostles, Parsons was concerned with the individual's overall development, morally and intellectually as well as vocationally. A descendant of the genteel tradition, he sought to mold character and civic virtue. "You must be a good citizen," he counseled, "as well as a good worker."

> A man who exerts himself only to get his bread and
> butter, and not at all for the social good has not de-
> veloped much beyond the oyster stage of civilization,
> although in outward appearance he may resemble a
> human being. (Parsons 1967, p. 105)

Parsons wanted his students reform-minded, and therefore broadly
knowledgeable in fields such as history, government, politics, and
social ethics. He provided a lengthy book list, recommended visits
to legislature and court sessions, and gave instruction on how to
research important public issues.

Parsons also made use of the scientific approach. With the
rudimentary psychological tests available at the time, combined
with extensive interviewing, he appraised the aptitudes and interests of his clients. He also researched and classified a long list of
occupations and the kinds of skills associated with them. Clients
were encouraged to read extensively in the literature of careers
that interested them. Parsons' comprehensive, humane system
became the early model for the vocational guidance that became
standard practice in major universities (Williamson 1964). It was
given a tremendous boost during World War I when the army developed "a full-fledged personnel system" characterized by "detailed
occupational specifications, trade tests, rating scales, and the
group intelligence test to supplement the interview" (Paterson 1950).
Some of these army psychologists filtered into the universities
after the war and began to establish vocational guidance centers
based more and more on the use of psychometrics. At the same
time, industry was developing similar classificatory personnel
procedures based on testing, as well as the new field of employee
counseling.

The army personnel movement, industrial psychology, and
higher education first came together when Colonel Walter Dill
Scott became president of Northwestern University in 1920. Scott
had been a professor of psychology at Northwestern and had served
as director of the army's Committee on the Classification of Personnel. Following the armistice, he had founded a consulting firm
specializing in industrial personnel. Under Scott's presidency
Northwestern established the first "student personnel" services
department. The office had a vocational orientation, with an emphasis on testing (Shay 1963). Scott's approach, however, was
narrowly focused on classification and placement. Others who
rose to prominence during the 1930s, such as E. G. Williamson at
Minnesota and Esther Lloyd-Jones at Columbia University Teachers College, with its Deweyan humanism, continued Parsons' emphasis on the whole individual (Williamson 1939; Lloyd-Jones and
Smith 1938; 1954).

In 1909, three years after Choosing a Vocation came out, Clifford Beers, another genteel New Englander, published A Mind That Found Itself, an account of his own mental breakdown and journey back to health. The work was a typical piece of Progressive muckraking, written with the purpose of exposing sadism and gross incompetence in the institutional care of the mentally afflicted. The idea was to arouse public outrage and galvanize support for a reformist crusade. Representatives of the declining gentry class spearheaded much of the humanitarian and scientific reform of the late nineteenth century and the Progressive age (Mann 1954; Lasch 1965). They had the breadth of education and the tradition of public service, and they were the class most sensitive to the ill effects of social massification—that is, urban corruption and economic exploitation.

Beers, like Parsons, was a highly gifted Yankee, with a vision of applied science and humane reform to revolutionize a neglected but vital area of social service. Founding the National Committee for Mental Hygiene, he became one of the great philanthropic organizers as his idea blossomed into a far-flung congeries of funds and agencies to promote public mental health. Community clinics, child guidance clinics, and programs to work with juvenile delinquents, veterans, the retarded, the disabled, and other special-needs populations have been developed under the aegis of the National Committee (Winslow 1956; Woodward 1956; Ridenous 1956).

The mental hygiene movement raised public support for preventive programs geared to training personnel to ferret out trouble spots in a number of institutional settings. One such setting was the college or university. At the same time the vocational guidance movement was bringing about the development of counseling bureaus in the universities, the mental hygiene movement was establishing clinics associated with student health services. University counseling and university mental hygiene thus developed prior to World War II as two separate but loosely coordinated movements.

The formative years of the psychological and psychiatric professions set the stage for a sharp demarcation of function. Because psychiatry grew out of the medical profession, personality disorders and other emotional disturbances were viewed as illnesses, to be diagnosed and treated much as any physical disease. Popular and institutional acceptance of the medical model gave physicians primary authority in attending to persons with mental and emotional disorders. Psychology in its early years was wrapped up in experimental study of behavior. Insofar as psychologists paid attention to human personality characteristics or mental development, they did so by constructing instruments of measurement. The early clinical psychologists functioned largely as psychometrists. On the college campus in the 1930s, clinical psychologists became involved in therapeutic treatment by serving as technical aids to psychiatrists in the health service. They administered and interpreted tests of personality and mental ability. The psychologist's counseling function was pretty much restricted to educational and vocational matters, though it was also proper to attend to general matters of personality development and even to stimulate emotional catharsis when necessary. But all "serious" matters of "emotional maladjustment" were turned over to the psychiatrist (Williamson 1939). Psychotherapy, or what came later to be known as personal counseling, was then considered a medical matter, the proper domain of the psychiatrist.

This manner of viewing mental and emotional dysfunction, besides creating rigid, artificial boundaries of competence and authority, served to sabotage the preventive purpose of mental hygiene. The notion of disease and abnormality requiring a physician's treatment, even for relatively mild symptoms, so stigmatized the process of psychotherapy on campus and throughout society that only a small percentage of those needing it referred themselves for such counseling. Even in the 1970s, well after the breakdown of the medical model and the growth of therapy as a prime function of the counseling center, students resisted bringing personal problems there. Tryon (1980), reviewing literature published between 1960 and 1979 on students' perceptions of counseling center services, found a consistent belief that educational and vocational concerns are more appropriate than personal ones to discuss with counselors. The idea of revealing personal problems to a counselor inevitably causes resistance, and thoughts of being "sick" or "abnormal," remnants of the medical model, keep a great many from seeking help. Even though this stigma continues to handicap counseling centers as they seek maximum contact with student bodies, their role on campus has indeed changed appreciably since the 1930s.

In order for counseling on the campus and in the community to begin to have the broad reformist impact envisioned by Parsons or Beers, it had to abandon the medical model. Only thus could all the different purposes of counseling come together in a new, more positive, and broadly attractive human growth model. The mental hygiene movement was limited in what it could offer because of its chiefly medical orientation. But its broad outreach in the community and its use of psychotherapeutic techniques in a variety of institutional settings opened the door to new influences. The child guidance clinics that came into being in the larger cities during the 1920s became a fertile ground for the interchange of ideas and the development of different psychotherapeutic techniques. Although the Freudians were dominant in the psychiatric profession at the time, they underwent accelerating challenge from others with alternative points of view. The centers were staffed by clinical psychologists and social workers as well as psychiatrists, thus providing a cross-fertilization of disciplines. Moreover, in the 1930s, many in psychiatric circles had begun to break away from Freud's emphasis on case history and diagnosis. Neo-Freudians, while not discounting personal psychodynamics, were much more attuned to the present life of the patient and the impact of his or her social environment. Otto Rank and his American students, Jessie Taft and Frederick Allen, broke with the medical model by laying stress on the patient's key role in effecting psychotherapeutic change (Kirschenbaum 1979). This point of view influenced a young clinical psychologist named Carl Rogers, who began to make use of it while heading a child guidance center in Rochester, New York, during the late 1930s. In the next decade, at Ohio State University and the University of Chicago, Rogers developed it into his nondirective, client-centered therapy.

Rogers' influence in shaping the counseling profession and transforming its role in higher education cannot be overestimated. While most therapists today, Rogers included, would acknowledge the limitations of a wholly nondirective approach, it was not in technique that he had his most revolutionary effect. It was in his conception of the counseling process. He saw in it an encounter of two human beings on an equal plane in an I-Thou relationship. The counselor's total acceptance of the client, his or her empathic commitment to walk in the client's world, acts to stimulate self-esteem and growth. Feeling the warmth of "unconditional positive regard," the client gradually relinquishes his or her defenses: "Thus to an increasing degree he becomes himself . . . not a facade of conformity to others, not a cynical denial of all feelings, nor a front of intellectual rationality, but a living, breathing, feeling, fluctuating process—in short, he becomes a person" (Rogers 1961).

As controversial as Rogers became, he revolutionized the field of psychotherapy, drawing it away from the private preserve of a medical elite. His relational basis of therapeutic change, supported by a wealth of research compiled by his students, served to democratize the counseling movement. Psychotherapy as a basis for mental hygiene became the province of social workers, clinical psychologists, counseling psychologists, family counselors, and even paraprofessionals. The potential for broadening public awareness of and participation in mental hygiene programs greatly increased as psychotherapy began to substitute a positive human growth model for the negative, medical-based concept of mental illness and emotional maladjustment. Not until the late 1960s and early 1970s did the new growth model, nurtured in the campus-

based counterculture, come of age as a full-blown national movement. In order for this development to occur, certain preconditions
had to be established. First and foremost, the college counseling
center had to broaden its approach beyond preoccupation with educational and vocational guidance to include more than passing attention to the personal problems of students.

The highly influential Minnesota school, led by E. G. Williamson, continued to stress psychometrics and vocational guidance,
though it did make gradually increasing room for consideration of
personal problems. Williamson observed that students are practically motivated. They want tangible goals that will relate their
"educational experience" to forthcoming "adult responsibilities."
Developing his thought in the economics-saturated atmosphere of
the Great Depression, he saw counseling strategy as centering on
the student's occupational goal and using it as a "motivating effect."
The idea was to deal first with the most pressing need by helping the
student "choose an achievable occupational goal . . . then the counselor may proceed to broaden the student's understanding of the
value of all phases of education as a means to this goal and also his
perception of other equally valid and satisfying values of education."
The counselor, in Williamson's formulation, played a rational, men-
toring role. Williamson emphasized the use of tests to "diagnose"
the student's aptitudes and interests. The counselor was to guide
the student in a direction consistent with optimum development in
all aspects of personality (Patterson 1980).

Whereas Rogers stressed the intuitive, personal, emotional
side of human development, Williamson accentuated its cognitive,
social, and rational aspects. He believed everyone should strive
for "the sovereignty of rationality" and for "enlightened self-
control." Those with a more psychotherapeutic orientation, he
thought, were apt to treat the individual in a social vacuum. The
self emerges, according to Williamson, only in the community.
Hence the counselor should encourage social responsibility while
discouraging all antisocial individuality.

Rogers' and Williamson's opposite viewpoints were not mutually exclusive. They simply represented the dialectical poles of
human nature. At various times in our culture, one or the other
mode of perception—the intuitive-affective or the rational-cognitive—
has been preeminent. Thus Rogers had his American precursors in
Emerson, Thoreau, and romanticism, while Williamson had his
forebears in Franklin, Jefferson, and the Enlightenment. Both perspectives exist simultaneously even while one may become dominant
in an individual, or periodically in a large-scale cultural movement.

Williamson and the Minnesota psychologists provided students
with useful information and role models for achieving effective inte-

gration with society. But their rationalism was of little help to the emotionally troubled student. Williamson recognized that counselors needed to pay attention to emotional concerns. Sometimes students needed catharsis or emotional support as a basis for consideration of practical matters. If, however, emotional difficulties became dominant, students were seen as in need of psychotherapy, a medical, not a counseling, matter.

Rogers challenged this notion that the emotional realm was the proper domain of the psychiatrist and not the university counselor. Under his leadership at the University of Chicago Counseling Center, clinical psychology on campus emerged from its preoccupation with psychometrics into the forefront of psychotherapy. The Rogerian approach enables clients to grow by gradually experiencing the full range and depth of their feelings. This emphasis on affective awareness provided a necessary balance to Williamson's rationalism. It also formed the basis of a new personal growth conception of psychotherapy that would gradually supplant the medical model.

Super (1955), in tracing the development of counseling psychology out of vocational guidance, gave Rogers credit for introducing psychotherapy into counseling and thereby making vocational counselors "more aware of the unity of personality, of the fact that one counsels people rather than problems." In addition, he pointed to the major difference between the new counseling psychology, which formally emerged about 1950, and the older clinical psychology:

> Counseling psychology concerns itself with hygiology, with the normalities even of abnormal persons, with locating and developing personal and social resources and adaptive tendencies so that the individual can be assisted in making more effective use of them. (p. 5)

Clinical psychology had traditionally concentrated its attention on hospital settings and the diagnosis of pathology. Super suggested that such preoccupation may have been "a serious error," and that clinical psychologists would have done better to have established their field as one "more independent of psychiatric tradition. . . ." Where the hygiological, growth, or developmental model became the special province of counseling psychologists, its influence also strongly affected persons in the clinical field, in which Rogers had had his training. Counseling psychologists moved into a number of institutional settings, most notably the universities, where since the late 1950s they have come to represent the majority of practitioners.

The overriding trend since 1954, when counseling psychology became a recognized profession with its own journal, has been away from preoccupation with vocational guidance and toward a broad, developmental form of "personal" counseling. At Minnesota, where the vocational guidance point of view was chiefly developed, one could observe broadening influence in the late 1940s. By that time the Student Counseling Bureau was cooperating with the Student Health Services in a well-defined mental hygiene program (Hinckley 1949; Berdie 1949; Fenlason 1949). It involved a partnership of three professional fields: clinical psychologist, psychiatrist, and psychiatric social worker. Of the three, only the psychologist worked in the Counseling Bureau. Functions of the three offices were fairly sharply defined, with the psychiatrist playing the prime therapeutic role, the psychologist doing the testing, and the social worker mobilizing community resources.

But overlap did occur, most notably in the therapeutic area. The psychologist in particular went well beyond the function of "testing technician." His or her role commonly involved diagnosis of personal problems and the application of preventive therapy in order that serious emotional conflicts would not develop. Many of the clients in whom counselors discovered personal problems had presented themselves only for vocational guidance. Psychologist counselors helped these students through such difficulties by "providing expressive situations" in which students could reveal their "motivations and conflicts." A study by Williamson and Bordin recorded "969 social, personal, and emotional problems . . . discovered by psychological counselors." Of these cases, only 53 were given psychiatric referrals (Berdie 1949). From such evidence it is reasonable to conclude that clinical psychologists working in the Counseling Bureau at the University of Minnesota in the late 1940s had moved well beyond their earlier role of psychometrist and vocational counselor.

During the next decade counselors gradually moved toward a more personal/developmental and less educational/vocational model. The client-centered approach had become so popular with counselors as to constitute a new orthodoxy. But many influential practitioners did not go all the way with nondirective counseling.

Gilbert Wrenn, educational psychologist at the University of Minnesota, advocated an eclectic approach. In his popular 1951 text on student personnel work, Wrenn cited the utility of Rogerian counseling in "holding up a mirror in which the student can see the meaning and significance of his deep-seated feelings." Rogerians, however, had objected to counselors' diagnosing their student clients because they feared such an objective procedure might hinder the empathic relationship (Tyler 1969). But Wrenn, like his Minnesota colleagues, upheld diagnosis as "the process of arriving at a specific and penetrating understanding of the student's characteristics within the context of his life pattern." As such it was a broader and more dynamic concept than simply extrapolating personality from test scores or labeling in accordance with a medical model. To buttress his eclecticism, Wrenn mentioned the work of the eclectic theorist Frederick Thorne. Thorne, who was both psychiatrist and clinical psychologist, systematized an assortment of directive and nondirective techniques for implementation in the context of an interview (Patterson 1980).

Since the early 1950s counseling psychologists on campus have experimented with a great variety of new therapies and techniques as they have increasingly come to view themselves as therapists and developmental counselors. Research has shown that since then counselors have gradually come to see helping clients' "adjustment to self and others," or personal counseling, as their most appropriate role. Thrush's early research (1957) detected significant movement away from vocational counseling and toward problems of personal adjustment at one university. But Warman's more comprehensive study (1961) found a persistence of "vocational choice" as primary, with personal "adjustment" issues making a strong showing. Kohlan's study (1975) was an attempt, nearly 15 years later, to duplicate Warman's. In 19 of Warman's 21 counseling centers, Kohlan found a decisive move toward personal counseling. He attributed this shift to "changes in theoretical orientation or training of counselors and . . . increased specialization and separation of student services such as financial aid, career planning and placement, and reading and study skills development." Cass and Lindeman (1978) verify this new specializing trend as they note the proliferation of career centers and study skills training centers.

Even though counselors have moved toward consensus about their therapeutic roles, students have not moved with them. Beginning with Warman's, studies have shown that students continue to regard educational and vocational counseling as more appropriate than the exploration of personal issues at campus counseling centers (Tyler 1969; Tryon 1980). Tryon cites student reluctance to appear "weak" or "disturbed" and concern about the confidentiality of their remarks as reasons given for not bringing personal problems to a counselor. She further notes that while students who know about the counseling center generally express favorable views of it, most are unaware of its existence. As the era of fiscal retrenchment came to public education in the early 1970s, publicizing their service and reaching a larger constituency became a leading priority of counseling centers. Much self-criticism, generated during the student activism of the 1960s, spilled over into the post-

Vietnam War period. Many leading centers and influential counselors began to critically reappraise counseling's purpose on campus.

Some intimations of new directions appeared in the fall of 1967, when a number of midwestern liberal arts colleges held a symposium on counseling at Albion College. They invited well-known counseling directors and theorists, such as E. S. Bordin, C. H. Patterson, and Sidney Jourard, to address them on important issues of the moment. Bordin placed alienation among college youth within a developmental framework, treating it as a positive aspect of "identity formation." Recognizing the value of alienation as a basis for positive institutional change, the counselor should guide students through this developmental crisis by helping them to find meaningful values and social involvement. Patterson also called for openness to change, accentuating the relational aspects of counseling. He advocated more attention to group therapy as a means of attending to the powerful affiliative needs of young college adults. Instructing his colleagues to take the complaints of the young seriously, he criticized the persistence of an authoritarian medical model that worked to discourage students from coming for counseling.

Jourard's talk further expounded the evils of counseling based on unequal relationships. He too blasted the medical model, invoking an alternative concept of counselor and student as "fellow seekers." In the terms of existential humanism, a theoretical perspective that has been growing in popularity among counseling psychologists since the 1950s, Jourard called for totally honest communication. Deep self-disclosure implies risk taking, which generates anxiety, but genuine human growth can occur only as both counselor and client shed their protective armor and really experience one another. This cry for authenticity and spontaneity in human relationships pervaded the counterculture of the late 1960s. With exposure to Regerian concepts, many counselors were sensitive to such crosscurrents. Much of the inner, personal-growth side of the youth movement was reflected in the popularity of practical humanistic psychology—Gestalt therapy, sensitivity training, and encounter groups—on campus.

The movement of many youths together with their psychologist gurus—toward self-exploration and self-awareness, consciousness expansion, and cultivated naturalness—came in reaction against the dominant consumer culture. The atrocities of Vietnam belied the humane and egalitarian pretensions of American society and pushed the young toward cultural alienation and a quest for alternatives. Nonconformity became popular, as college students reacted against being molded, processed, and standardized by the corporate state. As the "human potential" movement exerted influence on many counselors and students, a powerful reaction ensued against the traditional therapy of "adjustment."

Much of the intense criticism of the medical model that occurred during the late 1960s and early 1970s was in reality a large-scale repudiation of adjustment psychology. A true medical model was no longer standard practice in university counseling centers. Rogerian influence, as well as the impact of behavioral and other nonmedical schools of thought, upon the counseling profession had done much to break down psychiatric diagnosis and labeling. But adjustment psychology, which had been influential since the 1930s, retained a crucial aspect of the medical model. It viewed the client's environment as the normative standard and the troubled client as "maladjusted." Therapy consisted in helping the client "adjust" to the environment. Humanistic psychoanalyst Erich Fromm had attacked the notion that conformity to social norms is any indicator of personal psychic health back in the mid-1950s. He saw in it a tyrannical authoritarianism denying the person any right to his or her feelings if they are at odds with those of the multitudes: "I must not ask whether I am right or wrong, but whether I am adjusted, whether I am not 'peculiar,' not different . . . virtue is to be adjusted and to be like the rest. Vice, to be different. Often this is expressed in psychiatric terms, where 'virtuous' means being healthy and 'evil' means neurotic." Fromm suggested that a society that makes such demands for "robot conformity" is the locus of illness, not the "maladjusted" individual, who is fighting to retain his or her personhood (Fromm 1955).

While young men and women of the 1950s did not as a rule adopt this perspective, many in the Vietnam era did. Terms like "adjustment" and "maladjustment" were replaced by "authenticity," "awareness," "self-actualization," and other existential humanistic concepts. The ensuing personal-growth movement has recently been criticized for its exploitative and narcissistic excesses (Lasch 1979), but it has generally served as an important avenue to self-discovery. Counselors have used its psychology effectively to help students out of introjected conformity and toward an active search for their own deepest feelings and life-enhancing values. Even though the counterculture faded and students returned in the 1970s to preoccupation with practical matters, the personal-growth movement has continued in somewhat less flamboyant form. Existential humanism grows more influential among counselors as the medical model continues in retreat.

If the inner, or personal-growth, side of the social ferment of the late 1960s influenced the process of counseling, its outer, activist side addressed counseling's structure and program. Warnath (1973) criticized counselors for assuming the role of private practitioners, immersed in individual therapy and isolated from the university community. Having fought so long to become therapists, counselors had taken over the old psychiatric role. The health service psychiatrist had in turn become a technical consultant. Matters demanding specialized medical knowledge, such as use of psychoactive drugs or hospitalization, were now prime psychiatric involvements (Panagon 1970). Becoming primarily individual therapists, counselors had cut themselves off from a reformist perspective aimed at the campus as a whole.

In the 1960s and 1970s many universities and colleges broadened their student constituencies by reaching out to ethnic minorities, including ghetto blacks and Hispanics. These nontraditional populations expressed cultural values and patterns of communication different from those of the white middle class. Brown (1973) contended that the very process of counseling as verbal dialogue in an office is a middle-class practice wholly alien to blacks of the inner city. He further suggested that blacks generally shunned the counseling center as another form of "going to see the Man." Calling for more minority counselors, who could fully empathize with and provide role models for members of these new student populations, Brown also advocated more outreach and training of peer counselors.

Female students and counselors affected by the ideas of the women's movement expressed similar concerns. Berry (1973) inveighed against traditional-minded counselors of both genders who function as "gatekeepers for a sexist society." She called upon counselors to support and participate in the new campus programs and groups devoted to women's issues.

This notion of the counselor as an agent of social change generated much debate in the early 1970s. Some directors expressed concern about the potential divisiveness inherent in accepting the confrontational ideas of the more militant representatives of special populations (Grummon 1970; Ewing 1973). Gilbert (1973) observed: "Change based on social or political biases is not necessarily psychology." For their part, the activists objected to the remedial quality of existing counseling practices. Their preventive program called for humanizing the university, which they saw as a key instigator of student troubles. Here was the exact reverse of adjustment psychology. Stubbins (1973) saw most individual counseling as serving the institution. The student is invariably encouraged to assume responsibility for the problem, whereas the university's self-serving rigidity is usually at fault. Halleck (1973) pointed out that students frequently do not trust counselors because they fear betrayal of their confidences to the administration, faculty, or outside authorities. In short, they tend to view the counselor as an institutional functionary with a role of insuring stability. Harmon (1973) also alluded to student distrust of counselors, pointing out that counselor ambiguity, generally deemed essential to the counseling process, often betrayed an avoidance of commitment and involvement.

Counselors espousing social activism were able to gain a hearing for their views, partly because counseling centers were facing ever tighter budgets and were under pressure to expand their student constituency. Recent years have seen the rise of a new concept of the counseling center, based more on outreach and developmental skills training than on individual remedial therapy. While the latter still predominates, steady nationwide growth is occurring in outreach programs and counselor consultative work throughout the university (Domke, Winkelpleck, and Westefeld 1980).

The "human development" center, specializing in preventive outreach, first came into being in the late 1960s. Colorado State University inaugurated a program for comprehensive student development including a "crisis projection team" to study potential campus crises; stress conferences, featuring student "encounters" with faculty; and campuswide developmental skills training (Morrill, Ivey, and Oetting 1968). "A mental health problem," in this model, was defined as "anything that interferes with the use of the developmental tasks that are available in the environment for personal growth." The role of the counselor was thus broadened to include the human growth of all students, rather than merely the remediation of those with particular difficulties. Larson (1973) and Southworth and Slovin (1973) describe developmental outreach programs at South Dakota State University and the University of Massachusetts. Women's centers, human sexuality forums, career development programs, drug dependency centers, and ethnic minorities programs are a few of the activities sponsored by such counseling centers. Chaney and Hurst (1980) describe an approach to outreach through the ombudsman program at the University of Texas. The ombudsman compiles complaints from all sectors of the university community. Such a program can become the basis for effective counseling outreach programs in areas of real student concern.

One development since the 1960s that has contributed greatly to the developmental outreach movement is "the cognitive revolution" (Blocher 1980). The rise of cognitive behavior therapy has spurred a rapprochement between behaviorism and humanism among counselors. A rich eclecticism has developed as humanistically inclined psychologists lead cognitive behavioral groups and workshops in assertive training, coping skills, stress management, and self-hypnosis. The common theme is taking control over one's life in a time of institutional instability and increased personal stress.

As campus counseling centers slowly broaden their services, they frequently encounter an ironic resistance from administration. Lombardi (1974) notes the double bind in which counseling centers become trapped when they try to expand the scope of their campus involvement, partly to justify their continued existence in a period of fiscal conservatism. They hesitate to increase counselors' outreach time and thereby decrease their caseloads, since accountability formulas base funding on the size of individual caseloads. Lombardi's survey of 128 counseling centers showed that such constraints hampered the rate at which they could move toward a more preventive emphasis.

Yet, on the whole, counseling has continued to make steady progress in expanding the breadth and sophistication of its operations. Such positive change comes about largely because of the profession's remarkable openness to self-criticism. From the nondirective movement to the radical criticism of social activists and the current prominence of cognitive and developmental methods, counseling has continually absorbed new ideas while not abandoning valid old ones. Broad-based vocational counseling in the Williamson tradition, for example, persists in today's counseling centers as they work in conjunction with the more strictly functional career centers.

Critical self-evaluation today centers on the trend toward greater involvement with the university community as a whole. While important strides have been made in this direction, Aubrey (1980) finds counselors as therapists acting the role of "highly trained technocrats, mechanically adept at their craft but desperately wanting in perspective and purpose." Reminiscent of Parsons' catholicity, Aubrey's concept is of a new interchange between counseling and related academic disciplines, including political science, developmental and social psychology, learning theory, and linguistics. He calls for counselors to cease being mere technicians and to "seek purpose and perspective through greater use of the social and behavioral sciences, the humanities and philosophy."

In quite another vein, but also related to the present outthrust of counseling centers, developmental theorist Robert Havighurst (1980) asks counselors to pay attention to demographic trends that are bringing a huge new population of students with limited cognitive development into the universities. Such individuals are "passive learners" who "avoid intellectually complex tasks." "They need a simple and easily perceived structure in their curriculum," says Havighurst, and learning through "concrete, direct experience."

Counseling thus continues to grow and adapt to a changing environment. Having spent some time acquiring strong therapeutic skills, the profession on campus is now looking outward, toward the broad social amelioration envisioned by its Progressive originators. A thoroughly preventive psychology for the student body at large has had to await the maturation of a counseling profession completely devoted to a growth model.

Something over a century ago, when American higher education left a gap in student nurture with the rise of the secular university, the counseling movement arose to meet the challenge. Counselors shouldered the difficult task of adapting their service to a world of constant change where value consensus was fast evaporating. As they have grown on campus, counseling centers have retained high sensitivity to changing student needs. Such capacity to grow and adapt in a shifting environment indicates a vitality that should keep counseling with us for years to come. An ongoing quandary that counseling centers face, however, is how to approach today's pluralism of value systems. This question can likely be addressed only on the most personal level, as counselor and client or counselor and group work it out in self-disclosing dialogue.

## REFERENCES

Aubrey, R. F. 1980. Technology and the science of behavior. Personnel and Guidance Journal, 59: 318-327.

Beers, C. W. 1956. A mind that found itself. New York: Doubleday and Company.

Berdie, R. F. 1949. The clinical psychologist and mental hygiene counseling. In E. G. Williamson, ed., Trends in student personnel work. Minneapolis: University of Minnesota Press.

Berry, J. B. 1973. Women: Clients and counselors. In C. F. Warnath, ed., New directions for college counselors. San Francisco: Jossey-Bass.

Blocher, D. H. 1980. Some implications of recent research in social and developmental psychology for counseling practice. Personnel and Guidance Journal, 59: 334-336.

Borden, E. S. 1949. Counseling points of view, non-directive and others. In E. G. Williamson, ed., Trends in student personnel work. Minneapolis: University of Minnesota Press.

Bordin, E. S. 1968. The role of alienation in identity formation of college students. In J. C. Heston and W. B. Frick, eds.,

Counseling for the liberal arts campus. Yellow Springs, Ohio: The Antioch Press.

Brown, R. A. 1973. Counseling blacks: Abstraction and reality. In C. F. Warnath, ed., New directions for college counselors. San Francisco: Jossey-Bass.

Cass, W. A., and J. C. Lindeman. 1978. Trends and directions. In B. M. Schoenberg, ed., A handbook and guide for the college and university counseling center. Westport, Conn.: Greenwood Press.

Chaney, A. C. B., and J. C. Hurst. 1980. The applicability and benefits of a community mental health outreach model for campus ombudsman programs. Journal of College Student Personnel, 21: 215-222.

Cowley, W. H. 1964. Reflections of a troublesome but hopeful Rip Van Winkle. Journal of College Student Personnel, 5: 66-73.

_____. 1949. Some history and a venture in prophecy. In E. G. Williamson, ed., Trends in student personnel work. Minneapolis: University of Minnesota Press.

Davis, H. V. 1969. Frank Parsons: Prophet, innovator, counselor. Carbondale, Ill.: Southern Illinois University Press.

Domke, J. A., J. M. Winkelpleck, and J. Westefeld. 1980. Consultation and outreach: Implementation at a university counseling center. Journal of College Student Personnel, 21: 211-214.

Ewing, T. N. 1973. Perspectives on counseling 1938-1973. In Twenty-second annual conference of university and college counseling directors: Proceedings. Morgantown, W. Va.: West Virginia University.

Fenlason, A. 1949. The social workers in the mental hygiene clinic. In E. G. Williamson, ed., Trends in student personnel work. Minneapolis: University of Minnesota Press.

Fromm, E. 1955. The sane society. Greenwich, Conn.: Fawcett Books.

Gilbert, W. M. 1973. Perspectives in counseling and psychotherapy 1940-1973. In Twenty-second annual conference of university and college counseling center directors: Proceedings. Morgantown, W. Va.: West Virginia University.

Grummon, D. L. 1970. An overview: Prospect in retrospect. Twenty-fifth anniversary share-in, proceedings. East Lansing: Counseling Center, Michigan State University.

Halleck, S. 1973. Counselor as double agent. In C. F. Warnath, ed., New directions for college counselors. San Francisco: Jossey-Bass.

Harmon, L. W. 1973. Credibility and the counseling center. In C. F. Warnath, ed., New directions for college counselors. San Francisco: Jossey-Bass.

Havighurst, R. J. 1980. Social and developmental psychology: Trends influencing the future of counseling. Personnel and Guidance Journal, 59: 328-333.

Hedahl, B. 1978. The professionalization of change agents: Growth and development of counseling centers as institutions. In B. M. Schoenberg, ed., A handbook and guide for the college and university counseling center. Westport, Conn.: Greenwood Press.

Hinckley, R. G. 1949. A social movement and a clinical service. In E. G. Williamson, ed., Trends in student personnel work. Minneapolis: University of Minnesota Press.

Jourard, S. 1968. Counseling for the healthy personality. In J. C. Heston and W. B. Frick, eds., Counseling for the liberal arts campus. Yellow Springs, Ohio: Antioch Press.

Kirschenbaum, H. 1979. On becoming Carl Rogers. New York: Delta Books.

Kohlan, R. G. 1975. Problems appropriate for discussion in counseling centers: 15 years later. Journal of Counseling Psychology, 22: 560-562.

Larson, C. E. 1973. A student development center. In C. F. Warnath, ed., New directions for college counselors. San Francisco: Jossey-Bass.

Lasch, C. 1979. The culture of narcissism. New York: Warner Books.

_____. 1965. The new radicalism in America: 1889-1963. New York: Random House.

Lloyd-Jones, E. M., and M. R. Smith. 1954. Student personnel work as deeper teaching. New York: Harper and Brothers.

_____. 1938. A student personnel program for higher education. New York: McGraw-Hill.

Lombardi, J. S. 1974. The college counseling center and preventive mental health activities. Journal of College Student Personnel, 15: 435-437.

Mann, A. 1954. Yankee reformers in an urban age. New York: Harper and Row.

Morrill, W. H., A. E. Ivey, and E. R. Oetting. 1968. The college counseling center: A center for student development. In J. C. Heston and W. B. Frick, eds., Counseling for the liberal arts campus. Yellow Springs, Ohio: Antioch Press.

Noble, D. W. 1981. The Progressive mind 1890-1917. Minneapolis: Burgess Publishing Company.

Panagon, N. 1970. The psychiatric consultant. In P. J. Gallagher and G. D. Demos, eds., The counseling center in higher education. Springfield, Ill.: Charles C. Thomas.

Parsons, F. 1967. Choosing a vocation. Repr. New York: Agathon Press.

Paterson, D. G. 1950. The genesis of modern guidance. In A. H. Brayfield, ed., Readings in modern methods in counseling. New York: Appleton-Century-Crofts.

Patterson, C. H. 1980. Theories of counseling and psychotherapy. New York: Harper and Row.

_____. 1968. Some problems and proposals in college counseling. In J. C. Heston and W. B. Frick, eds., Counseling for the liberal arts campus. Yellow Springs, Ohio: Antioch Press.

Persons, S. 1973. The decline of American gentility. New York: Columbia University Press.

Ridenous, N. 1956. The mental hygiene movement 1948 through 1952. In C. W. Beers, A mind that found itself. New York: Doubleday and Company.

Rogers, C. R. 1961. On becoming a person. Boston: Houghton Mifflin.

Shay, J. E. 1963. Needed: A new professional name. Journal of College Student Personnel, 4: 236–239.

Southworth, J. A., and T. Slovin. 1973. Outreach programming: Campus community psychology in action. In C. F. Warnath, ed., New directions for college counselors. San Francisco: Jossey-Bass.

Stubbins, J. 1973. Social context of counseling. In C. F. Warnath, ed., New directions for college counselors. San Francisco: Jossey-Bass.

Super, D. 1955. Transition: From vocational guidance to counseling psychology. Journal of Counseling Psychology, 2: 3–8.

Thrush, R. S. 1957. An agency in transition: The case study of a counseling center. Journal of Counseling Psychology, 4: 183–190.

Tryon, G. S. 1980. A review of the literature concerning perceptions of and preferences for counseling center services. Journal of College Student Personnel, 21: 304–310.

Tyler, L. E. 1969. The work of the counselor. Englewood Cliffs, N.J.: Prentice-Hall.

Warman, R. E. 1961. The counseling role of college and university counseling center. Journal of Counseling Psychology, 8: 231–237.

Warnath, C. F. 1973. Whom does the counselor serve? In C. F. Warnath, ed., New directions for college counselors. San Francisco: Jossey-Bass.

Williamson, E. G. 1964. Student personnel work in future years. Journal of College Student Personnel, 5: 194–201.

_____. 1939. How to counsel students. New York: McGraw-Hill.

Wrenn, C. G. 1951. Student personnel work in college, with emphasis on counseling and group experiences. New York: Ronald Press.

Winslow, C. E. A. 1956. The mental hygiene movement and its founder. In C. W. Beers, A mind that found itself. New York: Doubleday and Company.

Woodward, L. E. 1956. The mental hygiene movement—more recent developments. In C. W. Beers, A mind that found itself. New York: Doubleday and Company.

# 4

# EVALUATION OF SERVICES
## *Edmund Bourne*

INTRODUCTION

In recent years the mental health field has experienced an increasing and persistent demand for accountability. Pressures for evaluation of human services programs have arisen from government funding agencies, state legislatures, third-party insurers, professional organizations, and consumers. In California community mental health programs have been required since 1971 to evaluate their services in order to continue receiving state support. On a national scale, funding permitting hospitals to provide Medicaid coverage to clients has been contingent on agencies' reporting in detail their utilization of resources. More recently the Community Mental Health Amendments of 1975 specified that community services programs must set aside at least 2 percent of their funds for evaluation.

The context of this growing demand for accountability arises from two conflicting circumstances: social concern for increasing the availability of mental health services to a wider range of the population—an initiative that began with the community mental health movement of the 1960s, and dwindling economic resources and opportunities for state or federal support—a condition more particularly associated with the anti-inflationary consciousness of the 1970s. In such an atmosphere no self-conscious mental health delivery service—including university counseling programs—can avoid confronting the issue of evaluation.

The purpose of this chapter is to examine program evaluation in the context of the university counseling center. In the course of the discussion, a number of specific recommendations and proposals for actually implementing an evaluation study will be presented. The chapter is divided into three major sections. First, some general considerations about program evaluation in regard to its basic principles and strategies will be discussed. It is suggested here that an evaluation study may be oriented toward any (or all) of three major aspects of a program: relevance, impact, or effectiveness. The second section of the chapter focuses on literature pertinent to the evaluation of the university counseling center, emphasizing counseling outcome studies and methods of assessing outcome in particular. In the third section, which forms the body of this chapter, a number of issues and problems connected with evaluating the relevance, impact, and effectiveness of university counseling services are discussed in some detail. Five alternative methods of measuring counseling effectiveness are considered.

## MENTAL HEALTH PROGRAM EVALUATION: GENERAL CONSIDERATIONS

Since the early 1970s the field of program evaluation and its accompanying literature has grown vast, leading to two journals (Evaluation and Journal of Evaluation Research), a major handbook (Guttentag and Struening 1975), an annual review (Glass 1976), numerous books and monographs (such as Coursey 1977; Hargreaves, Attkisson, and Sorensen 1977; Neigher, Hammer, and Landsberg 1977), and hundreds of articles, only some of which are listed in this chapter's "References" section. The introductory discussion of evaluation that follows is thus quite condensed and sketchy, though it attempts to distill the perspectives of several different authors (Coursey 1977; Keenan 1975; McIntyre, Attkisson, and Keller 1977; Mitchell 1977; Riecken 1977; Tarial 1977).

For purposes of this chapter, "evaluation" may be defined generally as the measurement of desirable or undesirable consequences of an action designed to achieve some objective, where "action" refers to a conscious attempt to change individual or group behavior or a psychological state in a valued direction (Riecken 1977). More specifically, "program evaluation" is understood as the determination of the relative worth of a program—or parts of a program—by examining some salient aspects of it. A "program," in turn, may be defined as any enterprise involving a staff that engages in certain specified activities (such as counseling) with certain types of clients (such as children, students, or parents), using certain resources (time, money, materials) to achieve some specified goal (such as improved client adjustment, reduced recidivism, prevention of mental health problems).

In undertaking any program evaluation, at least five basic questions can be raised (Stockdill 1976):

1. Why is the evaluation to be conducted?

2. What is to be evaluated? Alternatively, what are the objectives of the program that are to be evaluated?

3. What are the standards or criteria that provide the basis for a favorable or unfavorable evaluation of program objectives?

4. How are these criteria to be operationalized?

5. What is involved in actually implementing the evaluation?

Each of these questions is briefly considered below.

Why Conduct a Program Evaluation?

There are both external and internal reasons for undertaking an evaluation. Externally, the initial impetus for a program evaluation is almost always accountability to persons or parties outside of the program. These groups typically request accountability in somewhat different forms. While federal and state funding sources want information on program effectiveness—both literally as well as in the sense of cost-effectiveness—consumers may be more concerned with, for example, the availability or confidentiality of services. In any case, a preliminary question for any evaluation involves for whom it is to be.

Usually the evaluation provides as much useful information for administrators and staff within the program as it does for external agencies and groups. Hence a second major purpose of an evaluation is to provide internal feedback. In addition to global feedback on program effectiveness, administrators want to know which components of a human services program need to be emphasized, curtailed, or otherwise changed. And of course program staff, the counselors, would like feedback on the effectiveness of their various activities. It is important, then, to keep in mind that program evaluation not only serves to meet demands for accountability but also is a major basis for constructive self-scrutiny and program change.

What Is to Be Evaluated?

Before undertaking an evaluation, it is important for there to be a clear consensus among program staff about which of the pro-

gram's components are in need of examination. Usually this entails a formal and agreed-upon statement of the programs' goals
and objectives, and—perhaps more difficult but no less important—
agreement on the relative priority of these goals. Precise delinea-
tion and attainment of consensus on specific objectives is of course
a matter that needs to be handled by each individual program. Still,
it is possible here to indicate several basic dimensions in terms of
which more specific program objectives might be formulated. These
may be seen as fundamental issues that any human services program
might address in attempting to conduct an evaluation.

### Relevance or Significance

How relevant or significant are the program's activities and
functions to its recipients? In short, to what extent is the program
genuinely meeting the needs of those it seeks to serve? Immediately this leads to another question: What are the needs of the service
population?

### Impact

What proportion of the intended service population does the
program actually reach? More particularly, to what extent does
the program reach minority groups whose financial, cultural, or
logistic disadvantages relative to the population at large may make
them relatively more in need of program services? How available
is the program on a daily basis? Do its hours of operation discriminate against the working segment of its population?

### Effectiveness

In essence, this is the basic matter of "How well are we doing?" A program's effectiveness is the most fundamental and frequently addressed issue in its overall evaluation. It is necessary,
of course, that its staff first define and agree upon what constitutes
"effectiveness," an issue dealt with below. The meaning of effectiveness may vary depending upon who is asking and according to
what is the expected duration of "effects." In the context of evaluating a counseling program, this question leads to the complex array
of issues associated with the assessment of counseling outcome.

### By What Standards or Criteria Is a Program to Be Evaluated?

Briefly, this question can be answered in a general way for
each of the substantive dimensions of evaluation described above.

## Relevance

If a program is to be relevant or significant to its recipients, it is they who need to define the standards of relevance. Just how the consumer's view of a program's relevance might be assessed is taken up later in the chapter.

## Impact

The adequacy of a program's impact depends upon whether it is actually serving as many people as are expected to need its services within its total reference population. Adequate impact also implies that the proportions of minority clients seen by the program are comparable with the proportions of these groups in the reference population.

## Effectiveness

In the case of human services programs, the usual standard of effectiveness is whether the program assists its recipients in ameliorating the problems or concerns they bring to it. An alternative, usually supplementary standard involves the assessment of the competence and performance of individual staff members by administrators, outside observers, or consumers. Other standards of effectiveness, particularly in regard to "indirect" or consultative program services, are possible but usually difficult to operationalize.

## How Are Evaluation Standards to Be Operationalized?

Again, this question can be considered in a general way with respect to each of the major dimensions of evaluation.

## Relevance (Significance)

Appraising a program's significance from the standpoint of its recipients is frequently referred to in the evaluation literature as "needs assessment." Numerous approaches have been tried (see Mitchell 1977; Siegel, Attkisson, and Cohn 1977; Warheit, Bell, and Schwab 1974). There are briefer, cheaper, and less rigorous methods, such as interviewing several key informants from a total population or having a series of open forums or workshops enabling population members to vocalize their needs. On the other hand, an extensive sampling of a population's needs may be obtained from a systematic survey. This is a procedure compelling for its scientific accuracy, though perhaps likely to miss some of the information that could be obtained from the briefer approaches. Thus, an optimal needs assessment strategy would incorporate both types of approach.

## Impact

Evaluating impact depends upon first obtaining demographic statistics for a program's total service population. Total population characteristics can then be compared with the program's statistics on service utilization by clients of different age, sex, race, ethnic group, and occupation.

## Effectiveness

Three questions are of central importance in implementing an evaluation of the effectiveness of a mental health or counseling program.

1. Whose perspective on effectiveness is to be considered? The counselor's? The client's? Significant others of the client?

2. Once appropriate perspectives have been decided upon, what type of instrument(s) is to be chosen to measure counseling outcome? Global ratings versus concrete behavioral indices? Should measurement procedures involve self-administered questionnaires or utilize interviews? If multiple perspectives are employed, should different instruments or different versions of the same instrument be used?

3. What is the most adequate design for an evaluation study of counseling outcome? Experimental—involving control groups that receive no treatment or an alternative treatment? Quasi-experimental—involving a pre-post comparison of client status? If the latter, should the "post" comparison involve both termination and follow-up assessments? Instead of an experimental or quasi-experimental design, might a behavioral, goal attainment design be more desirable?

This enumeration of methodological issues in outcome assessment could easily be extended. A more detailed consideration of many of them may be found in "Dimensions of Program Evaluation for the University Counseling Center."

How Is the Evaluation to Be Implemented?

Twain (1975) considers several major problems associated with conducting an evaluation study. Ideally, these problems should be taken into account before implementation, rather than in midflight:

1. How will budgeting and funding for the research program be ensured?

2. How will the research staff be selected and trained?

3. What are the structural arrangements for "quality control" (for instance, how to maintain reliability and care in ratings)?

4. How will research and program integrity be maintained (for instance, how to guarantee that staff do not change their interventions during the project)?

5. How will the ongoing collaboration with staff, administrators, and others involved in the program be maintained?

6. What are the specifics of data collection and analysis? This will include developing a client identification system, coding the data, handling missing data, developing algorithms for classification and data conversion, preparing computer input, and developing backup tapes and files (Sells 1975).

EVALUATION STUDIES OF UNIVERSITY
COUNSELING PROGRAMS: A REVIEW OF
THE LITERATURE

Before indicating more detailed guidelines and proposals for program evaluation in the context of the university counseling center, it seems pertinent to describe previous evaluative efforts in this area. There are very few published reports of attempts to evaluate the effectiveness of university counseling services. A survey over 1970–78 of the two journals in which such studies are likely to appear—Journal of College Student Personnel and Journal of Counseling Psychology—yields only six (Hurst and Weigel 1968; Harman 1971; Thompson and Miller 1973; Thompson and Wise 1976; Davidshofer, Borman, and Weigel 1977; Rosen and Zytowski 1977). This is in marked contrast with the number of program evaluations of community mental health centers (see, for example, Ciarlo and Reihman 1977; Truitt and Binner 1969), as well as needs assessment studies of college students on various campuses (see "Dimensions of Program Evaluation," subsection "Which Segments of the University Student Population Are to Be Assessed?").

Three different instruments have been used to ascertain effectiveness of university counseling services. All three have involved only one of several possible perspectives* on effective-

---

*Major perspectives in evaluating the effectiveness of counseling include that of the counselor, the client, significant others of the client, and an impartial outside observer.

ness, albeit an important one, that of students. Each is described below.

## The Counseling Services Assessment Blank

The Counseling Services Assessment Blank (CSAB; see Hurst, Weigel, Thatcher, and Nyman 1969), used by Harman (1971), obtains a retrospective appraisal by the student of the counseling experience. The student is first requested to classify his/her presenting problem by area (educational, vocational, personal) and then by type or cause (lack of information about self, lack of information about environment, conflict with self, conflict with other, or lack of skills). Then the client is asked to make a global rating of how much improvement he/she obtained in the relevant problem area and type(s) on a five-point scale ranging from 1 ("not at all") to 5 ("very much"). Additional scales involve global satisfaction ratings of the client's individual and/or group counselors. These scales consist of five points ranging from 1 ("extremely negative") to 5 ("extremely positive").

Harman used the CSAB to assess the counseling service at the University of Kentucky. A total of 181 clients completed and returned the instrument at an unspecified time after termination of counseling. The clients' mean rating of their improvement over the five problem-type scales was 3.45 (out of 5). On the scales evaluating their satisfaction with individual or group counselors or experiences, the mean was 4.16. Davidshofer, Borman, and Weigel (1977) reported similar findings in a one-month follow-up study of Colorado State University students, the problem-type scales averaging around 3.2 and the global satisfaction scales around 4.0.

These results led investigators to conclude that most students favorably endorsed their counseling experiences. However, an equally plausible explanation is that the very global nature of the CSAB made it vulnerable to the so-called "hello-goodbye" effect (Hathaway 1948), in which a respondent gives an overly favorable assessment because he/she feels it is more socially acceptable, wishes to please or gain the approval of the investigator, or to rationalize his/her investment in the experience that is assessed. Global satisfaction ratings, in fact, say very little about whether a client has actually experienced an amelioration of personal problems (Ciarlo and Reihman 1977; Krumboltz 1966; Littlepage 1976). The data mentioned above corroborate this point, for client ratings on scales measuring growth respective to particular problem types were lower than their global ratings of satisfaction with services.

The lesson to be learned from studies employing the CSAB is that a probably more valid assessment of counseling effectiveness can be obtained if clients rate outcome with respect to specific target problems or problem areas.

### The "Target-Complaint" Technique

Rosen and Zytowski (1977) attempted to improve on the CSAB by employing a procedure that in essence did just that. Adopting the "target-complaint" technique of Battle, Imber, Hoehn-Saric, Stone, Nash, and Frank (1966), they asked clients, at the time of their first interview, to write down in their own words the problems for which they were seeking help, and to rate their severity. At a certain interval after termination of counseling, each client's problem statement was transferred to a follow-up questionnaire, and he/she was asked to rerate each problem's severity. The degree of change in rated severity of the problem was taken as an index of the impact of treatment. The procedure permitted clients to indicate no change or negative change, as well as positive change. Its chief advantage was that it didn't ask the client simply to make a retrospective appraisal of the counseling experience, but to rate his/her present status at two separate times (intake and follow-up), thus reducing the potential of a hello-goodbye effect.

Out of 460 follow-up questionnaires mailed to former clients of the counseling center at the State University of Iowa, 263 (57 percent) were returned. There was no set period of follow-up, since questionnaires were mailed at the end of the academic year to clients who had used the counseling service at various times. In contrast with the unqualifiedly favorable endorsements obtained by CSAB, Rosen and Zytowski found that 23 percent of the clients reported either no change or deterioration at the time of follow-up. Another 46 percent reported positive changes of 1-3 on a total scale of 10, while 27 percent indicated a change in the 4-6 range and only 4 percent in the 7-9 range.

This approach would seem to provide a more realistic, less inflated appraisal of counseling outcome. Rosen and Zytowski's study represents a clear improvement over those using the CSAB. Nonetheless, the study has several noteworthy methodological difficulties:

1. Because there was no control group (who received no counseling), it is difficult to know to what extent clients' ratings of improvement (or lack thereof) were actually attributable to counseling versus outside experiences in the time between termination and follow-up.

2. The follow-up ratings were not comparable because the period between termination and follow-up varied for different clients.

3. It is unclear whether the authors obtained change scores by simply subtracting intake ratings from follow-up ratings for individualized problems. Change scores obtained in this way are likely to be inflated due to statistical regression of intake scores toward their mean (see Nunnally 1975).

All in all, Rosen and Zytowski's use of ratings on individualized problems is commendable, and approximates to a major type of procedure gaining increasing recognition in evaluation research—goal attainment scaling. In terms of utility, their approach may be considered by some to be cumbersome because it requires a unique, individualized assessment for each client. A more convenient alternative—the use of a standardized list of target problems and problem areas—has been developed by Andrew Thompson and associates.

Thompson-Wise Questionnaire

On the basis of previous exploratory work attempting to identify both types of problems presented and changes reported as a result of counseling (Thompson and Zimmerman 1969; Miller and Thompson 1973; Thompson and Miller 1973), Thompson and Wise (1976) developed a closed-end, rating-scale type of questionnaire representing 17 types of problem areas, each containing 3-10 more specific questions. These 17 areas fall, roughly, into four broad categories: grades, vocational concerns, individual relationships, and feelings regarding self. Clients were asked to respond to all items in terms of the degree of change that had occurred since they had come for counseling, an interval ranging from 2 to 12 months (note that the questionnaire was used only for follow-up). Most interesting, there was also a question, for each problem area, asking the client to rate the effect of counseling on such change. Thus the investigators relied on clients themselves to assess the degree to which any positive/negative personal changes experienced were due specifically to counseling rather than to other factors in their lives. To the author's knowledge, this is the only study in the entire psychotherapy/counseling outcome literature that has attempted to have clients rate the effect of counseling on outcome.

An example of questions pertaining to one of the 17 problem areas, work-study skills, is presented below:

At the time you came to counseling, were you concerned about your work-study skills?

Definitely _____ Somewhat _____ Not Sure _____ Not Really _____
Definitely Not _____

Are you concerned about your work-study skills now?
Definitely _____ Somewhat _____ Not Sure _____ Not Really _____
Definitely Not _____

How have your work-study skills changed?
Much Better _____ Better _____ Not Sure _____ Worse _____
Much Worse _____

Effect of counseling?
None _____ Not Sure _____ Definitely Some _____ Quite a Bit _____

Other items on the questionnaire asked the client to indicate who was responsible for the termination of counseling (self, counselor, or both) and to make a global rating of his/her satisfaction with the overall counseling experience.

As is apparent from the above section of the questionnaire, it was designed primarily to obtain a single, retrospective follow-up evaluation from clients. Approximately 210 (62 percent) of a sample of 372 clients using the University of Oregon counseling center returned the questionnaire at follow-up. On the average, clients indicated small to significant positive changes in their functioning in most areas. Only one item—asking whether the client was more/less close to quitting school than before attaining his/her goals—elicited negative change. The smallest average positive change was observed for the four items dealing with work-study skills listed above.

In addition to determining mean change scores, the investigators used a multivariate procedure—discriminant function analysis*—to ascertain which items in which problem areas (including items on the effect of counseling) were most predictive of client's overall satisfaction with counseling. Rather than merely measuring client satisfaction with counseling, the intent was to explain which specific types of personal change, as well as the effect of counseling on such changes, were most highly associated with client satisfaction. In order of their relative predictive weight, items that best predicted client satisfaction were level of ability to express emotion†, level of maturity and/or capacity for independent

---

*Discriminant function analysis is a method of selecting from a large number of variables the optimum combination for predicting a particular criterion, in this instance client satisfaction.

†Emotional expressiveness may have attained the highest predictive weight because the sample consisted of 60 percent women.

action, effect of counseling on level of satisfaction with close other-sex friends, effect of counseling on changes in living situation, effect of counseling on acceptance of feelings of uncertainty about vocational future. On the other hand, items dealing with changes in grades, work-study skills, and vocational-educational choice were least predictive of client satisfaction. Out of nine items that did predict client satisfaction, six were "effect of counseling" items. In short, as might be expected, clients' assessments of the effect of counseling on particular changes were more predictive of their overall satisfaction with counseling than were the changes themselves.

Thompson and Wise's attempt to separate the effect of counseling from other life-situation factors, in terms of long-term outcome, is ingenious. Its credibility, however, depends upon the extent to which one is willing to believe clients can genuinely discriminate which factors are instrumental to their own growth or change. (Certainly, if anyone can, they are in the best position to do so.) A methodological limitation of the study was its failure to make pre-post comparisons of clients' views of their status. As with any solely retrospective study of counseling outcome, we do not know to what extent clients were inflating their estimates of change either to please the investigators (who were counselors themselves) or to justify their participation and involvement in counseling. The investigators were aware of this, and are planning to develop an intake and follow-up questionnaire for a forthcoming study. That they had clients assess themselves in terms of individualized problem areas gives their instrument an advantage over the more global CSAB. That the instrument involved a standard format, on the other hand, gives it an advantage in terms of convenience over the individualized target-complaint approach used by Rosen and Zytowski.

## DIMENSIONS OF PROGRAM EVALUATION FOR THE UNIVERSITY COUNSELING CENTER

### Needs Assessment

An important component of the evaluation of any program is the assessment of its significance or relevance to the population it is attempting to serve. In evaluation research this stage of appraisal is usually referred to as "needs assessment." It may be defined as follows:

(1) the application of a measuring tool or assortment of tools to a defined social area; and (2) the application

> of judgement to assess the significance of the informa-
> tion fathered in order to determine priorities for pro-
> gram planning and service development. (Blum 1974,
> p. 222)

Ideally, a needs assessment study is conducted before a program
develops its major goals and objectives. In practice, such studies
often provide crucial feedback contributing to a program's ongoing
reshaping of its major priorities and goals.

A number of approaches to needs assessment have been tried,
varying in comprehensiveness, complexity, cost, the length of time
involved, amount of information received, and relative utility. Bell,
Warheit, and Schwab (1977, p. 98) describe at least four methods:
key informant approach (securing information from a small number
of people having an intimate knowledge of a population), community
forum approach (open-forum meetings where community leaders
and members can freely voice their opinions and feelings about the
community's needs) social indicators approach (inferences about
community needs drawn from descriptive statistics found in public
records and reports), and the survey approach (systematic collection of information from a sample of the population of people living
in a community).

Among needs assessment studies conducted specifically for
college campus populations, the key informant, community forum,
and (especially) survey approaches have typically been used. While
the key informant and community forum approaches are cheap, ex-
pedient methods for obtaining information about student needs, the
campus survey approach remains the best available means for doing
rigorous, scientifically valid needs assessment research. Its rep-
resentativeness with respect to the population at issue is unquestionably greater. On the other hand, student responses to survey questionnaires or telephone interviews may neglect to mention certain
types of needs that can come out only in a public forum. Thus, the
optimal strategy for a comprehensive needs assessment would employ both community forum and survey approaches.

As would be expected, published needs assessment studies
conducted on large college campuses are almost exclusively of the
survey type (Fullerton and Potkay 1973; Carney and Barak 1976;
Gallagher and Scheuring 1978; Friedlander 1978; Westbrook, Moyares,
and Roberts 1978; Webster and Fretz 1978; Carney, Savitz, and
Weiskott 1979; Buck 1979). Variations among these studies with respect to populations assessed, procedures and methodologies employed, and types of needs assessed raise several key questions that
need to be addressed before making specific proposals for conducting a needs assessment survey. Three central questions are discussed below.

## Which Segments of the University Student
## Population Are to Be Assessed?

Clearly, the structure of needs for entering freshmen is going to differ from that of upper classmen (Carney et al. 1979; Buck, 1979), as it will for male versus female students (Gallagher and Scheuring 1978; King et al. 1973; Carney et al. 1979), black versus Caucasian versus Asian-American students (Westbrook et al. 1978; Carney et al. 1979; Webster and Fretz 1978), students with high versus low grade-point averages (Carney et al. 1979), and single versus married students (Carney et al. 1979). A comprehensive study, then, would preferably draw a large, stratified sample of students from all four undergraduate classes as well as from grauate students, and have numbers in groups varying by sex, race, ethnic group, grade-point average, marital status, employment status (and whatever other demographic variables are of interest) large enough to permit systematic comparisons.

## How Are Students to Be Solicited?

Once a sampling procedure has been developed, it is important to consider how the survey is to be distributed to students. In university surveys, three different methods of contacting students have been tried. In his survey of student needs at California State University at Fullerton, Buck mailed out survey questionnaires toward the end of the academic year. Approximately 32 percent of the questionnaires were returned, a not untypical result for surveys conducted by mail. This necessitated a detailed comparison of subjects in the total mail-out sample with those in the respondent sample to ascertain any systematic differences.

Using the more laborious telephone interview technique, Carney et al. (1979) obtained replies from close to 100 percent of their original random sample at Ohio State University. However, the final sample was much smaller than Buck's (801 versus 3,410).

Another procedure, difficult to implement without cooperation from both university administration and faculty, is to administer questionnaires to the total student population in the classroom setting. This type of contact procedure is commonly used in teacher evaluations, and it was successfully employed in a 1972 statewide survey of counseling and advice services in California. Short of surveying an entire student population in the classroom, the preferred strategy, in the author's opinion, is to mail questionnaires, then have sufficient follow-up to improve response rates beyond 50 percent. This involves sending nonrespondents not only reminder postcards but also a second copy of the survey questionnaire.

## Needs Assessment of What?

This is the most crucial question in designing a needs assessment study. Previous campus surveys suggest three possibilities:

1. Campuswide student services (see Carney and Barak 1976; Friedlander 1978; Carney et al. 1979; Buck 1979)

2. Major student concerns (see Fullerton and Potkay 1973; Carney and Barak 1976; Westbrook, Moyares, and Roberts 1978)

3. Sources of help (see Webster and Fretz 1978).

Each of these is considered below.

Campuswide Student Services. One would first like to know which university services (such as counseling center, student health, financial aid office) are deemed most important by students. Immediately the question arises: "Important in what sense?" If you ask students to rate how important a service is in general, they will tell you how important it is for their college to offer such a service—not how important such a service is to them personally, and even less how likely it is that they will actually use the service. In an excellent study done by Friedlander (1978) at UCLA, it was found that students' ratings of the importance or significance of services was not related to their ratings of the likelihood of actually using such services.

For example, while 43 percent of the students said it was "absolutely essential" or "very important" for UCLA to provide services that would enable students to "become better able to listen to, respect, and value others' feelings, intuitions, and preferences," approximately 13 percent said "I plan to use UCLA Student Services to assist me to become better able to listen to, respect, and value others' feelings, intuitions, and preferences." This type of finding was observed repeatedly across a variety of student services. It indicates the importance of separating the question of students' perceptions of how important a service is from their feelings about how personally relevant it is or how likely it is they would use it. A thorough needs assessment study ought to ask all three of these questions independently.

There are, furthermore, two other questions that can provide essential information on student needs. Before asking a student how important he/she feels a particular student service is, it is important to find out how much, if anything, he/she knows about the service. Also, it is important to ascertain whether the student has used the service in the past, and, if so, whether he/she found it helpful. Surely the perceived relevance of a service depends upon the amount of information a student has about such a service and any actual experience the student has had with the service.

In sum, it is suggested that a comprehensive needs assessment study ask at least the following four questions in regard to each student service program:

1. How much would you say you know about _____?
   A lot _____ Some _____ Little _____ Nothing _____

2. Have you used the services offered by _____?
   No _____ Yes _____
   If yes, indicate how helpful these services were to you.
   Very _____ Somewhat _____ Slightly _____ Not helpful _____

3. How important is it that this university offers _____?
   Absolutely essential _____ Very important _____ Moderately important _____ Slightly important _____ Not important _____

4. How likely is it that you will participate in or utilize
   _____ in the next year or so?
   Definitely _____ Probably _____ Possibly _____ Only
   slightly possible _____ Definitely not _____

Each type of question provides a distinct and useful type of information pertinent to needs assessment: general knowledge versus ignorance of the service, degree of utilization of the service, perceived importance of the service for the campus in general, and personal relevance of the service. It is only in the light of reviewing students' responses along all four dimensions that appropriate feedback for reformulating, extending, or curtailing particular student services can be obtained.

Student ratings of university service programs, although highly specific in terms of types of question asked, remain relatively global and unspecified in relation to the diversity and variety of existing student needs. Any university service program consists of numerous, more specific service functions that meet relatively specific student needs. For example, most counseling centers meet needs for vocational, educational, personal, and crisis-intervention counseling, as well as interpersonal communication and stress-reduction needs. A more "fine-grained" analysis of student needs, then, would break each basic service program down into its constituent functions.

If one follows the example set by Buck's (1979) study, one can describe upwards of 100 separate service functions, each of which can be rated with respect to general importance as well as personal relevance (in addition to knowledge and utilization).

Perhaps one of the reasons why Buck (1979) refrained from asking students all four of the questions suggested above is that it would have been too cumbersome for students to rate 85 service functions on four different dimensions. (One can imagine the response rate that would have been obtained had this been tried.) Thus, it is preferable to develop a survey format that acknowledges the need for sufficiently specific questions while recognizing the large number of service needs that might be assessed.

Certain features of Buck's report are worth noting. When ranked, students' ratings on 85 campus functions are rather cumbersome to follow, though they provide interesting comparisons for constituent services within a given program (for instance, counseling in regard to career goals ranked 16, personal counseling ranked 42, and group counseling ranked 78). Fortunately the functions were ordered into broader categories, and these categories were subsequently ranked. Buck found that academic advice and career planning/job placement services obtained the highest average ranks; testing and learning assistance were ranked around seventh or eighth; and counseling-related services ranked about tenth. These findings corroborate the results of other surveys of salient student concerns. In the late 1970s students appear to have been most concerned about problems relating to career selection and jobs (Carney and Barak 1976; Gallagher and Scheuring 1978), while problems with academic effectiveness, finances, and negotiating the university system constitute a second-ranked problem group for many students (Carney and Barak 1976; Fullerton and Potkay 1973; Gallagher and Scheuring 1978).

Major Student Concerns. A second approach to student needs assessment is perhaps simpler, and definitely more direct. Instead of asking students about knowledge, utilization, importance, and relevance of various university services—a type of information undoubtedly useful for purposes of program planning and setting of goals—one simply asks them what are their most pressing problems or concerns. Such a survey of salient student concerns is a useful adjunct, but probably ought not to replace ratings of services (or service functions). If anything, one would like to know whether services that students deem most important or personally relevant are those that meet what they indicate are their greatest concerns and problems. A mismatch would raise questions about the validity of both types of surveys.

Several studies of student concerns have appeared in the literature. Fullerton and Potkay (1973) went around the campus at Western Illinois University, asking students what they felt were the three greatest pressures on them personally. Grades, money,

and social problems were—in that order. Of all students inter-
viewed, 91 percent felt counseling services ought to be offered,
though only 63 percent (56 percent of the males, 73 percent of the
females) said they would actually use those services. When asked
by the interviewers what gave them the most help in dealing with
their pressures, the students replied in terms of "self," "friends,"
and "escape"—in that order.

Westbrook et al. (1978) administered a target-problem questionnaire to white and black students at the University of Maryland.
The instrument contained 20 problem areas (with examples of specific problems) that respondents were asked to rate according to
how frequently they needed assistance. It turned out that black students' three greatest concerns were academic difficulties, campus
facilities, and negotiating the university system, whereas for white
students they were negotiating the university system, campus facilities, and setting career goals.

Carney and Barak (1976) used a questionnaire with prescribed
problem areas to ascertain what Ohio State University students considered to be their most pressing personal problems. Choice of
major and career headed the list by a wide margin, followed by
negotiating the university system, financial problems, and scholastic concerns. (The authors did not indicate the proportions of males
versus females or of blacks versus whites in their sample.)

An evaluation of salient concerns of students would be pertinent as an additional, auxiliary source of needs-assessment information useful to administrators at the university level as well as
within specific programs. Comparisons might be made by sex,
class, race, ethnic group, and academic variables if a large enough
sample could be obtained. For this type of survey in particular,
personal interviews, conducted by trained interviewers, would be
superior to self-report questionnaires (probably more so than in
the case of surveying attitudes toward university services and service functions).

A proposed list of major student concern areas, extending
those developed in the above three studies, is presented below.

## SOME PRINCIPAL CONCERNS OF STUDENTS

1. Negotiating the university "system"
2. Academic pressure
3. Reading/study skills
   a. Need to better allocate time for study
   b. Deficiency in basic academic skills (reading, writing,
      computation)
4. Selecting an appropriate major

5. Deciding whether to stay in or leave school
6. Choosing and/or planning an appropriate career
   a. Undecided or conflict among alternatives
   b. In need of information on jobs and how to obtain them
7. Problem with current employment
8. Financial problems
9. Personal relationships—concern about relationship with
   a. Parents
   b. Boyfriend or girlfriend
   c. Spouse
   d. Teacher
   e. Same-sex friend(s)
   f. Roommate(s)
   g. Employer
   h. Other
10. Problem with meeting people—loneliness, isolation
11. Sexual issues
12. Personal identity
    a. Improve self-image, self-confidence
    b. Deciding "who I am"—setting value priorities; choosing lifestyle
    c. Accepting limitations
13. Body image
14. Time utilization
15. Symptomatic complaints (anxiety, depression, insomnia, headaches)
16. Alcohol or drug problem
17. Social stereotypes problem
18. Existential problem (concern about meaning of life, religious concerns, concerns about death).

Sources of Help. A final method for assessing the significance of university services—and especially counseling services—is to ask students whom they would seek out first if they had a pressing problem or concern they needed to talk about. The basic question is how willing students are to utilize university counseling services in times of personal stress, confusion over academic requirements, or vocational indecision, as opposed to consulting their parents, friends, relatives, or teachers.

Of course, who is sought first depends upon the type of problem (Gelso and Karl 1974) and on who is doing the seeking. For example, students genuinely wanting personal insight seek counseling psychologists rather than guidance counselors (Getsinger and Garfield 1976). On the other hand, low-income and foreign families view psychological services as potentially shameful and threatening (Leavitt, Cary, and Swartz 1971). Ethnic identification, particularly in the case of Asian-American students, affects preferred help sources (Sue and Sue 1974; Sue and Kirk 1975). A study by Webster and Fretz (1978) found slight (though nonsignificant) differences in preferred sources of help among blacks, Asian-Americans, and whites. Their sample was divided between students with vocational-educational concerns and those with personal concerns. The vocational-educational group ranked the university counseling center third after parents and teachers as a source of help, while the group with personal concerns ranked it fifth after parents, friends, relatives, or a physician. It should be noted that more than half of the sample consisted of black and Asian-American students.

Data on students' preferred resources for obtaining assistance would provide information useful in assessing the impact of counseling services on the student population, a topic taken up below. A list of help sources that might be surveyed includes the following:

Who would you go to first if you needed to talk to someone about a difficult personal concern or problem?*

1. Parent
2. Friend
3. Teacher
4. University counseling center
5. Relative
6. Clergyman/minister
7. Private counselor or therapist
8. Local community mental health center
9. Person on a crisis "hotline"
10. Physician
11. Other _____

## Impact

A program's impact has to do with the degree to which it reaches its intended service population. Impact is dependent upon two factors: the quality of communication between the agency and its consumers, and the availability of agency services. A program's quality of communication and availability result in its degree of utilization, which is simply another way of describing its "impact."

A comprehensive evaluation of any counseling service will seek to assess that service's visibility to students and its availability, and must compare existing rates of utilization (including utilization by minority groups, in particular) with expected frequencies of utilization for the campus population at large. Each of these issues is considered below.

---

*More forms of the list might be developed to control for potential bias due to "order effects."

## Communication

Are the university's catalog description of the counseling center, counseling center flyers, and articles on the counseling center that appear in campus newspapers sufficient to inform students of its existence, nature, and scope? Probably the most direct way of answering this question is through the first of the four questions in the needs assessment survey proposed above—How much do you know about the university's counseling services?

## Availability

A briefer and frequently used strategy is to ask clients at intake how they learned about the counseling center. This would provide some idea of the range and scope of dissemination of information about the center on campus. Nonetheless, the needs assessment survey approach would provide more systematic information and indicate the knowledgeability of the entire student body about counseling services.

## Utilization

The first question here concerns whether a counseling center is reaching as many students on campus as might be expected to be in need of counseling. Of course this depends upon what criteria are used to define "in need of counseling." To come for counseling because of logistic problems in negotiating university curriculum regulations is quite different from coming because of disruptive emotional difficulties.

Considering those clients in the latter category, there are numerous shades of severity of disturbance. As a result, counselors, teachers, parents, administrators, and friends of a student typically disagree on the degree of severity of problems necessary for him/her to be "in need of counseling." Blaine, McArthur et al. (1961) argue that among the average student population, roughly 10-15 percent may be expected to experience emotional disturbance severe enough to result in clinical symptoms and disturbed life efficiency. (It is unclear, though, what more detailed criteria these investigators used to define "disturbed life efficiency.") There is no easy way to assess whether a counseling center is reaching a high proportion of students with moderate to severe emotional problems, short of conducting an extensive survey of the mental health status of the campus at large—an initiative that is likely to be infeasible for practical, financial, and ethical reasons.

In spite of these limitations, one valuable piece of information on students' willingness to use counseling services can be obtained from the needs assessment survey. Given a high frequency of response to such a survey, it would be possible to compare the number and types of students who say they plan to use the counseling center with actual utilization statistics.

A second basic question concerns utilization by minority groups. Is the counseling center reaching these groups to the same extent it is reaching American/Caucasian students? A very direct estimate can be made by comparing race/ethnic group proportions within the total student population with the proportions of black, Mexican-American, Asian-American, Native American, and other minority students within the total number of clients seen at the counseling center in a single year.

More detailed information could be obtained from a needs assessment survey. The relevant questions here would be the following:

1. What proportions of minority groups (relative to the majority "Anglo" group) know about the various services of the counseling center?

2. What proportions of minority groups have used the center's services? What proportions have found them helpful?

3. What proportions of minority groups intend to make use of the services?

4. What proportions of minority groups regard the counseling center as important to have on the campus?

Given the results of previous studies, which show a tendency among black and Asian-American students to regard counseling as a sign of weakness (Sue and Sue 1974; Sue and Kirk 1975), it might be expected that proportions of these groups planning to utilize a counseling center would be lower than in the case of the majority Anglo group. In any case, responses to such questions would provide essential feedback necessary to determine how and to what extent a counseling center should strive to improve its communication and public relations with minority groups.


Effectiveness

Appraising a program's effectiveness is the most central and frequently raised issue in its evaluation. In the case of human service delivery programs, it is also easily the most complex. In considering how to optimally evaluate the effectiveness of a counseling

program, it is necessary to define what is meant by "effectiveness."
This in turn requires confronting a veritable thicket of methodologi-
cal issues associated with the assessment of counseling (or psycho-
therapy) outcome (see, for example, Cartwright, Kirtner, and
Fiske 1963; Kiesler 1966; Fiske, Hunt, Luborsky, Orne, Parloff,
Reisler, and Tuma 1970; Mintz 1972; Green, Gleser, Stone, and
Seifert 1975; Garfield, Prager, and Bergin 1971; Fiske 1971;
Nunnally 1975; Cowan 1978).

## What Are the Criteria of "Effectiveness"?

If counseling is "effective," we ordinarily expect it to ameliorate the problems/concerns a client initially presents. As a first
approximation, then, what is meant by "counseling effectiveness"
is some kind of improvement in the client's status. However, it is
quite possible, alternatively, to define effectiveness in terms of the
assessed competence of the counselor over many clients, without
reference to the outcome of any particular client. For the purposes
of this discussion, it will be important to keep these two senses of
"effectiveness" separate: effectiveness as successful client outcome
and effectiveness as counselor competence. The former represents
by far the more common criterion used in evaluating human service
program effectiveness, yet it is not necessarily the only criterion.
In fact, both criteria will be recommended in the discussion to
follow.

## What Is Meant by "Successful" Client Outcome?

Taking up the question of how counseling outcome might be
assessed, a first critical issue concerns what we mean in saying
counseling has "succeeded" with any particular client. This raises
the rather involved question of what we mean by "mental health" or
"improvement in mental health status" (see, for example, Jahoda
1958). Among the numerous possible definitions of "success" we
might include the following: global client satisfaction with counseling, alleviation of symptoms (anxiety, phobias, depression, insomnia), increase in self-esteem and/or self-reliance, improved
social adaptation, better handling of personal relationships, reduc-
tion of problem behaviors (such as drug dependency, delinquent or
violent acts), or any combination or all of the above. To enter into
a discussion of the normative and philosophical issues connected
with the definition of "mental health" is well beyond the scope of
this chapter. It must suffice here merely to note that defining what
is meant by "successful outcome" is one of the first issues that
must be addressed in evaluating a counseling program's effectiveness.

Success from Whose Standpoint?

A third critical issue in counseling outcome evaluation concerns the question of success from whose standpoint. The client's? The counselor's? The client's friend? An outside observer? If the client reports that he/she has been "satisfied," has "benefited," or even has "improved" as a result of counseling, is this sufficient to indicate that counseling has been effective?

Few would disagree with the idea that the client's view of how he/she has done in a counseling program is one way to evaluate the effectiveness of that program. But there are numerous reasons why it would be misleading to regard the client's view as the only criterion of effectiveness. Cowan (1978, p. 794) makes this point in a compelling way:

> When a program ends, the client is asked in 20 different guises: "So, how'd you do?" His (or her) response, also in 20 ways, is "Terrific!"
> Problem No. 1: Did he respond that way because that's how he feels or because he senses that's what the experimenter (or counselor) wants to hear? (the so-called "hello-goodbye" effect)
> Problem No. 2: If he truly does feel better, is it due to the program or because he has just struck oil or won the Irish Sweepstakes?
> Problem No. 3: If indeed he does feel better because of the program, has his behavior changed in a parallel way?

The first problem concerns the fact that the average questionnaire respondent, when asked to evaluate a program or treatment in which he/she has been involved, is likely to respond in a socially desirable manner, unless he/she has had an unequivocally bad time, either out of a desire to be a good respondent (to be pleasing) or out of the need to rationalize the time and personal investment involved in committing himself/herself to the program. It is especially difficult to avoid this "hello-goodbye effect" (Hathaway 1948) in evaluating counseling outcome. In order to have sought counseling in the first place, the client must have felt abnormally low or troubled. By the time of leaving the program, he/she is almost bound to feel better, regardless of what happens during counseling. Most likely, though, this feeling better will be attributed to the counseling. The second problem, on the other hand, refers to the difficulty of separating the effect of counseling itself from other ongoing factors in the client's life during counseling, in terms of being a potential determinant of outcome.

The traditional solution to both of these problems is to have a randomly assigned control group of clients who have comparable difficulties but do not receive counseling during the period that an experimental group does. Thus all variables except the counseling "treatment" itself can be held constant and the effect of counseling alone may be observed. Unfortunately, ethical and (even more so) practical considerations often preclude using this type of control group. Furthermore, even when it is possible to have a "no-treatment" control group, it is questionable whether this constitutes an adequate control because "no treatment" is really a special form of treatment with its own special effects on outcome variables. (More will be said about this later.) The third problem pertains to the fact that a client may feel better without acting better. Such a circumstance argues for the use of behavioral instead of global criteria of counseling effectiveness, an issue that will be taken up shortly.

The point of these considerations is to suggest that the client's view of counseling outcome represents only one perspective—one that is certainly necessary but not sufficient because of several inherent limitations. An adequate assessment of client outcome needs to take into account the perspectives of other persons in a position to judge (Fiske et al. 1970; Garfield et al. 1971). After the client, the individual probably in the best position to assess the client's relative improvement is the counselor. In fact there is a running argument in the literature on counseling outcome whether the counselor is in a better position to judge (Auerbach and Luborsky 1968; Luborsky, Chandler, Auerbach, Cohen, and Bachrach 1971). Those favoring the counselor's judgment argue that professional training and capacity for detached observation place him/her in the best position to appraise whether the client has genuinely improved. Those favoring the client's judgment argue that clients alone are privy to their most intimate and internal reactions, and certainly are most apt to be available to observe their public reactions. Those favoring the client's perspective also argue that the counselor usually is not around to observe the effect of counseling beyond termination.

More crucially, the counselor, professional training notwithstanding, can be just as biased as the client in evaluating counseling effectiveness, especially to the degree that his/her self-esteem, personal acceptance by the client, reputation among peers, or job is at stake. To take both the client's and the counselor's perspective into account in assessing counseling outcome is better than either one alone—yet both may be biased.

For this reason numerous investigators have proposed that an adequate outcome study must include a third perspective, that of significant others of the client (see Cartwright et al. 1963; Katz 1977).

Some have even suggested that this perspective is most likely to be valid in appraising counseling outcome. However, there are several difficulties. First, the client's near relatives or friends may be just as likely as the client to provide socially desirable responses concerning the client's outcome, particularly if they want to believe the client has improved (or if they want to stay friends with the client). Second, significant others' criteria of successful outcome may be quite different and in disagreement with those of the client or counselor (for instance, for the client, "success" means reduced anxiety and depression, while for the client's spouse, "success" means reduced alcohol consumption or tendency to argue). Third, even if significant-other evaluations are mostly unbiased, the difficulty of tracking down these people, especially in studies employing follow-up assessments, often constitutes an obstacle to their inclusion.

Suppose, at any rate, it were possible to design a study of counseling outcome that incorporated the perspectives of client, counselor, and significant others of the client. Even more ideally, suppose the study somehow managed to control for potential sources of bias in each perspective. Would such an outcome study be home free? In the light of all previous studies that have attempted to do just this, the answer is an emphatic "no." The typical and notorious result of nearly all outcome studies employing multiple criteria of effectiveness from multiple perspectives is that these different perspectives disagree. Frequently the correlation between the client's and the therapist's ratings of outcome is zero or negative (Cartwright et al. 1963; Fiske et al. 1970; Garfield et al. 1971). The problem has been so persistent and frustrating that it has compelled some investigators to return to the use of only one perspective—most often that of the client (for instance, Thompson and Wise 1976). One has to question the meaning of a composite, multiperspective rating of +3 if it is composed of, say, a client's rating of +5, a spouse's rating of +1, and a counselor's rating of -3. Certainly, to the degree that ratings across perspectives agree, one may have confidence in the assessment of counseling outcome. The problem is that it is very difficult to obtain such agreement.

## Methods of Measuring Successful Outcome

In addition to the problem of divergence among perspectives on client outcome, there is the further problem of divergence among different methods or instruments for assessing outcome. Suppose the outcome of 20 clients is assessed by the MMPI, a symptom checklist, and projective (TAT or Rorschach) responses. In the light of most previous research using multiple measures of outcome—even from a single perspective—such as self-report of the client, the correlations among these three measures would be expected to be around zero.

Cartwright et al. (1963) employed eight outcome measures from the client's perspective, four from the therapist's, and seven from the perspective of an independent diagnostician. The factor analysis of the correlation matrix among these diverse measures produced four orthogonal factors that the authors concluded were "method factors," each being associated with a particular observer-instrument combination rather than with a substantive dimension of client change. It turns out that even when one is attempting to measure a single construct—such as extraversion or ego strength—different types of measures of that same construct often correlate poorly or not at all (Mischel 1968). In fact, correlations among the same type of measuring procedure applied to several different constructs will sometimes be higher than correlations among different methods of measuring the same construct (Campbell and Fiske 1959).

This problem of "method variance" has a most important implication for outcome research attempting to assess counseling effectiveness from multiple perspectives. If a different type of instrument is employed for each perspective (client, counselor, and significant other), one would expect lack of covariance among perspectives on the basis of method variance alone. That is, if therapist, client, and client's spouse disagree in their assessment of the client's outcome, it may be more because they are using different types of assessment instruments than because they represent different perspectives. The solution to this problem (which will be adopted in one of the proposed evaluation models discussed later in this section) is to use different formats of essentially the same basic instrument in obtaining outcome assessments from different perspectives. Any divergence among perspectives that occurs, then, will be genuinely attributable to perspective variance and not to a confounding of perspective and method variance.

## Global Versus Concrete Indices of Outcome

Whether outcome is assessed from a single or from multiple perspectives, another major issue concerns the use of global versus behavioral outcome dimensions. An example of a global assessment procedure, from the client's perspective, would be to have him/her respond to questions such as "How would you rate your overall individual counseling experience?" and "Do you feel your counseling experience provided the assistance you sought?" (An example of a global assessment procedure for the counselor would be the Global Assessment Scale (GAS; see Spitzer, Gibbon, and Endicott 1977).

As has been discussed previously, the problem with global scales is their susceptibility to bias in a singularly positive (or occasionally negative) direction. By their very nature they tap only the respondent's overall, frequently emotionally tinged, impression of whatever he/she is being asked to assess. The fact that such impressions are usually one-sided was referred to as the "halo effect" (Thorndike 1920). On this basis alone, the author cannot endorse use of the CSAB (Hurst and Weigel 1968) in a prospective evaluation program. By inspection alone, the evaluative dimensions of the CSAB are too vague and global. This is not to say that global indices of client satisfaction are not a useful adjunct to an evaluation of program effectiveness. In fact, arguments for their inclusion in the evaluation proposed by this report will be presented later.

In sum, the more specific the dimensions in terms of which personal change is defined, the more the observer (whether client or counselor) should be able to differentiate his/her overall impression of change into its respective components. Consequently he/she can make a more balanced, and ultimately more valid, appraisal of what has occurred.

There are two degrees of specificity that can be attained in proposing instruments for assessing counseling outcome, each with certain merits and drawbacks. A first level of specificity is to differentiate outcome by specific problem areas. In the case of student counseling, this would imply asking the student client to assess outcome with respect to specific target problems, such as grades, choice of major, career plans, financial problems, academic/study skills, interpersonal problems, identity and/or value priorities, and so on. Each of these areas could, in turn, be further subdivided. To date, only one questionnaire specifying target-problem areas has appeared in the literature on the assessment of student counseling outcome (Thompson and Wise 1976).

A second and more extreme degree of specificity involves differentiating outcome into highly concrete, reliable behaviors. In this case there is no room for bias entering into either the client's or the counselor's assessment of outcome because such outcome is defined in terms of very concrete, in many cases countable, behaviors or events. An example of a standardized instrument employing this degree of specificity—one that has been used with relative success in the evaluation of several community mental health programs—is the Denver Community Mental Health Questionnaire (DCMHQ; see Ciarlo and Reihman 1977 for a full description of the development and implementation of this instrument). Typical questions from the DCMHQ are "In the last couple of days, how often have you felt sad or depressed? Never ____ Once or twice ____ Often ____ Almost always ____" and "How many close friends do

you have? Six or more ____ 3-5 ____ 1 or 2 ____ None ____."
When administered by interview at intake and follow-up, as suggested by its authors, the DCMHQ is an especially reliable outcome assessment instrument. It is not, however, entirely free of certain faults and limitations (Speer 1977).

Specifying outcome in terms of precise, concrete behaviors or events is an innovation introduced by behaviorally oriented psychologists in the 1960s (Battle et al. 1966; Krumboltz 1966). In a more recent form, goal attainment scaling (to be described below), it surpasses any other means of assessing counseling outcome in reliability and methodological rigor. The chief limitation of this sort of approach, from the standpoint of nonbehavioristic psychologists, is that definition of outcome in terms of countable behaviors or events may not reflect change along deeper, more dynamic dimensions (such as ego strength, flexibility of defenses, autonomy, self-esteem). This raises the perennial question of whether phenotypic behavioral changes necessarily reflect genotypic or personality-structural changes—a question to which the answer is "yes" or "no," depending, again, on one's basic theoretical orientation. (This issue will be discussed further subsequently.)

## Suggested Alternative Strategies for Counseling Outcome Assessment

With the above considerations in mind, several alternative strategies for the assessment of counseling effectiveness (defined as successful client outcome) are described below. First priority is given to a behavioral strategy, goal attainment scaling (Kiresuk and Sherman 1968; Sherman 1977), and second priority to the general approach of a standardized questionnaire defining client status in terms of distinct target-problem areas (for instance, Thompson and Wise 1976). Both advantages and drawbacks of each strategy will be noted in the course of the discussion.

Goal Attainment Scaling and Related Approaches. Goal-attainment scaling (GAS) developed largely in response to limitations inherent in assessing counseling outcome through standardized rating scales or questionnaires (Kiresuk and Sherman 1968). Frequently, such instruments define outcome so globally or vaguely as to be susceptible to halo effects. In particular, use of the same questionnaire or rating device for clients varying considerably in age, sex, socioeconomic status, ethnic group, and/or educational status entails appraising many individuals on certain variables that are irrelevant to their particular dilemmas or circumstances. The essential feature of GAS involves specification and measurement of highly concrete and individualized goals for each client.

More specifically, the procedure operates as follows:

1. After an initial diagnostic evaluation, a trained interviewer meets with the client and collaboratively assists him/her in deciding upon a realistic set of counseling goals.

2. For each goal a scale consisting of a graded series of likely counseling outcomes, ranging from least to most favorable, is constructed.

3. The graded outcomes are defined in highly concrete, behavioral terms to permit an unfamiliar observer, at a later time, to determine whether the client has attained above or below any given scale point assigned to a particular outcome.

4. The scale points are assigned numerical values, ranging from +2 for the most favorable outcome to -2 for the least favorable outcome.

Typically at least three points along the scale are defined. For example, for one client the goal "less dependency on mother" was established, with three of the scale points defined as follows: (-2) "Does not make even minor decisions without," (0) "Makes many of own decisions without feeling rejected by mother," (+2) "Consults with mother only on decisions that affect her."

In the course of working with a client, the counselor may decide to assign different weights to the various goals, although little information is lost by maintaining equal weighting. Also, the procedure has the built-in flexibility for allowing new goals to be added (or previous ones modified) during the course of counseling. Often, in the case of clients with highly circumscribed problems (such as weight control or alcohol consumption), the development and monitoring of a single goal is sufficient. However, there is no limitation on the number of goals that can be chosen for any given client.

At some interval after counseling is terminated, a trained interviewer contacts the client and reviews with him/her any progress toward achieving the goals specified prior to (or during) counseling, thus arriving at a composite goal-attainment score, which represents the overall success-failure of the counseling effort. The composite score is standardized on a scale having a mean of 50 and standard deviation of 10 (see Kiresuk and Sherman 1968).

What are some of the principal advantages of this procedure? First, the problem of the differing perspectives of therapist and client is resolved in two ways: the therapist and client mutually decide what the criteria of successful outcome are to be, and outcome criteria are so concrete as to leave little room for ambiguity. Second, GAS aids the counseling relationship itself by providing an organized, agreed-upon framework in terms of which both counselor and client obtain a relatively clear sense of where they are trying to go. Proponents of GAS often criticize both psychoanalysts and non-directive counselors on the ground that they provide little direction and sense of purpose for clients. Their procedure, on the other hand, can provide the client with a structured framework within which he/she can commit himself/herself to a "treatment contract" for any desired time period. In sum, effective counseling should have the quality of goal-directedness, and GAS helps make this manifest.

From the standpoint of conducting methodologically rigorous outcome research, GAS is without rival. As previously mentioned, standardized questionnaires or rating scales may not be equally interpretable or applicable to all clients. There can be no question that it is preferable, if one is trying to establish the most valid criteria of counseling outcome, to have individualized, tailor-made criteria for each client rather than applying the same criteria across a large number of clients. Problems connected with the reliability of more traditional measuring procedures are also circumvented, since outcome is specified in highly concrete, often countable terms. From the standpoint of program evaluation in general, finally, GAS has the advantage of making outcome evaluation a built-in part of the "treatment" itself. The goals of helping clients and evaluating the effectiveness of helping efforts are not separate (as they are in most attempts to evaluate counseling programs), but mutually facilitative.

It would be possible to conclude this section on the evaluation of program effectiveness without further discussion were it not for several limitations of GAS that need to be pointed out. First, there are some inherent difficulties with the procedure. Furthermore, the prospect of actually implementing GAS in a context such as a university counseling center raises some formidable problems.

There are at least three inherent limitations of GAS. First, without careful evaluation of the client, goals that are either too trivial or too difficult may be prescribed. The degree to which counseling is deemed a "success," then, depends entirely on what goals (and criteria of goal attainment) are selected. At first glance this appears to be a very arbitrary way of measuring counseling outcome (though it is probably no less arbitrary than the decisions involved in choosing an "appropriate" standardized questionnaire or rating scale of counseling outcome). This limitation is partially overcome if the same interviewer—or team of interviewers—develops and evaluates goals for all clients, to assure some standardization of the procedure in practice. Furthermore, with proper training, interviewers should be able to discriminate what constitutes the most realistic and expectable goals for each particular client. Of course, the problem remains that the client's goals often evolve or change over the course of therapy. Thus, an optimal GAS procedure would involve a continuous renegotiation of the client's goals, at regular intervals, for the duration of his/her involvement in the counseling program.

A second, more serious limitation of GAS, mentioned previously, involves the standard criticism made by all dynamically oriented therapists regarding behavioral approaches: that behavioral criteria of successful outcome do not necessarily reflect deeper, dynamic factors and dimensions involved in personality change. The author agrees with this criticism. Behavioral indicators do not necessarily measure personality structural changes and, in fact, the criteria prescribed by GAS may seem superficial to the client or to the therapist, depending on their respective attitudes. But with this, one comes upon the standard impasse between behavioral versus holistic-dynamic psychology: what can be measured often is not very personally relevant or significant, and what is most significant is usually not amenable to measurement. It is clear that GAS offers the most methodologically rigorous approach to the assessment of client outcome. In doing so, however, it cannot tap all that is encompassed in the full sense of the term "outcome."

Practically speaking, a major limitation of GAS is that at the stage of implementation it is unlikely to receive a favorable reception among counselors who object to such a behavioristic approach. And even if it were found acceptable, there is the issue of hiring trained interviewers to administer intake, termination, and/or follow-up interviews—or of training an entire counseling center staff in the use of the GAS procedure (which would involve some loss in standardization). The latter alternative would clearly demand a substantial degree of commitment in time, energy, and money on the part of a counseling center—a degree not likely to be attained unless the center were very enthusiastic about GAS as an aid to the counseling process per se.

Because of the real-life difficulties in instituting a full-scale GAS procedure at a university counseling center, the following two modified GAS procedures, less precise but considerably simpler, are suggested as practical alternatives. Each has, in fact, been tried at a university counseling center with moderate success.

In the first alternative, at the time of intake or during the first counseling session, the student is asked to write down in his/her own words, on a 4x6 card, what he/she feels are the principal goals he/she would like to attain during counseling. At the termination of counseling—or some time afterward (follow-up)—the student is sent a form on which the originally stated goals have been transcribed, and is asked to rate the degree of progress made toward each goal. This is a modification of the procedure used by Rosen and Zytowski (1977), who had clients rate the degree of severity of their own, self-reported concerns and problems at intake and follow-up on a ten-point scale. This type of pre-post comparison of ratings is commendable, though it has certain methodological difficulties that will be considered in the section on design.

The procedure proposed here would simply have clients write down their own goals and then rate their degree of progress for each goal on a negative-to-positive-keyed scale at follow-up. Such a scale might include the following points: (-1) worse off, (0) no change, (+1) slight progress, (+2), moderate progress, (+3) much progress, (+4) goal completely attained. By having a scale both negatively and positively keyed, there would be less tendency for clients to overrate their counseling experience ("hello-goodbye" effect). The major limitation of such a procedure would be the inconvenience of having clients write down their goals and then transcribing their written statements onto a follow-up questionnaire. Also, it should be noted that this procedure is not comparable with a formal GAS procedure, since goal scales are left undefined and are not specified in terms of concrete, countable events. On the other hand, the procedure permits the client to define what constitutes successful outcome in his/her own terms, rather than applying arbitrary categories that may be irrelevant to certain clients.

The second alternative, which has been used with some success (see Miller and Thompson 1973; Thompson and Miller 1973), is to provide a client at intake with a standardized list of goals from which he/she selects those he/she feels are most pertinent to his/her aims in seeking counseling. Later, at follow-up, the client is sent the same standard form, to which have been added scales for each goal, with the same intervals described in the first alternative. At that time the client is asked to rate his/her progress on goals specified at intake, as well as on any new goals that arose during counseling.

A further addition to the follow-up goal-attainment ratings introduced by Thompson and Miller is to have clients rate the effect of counseling on any change they have experienced for each goal. "Effect of counseling" is rated as follows: (1) "definitely of no help," (2) "perhaps of some help," (3) "definitely of some help," or (4) "of great help." In essence, the investigators have tried to separate the effect of counseling on outcome from that of other factors in the client's life by asking the client himself/herself to make the relevant discrimination. In their more recent studies, Thompson and associates have obtained positive correlations (about 0.4) between clients' ratings of the effect of counseling and their ratings of progress toward goals. (For a discussion of the development and standardization of this procedure, see Thompson and Zimmerman 1969; Thompson and Miller 1973 .

One advantage of a standardized list of goals is that it is easier to administer to large numbers of clients. Another is that with such an instrument it is relatively easy to have the counselor and significant others of the client specify what they feel are appropriate goals (for the client), so that goal attainment can be evaluated from multiple perspectives (Wilson 1977). On the other hand, a difficulty of a standardized goal list is its inevitable length and, hence, cumbersome to clients. And in spite of its length, it is likely not to include goals that certain clients would consider most relevant. Any standard instrument would need to be modified by having spaces at the bottom where clients could write in their own goals. A preliminary list of goals relevant to the construction of this type of instrument is presented below.

## A PROPOSED STUDENT GOAL CHECKLIST
### (partial listing)

A. Academic
1. To be better able to cope with academic pressures
2. To improve my grade-point average
3. To handle a particular course or courses better
4. To better negotiate the university system (get through administrative red tape)
5. To obtain clarification about university regulations
6. To decide to stay in versus leave school
7. To improve my study habits and skills
8. To budget my study time better
9. To select an appropriate major (resolve conflict between two alternative majors)
10. To receive assistance in improving my reading or writing skills
11. To overcome anxiety about exams or class participation
12. To deal with a rules and regulations problem I have with a teacher

B. Career-Vocational
1. To decide on the right career for me
2. To have a job that is relevant to my career choice
3. To become more sure about my vocational future
4. To obtain information on employment opportunities
5. To obtain information about effective job-search techniques

    6. To receive information on graduate or professional school programs and admission standards

    7. To learn about the relation between my college work and the requirements of the vocational area(s) in which I'm interested

    8. To deal better with problems occurring on my present job

    9. To change jobs

    10. To find a job

## C. Financial

1. To improve my financial circumstances
2. To learn more about what resources exist for financial support
3. To budget my money better

## D. Personal Relationships

1. To improve my relationship with a teacher (or teachers)
2. To improve my relationship with my mother, father, or other family members
3. To improve my relationship with my boyfriend or girlfriend
4. To improve my relationship with my spouse
5. To improve my relationship with one or more same-sex friends
6. To improve my relationship with my roommate(s)
7. To resolve a conflict on whether to get into a relationship
8. To resolve a conflict on whether to break off a relationship
9. To obtain greater independence from family domination and control
10. To find a boyfriend or girlfriend
11. To feel less lonely, isolated
12. To join a particular group
13. To improve my social skills
14. To be more open and trusting toward others
15. To be more sensitive toward others or be more aware of the impact I have on them
16. To be less competitive in social situations
17. To be less fearful about saying what I feel or think
18. To change behaviors (with others) that are troublesome to me

## E. Sexuality

1. To have a more satisfactory sex life
2. To resolve a particular conflict I have over sexuality
3. Not to feel caught up in sex-role stereotypes

## F. Self

1. To have a better sense of who I am
2. To have more of a sense of direction—know what I want

3. To know better what my values are
4. To accept my limitations
5. To have more self-esteem, self-confidence
6. To feel more mature, competent, adult
7. To be able to cope with stress or pressure better
8. To get rid of bad habits I don't need (specify)
9. To build new habits into my life (specify)
10. To have less tendency to distort reality—see things the wrong way
11. To have greater involvement and commitment to things outside myself
12. To lose weight
13. To increase in strength
14. To make myself more attractive

G. To learn how to allocate my time better among school, personal life, and (if applicable) work

H. To cope with or overcome an alcohol or drug dependency problem

I. Symptoms
1. To have more pep and energy
2. To have more motivation
3. To have less tension/anxiety
4. To feel less depressed, blue
5. To have less anxiety over a particular type of situation
6. To feel less guilty
7. To feel less angry, resentful
8. To sleep better
9. To deal better with a physical problem (headaches, ulcers)

J. Miscellaneous

Either of these two simplified GAS techniques might be incorporated into the regular procedures by which clients are handled at a university counseling center. The first procedure is relatively simple and straightforward for the client, but involves more work for those staff who are involved in transcribing clients' goal statements onto follow-up questionnaires. Conversely, the standardized goal checklist entails less work for staff engaged in program evaluation, but is relatively more inconvenient and potentially disruptive to the client. In either case, however, the client is compelled to verbally articulate his/her own outcome criteria in terms of concrete goals. Thus the client knows his/her own counseling goals, and knows the counselor knows them.

While this may provide an orienting frame of reference and direction for many clients, it could conceivably be an unwanted

source of pressure for others.  Some clients may prefer to avoid
setting concrete goals, feeling that the "real" benefits to be obtained from counseling are too subtle, intangible, or inexpressible
to be reduced to such terms.  The counselor too may be averse to
setting goals upon attainment of which the success of the counseling
relationship is contingent.  Perhaps it is in the role of being a sup-
porter or model that the counselor feels he or she can be on most
service to a client, quite apart from whether the latter achieves
specific goals.

The Target-Problem Questionnaire Approach.  Though GAS is without question a highly reliable means of evaluating counseling outcome, there remains the more traditional alternative of using some
type of standardized outcome questionnaire.  A number of considerations influence the choice of such a questionnaire.  First, the number of instruments that have been carefully developed and have demonstrated both high (retest) reliability and validity is quite limited.
Even these cannot escape the influence of response styles such as
social desirability and acquiescence.  An instrument that attempts
to elicit global assessments of clients' attitudes or feelings toward
counseling is especially likely to obtain inflated responses.  In the
light of contemporary disenchantment with nearly all types of global
personality inventories (Mischel 1968; Fiske 1974), it would seem
that any questionnaire used to evaluate client outcome should attempt to employ outcome dimensions much more finely differentiated
than global personality constructs such as ego strength, self-esteem,
resiliency, and tolerance for ambiguity.  The previously mentioned
DCMHQ has done just this, going to the extreme of developing items
keyed in highly behavioral terms.  Unfortunately the DCMHQ was
developed for use in community mental health centers, and is not
very useful for outcome assessment in a university counseling center.
    Perhaps the closest approximation to the DCMHQ that is rele-
vant to a college counseling center is the experimental questionnaire
used by Thompson and Wise (1976).  On the basis of results of several factor analyses of the goal checklist used by Thompson and
Miller (1973), a closed-end rating-scale type of questionnaire was
developed and sent to student clients following the termination of
counseling.  No psychometric data on this instrument's reliability
and validity have been reported, although the checklist from which
it was developed showed satisfactory psychometric properties.  The
questionnaire is divided into three content areas: academic-voca-
tional, interpersonal, and personal—each of which contains items
asking the client to rate changes that have occurred since he/she
entered counseling with respect to particular problem areas.  Note

that rather than using a pre-post assessment design, the instrument asks the client to compare his/her status at the time of entering counseling and his/her status at follow-up. Note also that clients are asked to estimate the effect of counseling on each separate outcome dimension. The study utilizing this instrument has been described. Its principal purpose was to establish, by way of discriminant analysis, which items were most highly predictive of client satisfaction with counseling.

One criticism of this particular questionnaire is that, to a certain extent, it is "geared" to elicit favorable responses—at least on items that are not strictly objective. That is, when one is asked to compare how things were at a past time with how they are now, there is a tendency to imagine them as better—especially if one has had some form of counseling in the meantime. And, in fact, it turned out that on most items concerned with interpersonal relations, mean change ratings averaged about +1 point, whereas on some of the less ambiguous items concerned with grades and work-study skills, mean changes were much smaller. In spite of the questionnaire's unusual format, its use of items referring to specific concern or "target-problem" areas is, in the author's view, a step in the right direction. It is less likely to be vulnerable to halo and hello-goodbye effects than instruments that do not compel the respondent to focus on specific facets of outcome.

Something like Thompson and Wise's problem-oriented questionnaire might provide a useful start for anyone planning to conduct an outcome assessment of a university counseling service. With adequate time and resources, however, a better instrument utilizing the same basic approach could likely be developed. It should be possible to develop a standard questionnaire that covers the total continuum of concerns students bring to counseling but, at the same time, is relatively brief and convenient, and scales in such a way as to minimize hello-goodbye effects. Two such instruments are suggested below—one lending itself to a "post" or follow-up design only, the other to a "pre-post" design in which the client's functioning at follow-up is compared with that at intake. It should be emphasized that adequate development, construction, and validation of either proposed instrument would require a considerable commitment in time and resources, utilizing large numbers of client subjects and taking several years to complete.

In the first alternative the scope of Thompson and Wise's questionnaire might be extended to encompass a wider range of areas of concern to students seeking counseling. A tentative listing of such areas is presented below. Note that the substantive areas are approximately the same as those of the Standard Goal Checklist above, except that the format has been changed from one of goal statements to one presenting types of concerns.

AREAS-OF-CONCERN INVENTORY
(a partial list)

1. Negotiating the University System
   a. Clarification of academic rules and regulations
   b. Rules and regulations problem with a teacher
   c. Registration procedures
   d. Other

2. Academic Pressure
   a. Improving my grades
   b. One or more problem courses
   c. Pressure to do well from parents or friends
   d. Overall competitiveness of the university environment
   e. Other

3. Reading/Study Skills
   a. Allocating more time for studying—being more disciplined about studying
   b. Inadequate study skills—textbook reading, listening, note-taking, exam preparation
   c. Lack of basic academic skills—reading, writing, computatation, typing
   d. Inadequate skill in using English
   e. Other

4. Selecting an Appropriate Major

5. Deciding Whether to Stay in or Leave School

6. Choosing and/or Planning Career/Job Situation After Graduation
   a. Deciding on an appropriate career
   b. Conflict between two alternative careers
   c. In need of information on employment opportunities and/or job application procedures
   d. In need of information on admission to graduate or professional school
   e. Other

7. Current Employment Situation
   a. In need of obtaining a job
   b. Concern about leaving present job or changing jobs
   c. Concern about dealing better with persons or conditions at current job
   d. Other

8. Financial Concerns
   a. Improving my financial circumstances
   b. Need information about grants, loans, or work-study program

    c.  Need to learn to budget financial resources better

    d.  Other

9. Personal Relationships
Concern about my relationship with

    a.  Parents

    b.  Boyfriend or girlfriend

    c.  Spouse

    d.  Teacher

    e.  Same-sex friend(s)

    f.  Roommate(s)

    g.  Other

    h.  Problem with meeting people—shyness

    i.  Loneliness, isolation

    j.  Conflict over entering into a relationship

    k.  Conflict about leaving/losing a relationship

    l.  Need to develop better communication and/or social skills

    m.  Need to be more
   1. Open
   2. Sensitive to others
   3. Trusting
   4. Tolerant

    n.  Need to have greater assertiveness in social situations

    o.  Other

10. Sexual Concerns

    a.  Concern about sex life

    b.  Concern about being more accepting of sexuality or certain aspect(s) of sex

    c.  Need to feel less caught up in sex-role stereotypes

    d.  Other

11. Personal Identity

    a.  Concern about improving my self-image, self-confidence

    b.  Deciding who I am—my priorities and values

    c.  Having more of a sense of direction in my life

    d.  Accepting my limitations

    e.  Becoming more competent, skilled at something

    f.  Getting rid of one or more bad habits

    g.  Building one or more good habits into my life

    h.  Changing my lifestyle

    i.  Other

11A. Body Image

    a.  Losing weight

    b.  Increasing my strength

    c.  Making myself more attractive

    d.  Other

12. Time Utilization—juggling school, personal life, and work

13. Overall School Environment
    a. Problem with impersonal quality of large, commuter university
    b. Physical impact of architecture
    c. Other

14. Symptoms
    a. Anxiety
    b. Depression
    c. Persistent fatigue, exhaustion
    d. Can't sleep at night
    e. Headaches
    f. Can't concentrate
    g. Other

15. Alcohol or Drug Problem

16. Social Stereotypes
    a. Feel stuck in male or female role
    b. Problem with racial/ethnic stereotypes
    c. Other

17. Existential
    a. Concern about meaning of life
    b. Religious concern
    c. Concern about death
    d. Other

The basic procedure would be to have clients check off pertinent areas of concern at intake (either through a separate intake interview or during the first session with a counselor). At termination and/or follow-up the client would complete a scaled version of the same list of areas of concern. For each concern indicated at intake, he/she would be asked at follow-up to specify whether he/she experienced a negative or positive change on either a seven-point scale—for example: (-3) "Considerably more difficult, " (-2) "Moderately more difficult, " (-1) "Slightly more difficult, " (0) "No change or Unsure, " (+1) "Slight improvement, " (+2) "Moderate improvement, " or (+3) "Considerable improvement"—or a five-point scale—for example: (-2) "Definitely worse, " (-1) "Somewhat worse, " (0) "No change" or "Unsure, " (+1) "Somewhat better, " (+2) "Definitely better. "

The client would also be asked to specify any changes that occurred in other areas not listed at the time of intake. Both seven-point and five-point scale formats could be tested in a pilot study to see if they elicited significantly different mean change scores and also to ascertain whether the seven-point scale provided more detailed information. Note that in both cases the "No change" or "Unsure" category is in the middle of the scale rather than toward the negative end, as in Thompson and associates' questionnaire. As such it parallels the procedure used in GAS approaches and is more likely to elicit an honest, uninflated response from clients.

One very significant way of further enhancing the client's honesty and impartiality in assessing outcome would be to provide him/her with an instructional format that encourages him/her to be as honest and forthright as possible. The most sophisticated psychometricians in recent times have advocated this (for instance, Fiske 1971; Nunnally 1975), and it cannot be emphasized too much. An example of an instructional format that would encourage a client's candor in assessing his/her own outcome might run as follows:

> In order to provide us with feedback on how we are doing and what we might improve, the Counseling Center would appreciate your candid response to the following questions. Please indicate, as honestly as you can, to what extent each concern or problem you had at the time you came to the Counseling Center has become more difficult, remained about the same, or improved since then. Also rate the extent to which you feel counseling (as opposed to other circumstances in your life) is responsible for any changes you have experienced. Your counselor will not see your responses to this questionnaire.

The second alternative would implement a pre-post design, in which independent assessments of a client's functioning would be obtained at both intake and termination or follow-up. The client would not be asked to give a single rating of the degree of negative-to-positive change for each "area of concern." Rather, he/she would be asked to rate his/her satisfaction with his/her situation in each area at two separate times, preceding and following counseling. Again, either a seven-point or a five-point scale could be used: either (-3) "Very dissatisfied," (-2) "Somewhat dissatisfied," (-1) "Slightly dissatisfied," (0) "Unsure," (+1) "Slightly satisfied," (+2) "Somewhat satisfied," (+3) "Very satisfied" or (-2) "Definitely dissatisfied," (-1) "Somewhat dissatisfied," (0) "Unsure," (+1) "Somewhat satisfied," (+2) "Very satisfied." Again, a pilot study would be needed to determine which scale was more useful.

Whether either alternative is adopted, it would seem important to have clients rate the effect of counseling on changes reported for each item. In fact, it would seem appropriate to have ratings of the effect of counseling made in the two GAS strategies described previously. Once again, the rationale is to try to have the client—the only person in a position to know—try to tease out the influence of counseling from other current factors in his/her life that might have influenced counseling outcome. Subsequent correlation of "effect of counseling" ratings with clients' ratings of goal attainment, positive/negative change in areas of concern, or change in satisfaction/dissatisfaction in areas of concern would provide highly useful information from the standpoint of evaluating program effectiveness.

A final issue to be addressed, if a standard questionnaire is to be used instead of a GAS strategy, is whether a "post-only" or "pre-post" design in assessing counseling outcome is preferable. Both designs were presented above because both have certain assets as well as liabilities. A full consideration of their relative merits brings up the final part of this section on outcome assessment, that concerning study design.

## Design Considerations

The first basic point in regard to the design of outcome studies of human service delivery programs is a pessimistic one. Without a true experimental design employing a true control group* (that is, involving random assignment of subjects to both experimental and control groups), a valid assessment of counseling outcome is difficult to achieve (see Nunnally 1975; Riecken 1977). On the other hand, the formation of a true control group within a mental health setting is ethically and practically infeasible (see Cowan 1978). To have a control group when studying the effectiveness of counseling is essentially to tell a randomly selected proportion of prospective clients to wait X amount of time (whatever is needed for experimental clients to complete counseling) before seeing a counselor, a manipulation that can't be justified simply for the sake of optimizing methodological requirements.

---

*Actually, a true control group does not imply "no treatment," but provides an alternative treatment that tries to match control subjects with clients on all service-related factors other than counseling per se. Thus a true control group would not be told simply to wait—this is actually a type of "treatment." Rather, they would be given "placebo counseling"—that is, permitted to rap one-to-one with another student an hour per week in the counseling center, with the understanding that this would not constitute counseling.

The alternative is not to have a control group. The notion that a control group might be composed of randomly selected non-client students matched with clients on age, sex, demographic, and academic variables is fallacious, since nonclient students differ from clients in the most crucial respect—they have not perceived themselves as being in need of counseling. Without a true control group, neither a post-only nor a pre-post experimental design is going to demonstrate that clients' outcomes are primarily due to counseling rather than to other factors in their lives. Perhaps the optimal course is to adopt Thompson's strategy of asking clients to rate the effect of counseling on various outcome dimensions.

Given this imperfect state of affairs, what are the relative advantages of a post-only versus a pre-post design? Pros and cons of each type of design are enumerated below.

Pre-Post Design. This type of design has two advantages. First, one has a baseline with which client's ratings at follow-up can be compared. (Otherwise it is necessary to phrase the format of the follow-up questionnaire in terms of "how much change has occurred?" since the beginning of counseling.) Second, by making two independent assessments of a client's functioning at two separate times, there is less room for intrusion of hello-goodbye effects. It is the difference between asking "How are you doing now?" at two separate times, which encourages the client to make a direct rather than a comparative self-assessment at follow-up, versus asking "How much improvement or deterioration has occurred since then?"—which may cue some clients to make ratings that implicitly say, for any number of reasons, "I guess I must have gotten something out of it."

There also are two disadvantages. First, the client's pre-counseling or initial self-appraisal is likely to be unusually low, so that in effect a pre-post design "builds in" the potentiality of favorable outcome ratings. (This is probably the most common criticism of pre-post designs.)

Second, there are problems associated with the calculation of change scores. It does not suffice merely to subtract the "pre" score from the "post" score. Suppose clients were given an initial self-report questionnaire, then given the same questionnaire two weeks later—both times before they started counseling. The phenomenon of statistical regression toward the mean alone would predict that certain clients (those having initial scores below the mean of all of the scores) would show an improvement. What is necessary is to calculate residual change scores, which consist of the deviations of "post" scores from a regression line that can be predicted from "pre" scores by linear regression. Unfortunately, even residual change scores are not very satisfactory because they do not take into account measurement error inherent in both "pre" and "post" scores. If "pre" and "post" assessments were only an hour apart, one would still get residual change scores due to random error in the measurement procedures.

To take account of measurement error inherent in residual change scores, it has been recommended that the correlation between "pre" and "post" scores be corrected for attenuation before residual change scores are computed. However, there is considerable dispute about how this is to be done (for instance, should one correct for measurement error only in "pre" scores, or make a double correction for random error in both "pre" and "post" scores?). A number of complex mathematical models have been proposed for handling change scores (Lord 1963). Cronbach and Furby (1970) suggest, however, that investigators, as a rule of thumb, should avoid working with change scores if possible. There is a way of getting around these difficulties if a true control group is used (Nunnally 1975, p. 115), but in the absence of the latter, it is unwise to try to work with change scores.

Post Design. This type of design has two advantages. First, it is more convenient and easier to implement, because it requires an assessment (scaled in terms of progress or change ratings) to be made only once. This is especially so when multiple assessments by client, counselor, and significant others are obtained.

Second, it avoids the possibly confounding influence of "practice effects." This is a problem that might have been mentioned under the disadvantages of pre-post designs. It involves the tendency of a subject responding to an instrument a second time to be influenced by his/her responses on the first administration of the test. Practice effects can be controlled for by the use of a Solomon design (Campbell 1972), but such a design involves two separate types of control groups and is generally infeasible in the context of counseling outcome studies.

The main disadvantage is the susceptibility to hello-goodbye and halo effects, though this can be minimized to the extent that highly specific, concrete outcome dimensions are used, and by instructing respondents to be as candid as possible in their ratings.

On balance, it would seem that the post design has a slight advantage over the pre-post design, both methodologically and in terms of convenience. However, a thoroughgoing program evaluation study might conduct pilot studies comparing both types of design in order to determine whether there was a significant difference between the two in subjects' ratings of favorableness of outcome.

Timing of Outcome Assessment. A second consideration is whether
to conduct outcome assessments at termination, when there is less
chance for factors outside of counseling to influence outcome, though
this in no way rules out the possible influence of extraneous factors
during counseling (which can be ruled out only by use of an adequate
control group). On the other hand, an assessment at termination is
by far the most susceptible to hello-goodbye effects. If you ask
someone to tell you how well he/she has done in your program just
before he/she leaves, that is the time he/she will be most likely to
pat you on the back. Finally, an assessment at the time of termination provides no information on the duration of the effects of counseling, if any.

A follow-up assessment does demonstrate the durability of
counseling effects, but may also be confounded by current, non-
counseling-related factors. As previously suggested, perhaps the
strategy of asking clients to rate the effect of counseling on any
changes they have experienced can help in this instance. The principal problems with follow-up assessments are, of course, logistic
and practical. Mailed-out follow-up questionnaires typically elicit
a response rate on the order of 30–40 percent. This rate often can
be raised to 60–70 percent, however, by mailing the questionnaire
out a second or third time, as well as by sending respondents personally signed reminder notes. More cumbersome follow-up procedures that tend to elicit higher response rates include telephone
and face-to-face interviews. It is critical that return rates be
raised to at least a majority level (two-thirds). Otherwise the respondent group is likely to be a biased sample of the total population
assessed.

What about the alternative of having both termination and
follow-up assessments? This would be useful—except for the per-
vasive influence of practice effects. If you ask a student twice over
the period of a month how much he/she has changed, and if he/she
is willing to return the second questionnaire, you're likely to be
told much the same thing you were told the first time. The author
recommends that a preliminary pilot study be conducted in order to
compare the results of outcome assessments conducted both at termination and one to three weeks afterward. From the standpoint of
gaining some estimate of the durability of counseling effects, however, a one- to three-week follow-up assessment is, in general,
preferable to one conducted at termination only.

An Alternative Outcome Criterion: Use of Grades and Continued School Attendance as Criteria of Counseling Effectiveness

Up to now "successful outcome" has been defined as the amelioration of concerns/problems a student initially brings to the counsel-

ing center. What about the possibility of defining outcome in terms of criteria that are external to students' stated concerns and needs, such as grades and/or continuance in school?

Such outcome criteria are ostensibly attractive in terms of the overall aim of university counseling centers to enhance students' adjustment and coping strategies vis-à-vis the academic environment. Surely improved grades and continuing in school subsequent to counseling would seem to indicate a favorable outcome.

While this may be generally so, it is not necessarily so. What about cases where the decision to leave school, perhaps only temporarily, is an indication of maturity and wisdom on the student's part? Or what about the case of the overachiever who, subsequent to counseling, has lower grades but has achieved a more balanced and less stressful coordination among the academic, occupational, and interpersonal sectors of his/her life? Furthermore, although improved grades and continuing in school may be appropriate criteria for students seeking only academic-educational counseling, the question remains to what extent these students' professed academic difficulties can be separated from personal and interpersonal concerns. In sum, improved academic performance is not invariably an indication of effective counseling and, even when observed, may be due to other factors independent of counseling.

If, on the other hand, one reviews the relatively few studies that have employed grades and graduation as criteria of favorable counseling outcome, one is hard-pressed to find much evidence for their utility. In an early study Williamson and Bordin (1940) matched counseling center freshmen clients with nonclient students on aptitude, achievement, and demographic characteristics. Effects of counseling on scholastic achievement were found at the end of the first quarter, but there was no effect for the rest of the freshman year. By reanalyzing Williamson and Bordin's data and examining student records, Campbell (1963) was able to identify a "better" control group of subjects among the original controls—those who sought counseling later in their college career. While this special group did not differ from the client and control groups in the original study with respect to grades, it did have (along with the original client group) a higher proportion of graduates (59 percent), compared with the original control group (47 percent). However, the chain of inference involved in assuming that counseling was responsible for an increased graduation rate is tenuous indeed.

In a more recent study by Hill and Grieneeks (1966), 479 University of Texas students who had sought counseling were compared with controls matched on precounseling grades and aptitude scores. No differences in grades were found. Furthermore, selecting only

clients seeking educational and vocational counseling during their
sophomore year and comparing them with controls matched on sex,
aptitude, and freshman grades, no difference in junior year grades
was found. Nor did rate of graduation vary between counseled students and matched controls. The authors concluded that grades and
graduation were inadequate criteria for assessing counseling effectiveness, even if counseling does have a favorable effect on academic
success.

In sum, grades and continuing in school may or may not indicate favorable counseling outcome. And even when it is assumed
that they do, researchers have usually been unable to differentiate
students seeking counseling from controls in terms of these criteria.
All in all, it is suggested that any attempt to utilize grades and/or
continuing in school as outcome criteria in an evaluation of the "effectiveness" of a university counseling service should be undertaken
with considerable caution and modest expectations.

## An Alternative Approach to Evaluating
## Program Effectiveness: Clients'
## Evaluations of Counselors

Up to now this discussion has been concerned with the evaluation of counseling outcome. The premise has been that a human
service delivery program's effectiveness can best be gauged by appraising the degree to which its recipients are actually helped or
facilitated—from their own point of view and preferably from the
perspectives of the counselor and significant others as well. In the
course of the discussion, numerous methodological difficulties associated with the assessment of counseling outcome have been
brought out.

An alternative approach to the evaluation of counseling effectiveness, intended not to supplant but to supplement that of outcome
assessment, is to obtain clients' assessments of counselors. The
focus shifts from how well clients do after counseling to how well
counselors are perceived to function, from the clients' standpoint,
during counseling. If a counselor has seen 20 clients during a week,
then there are 20 independent observers who should be capable of
rating some (though likely not all) aspects of his/her performance
(Grigg and Goodstein 1957). Certainly, because of their personal
involvement in counseling, clients are not unbiased observers.
Their objectivity may be confounded with their liking of the counselor and/or desire for his/her success. Moreover, ratings obtained at counseling termination may be spuriously inflated by
hello–goodbye effects. Yet, in spite of these limitations, the sheer
number of independent ratings of a single counselor will tend to in-

crease their composite reliability. As Grigg and Goodstein (1957, p. 31) summarize it:

> What exists here is a pool of independent observers of a fairly well-delineated job performance, namely a counselor as he goes about his assignment of entering into rapport with others, of attending to their problems, and of responding to these clients and their problems according to his own style of performing and according to his particular theoretical beliefs, dogma, and training.

Probably the most widely used and psychometrically adequate instrument for assessing counselors is the Counseling Evaluation Inventory (or CEI—Linden, Stone, and Shertzer 1965; Gabbert, Ivey, and Miller 1967; Haase and Miller 1968; Ivey, Miller, and Gabbert 1968). Though no less subject to social desirability response styles and halo effects than any other rating scale of its kind, the CEI has at least been carefully constructed and demonstrated satisfactory test-retest stability and discriminant validity. The instrument consists of 21 items that ask the client to rate the counselor on dimensions such as "accepted me as an individual," "acted as though my concerns were important to him," "was relaxed and at ease," "acted as if he were better than I." On each item the client rates the frequency with which it is applicable to the counselor: "Always," "Often," "Sometimes," "Rarely," "Never."

Numerous studies have examined the relationship between counseling effectiveness, measured by clients' global judgments or by some external criterion, and various items on the CEI pertaining to empathy, patience, trustworthiness, and relaxation. When used for purposes of evaluation, it would seem that some of the more relevant questions that might be asked would include the following: On which items is a counselor consistently high or low? For which types of clients (by sex, age, class, ethnic group) does a counselor obtain highest or lowest mean ratings? Are ratings on all or certain items for a given counselor affected by variations in his/her counseling technique, or by the duration of counseling? Which items having favorable mean ratings correlate most highly with favorable counseling outcome, measured by an independent procedure?

In actually implementing this form of evaluation, it is important that counselors not be made to feel defensive or under scrutiny, a circumstance that could readily interfere with the counseling process. An appropriate procedure would be to distribute copies of the CEI to each counselor and have him/her periodically administer them to samples of clients in order to obtain his/her own feedback. Evaluation of counselor effectiveness would thus become a matter of self-evaluation rather than of administrative monitoring.

## Should Global Measures of Client Satisfaction with Counseling Be Included in Outcome Assessment?

Throughout this chapter it has been suggested that overly abstract, global criteria of outcome do not provide reliable or valid indices of counseling effectiveness. That a client feels satisfied with the counseling experience does not imply that his/her problems have necessarily been assuaged. Is there any justification, then, for asking clients, at the termination of counseling, whether they feel counseling was "helpful" or whether they "received what they came for"? (This type of global appraisal would be conducted in addition to the more highly specified measures of outcome suggested in the various alternatives.)

Actually, there are several advantages to including a global satisfaction measure. From the standpoint of the client's welfare, it gives him/her a chance to articulate any reactions to the experience. It is especially open-ended questions, which ask the client to state in his/her own words the greatest strengths or shortcomings of the experience, that would provide the chance to express in detail any unfinished business. The importance of clients' overall satisfaction with a counseling service, as an aspect of program evaluation, has been discussed elsewhere (see Giordano 1977; Margolis, Sorensen, and Galano 1977).

From the standpoint of program evaluation, a global assessment of client satisfaction permits two kinds of comparisons. First, one can ask whether satisfaction ratings are related to ratings of goal attainment, change in status of salient problems/concerns, or effect of counseling on such changes. Though previous research has found satisfaction ratings to be unrelated to clients' perceptions of actual improvement, further cross-validation of this result would be of definite significance. Second, to the extent that any of the more differentiated outcome criteria were correlated with global satisfaction, it would be interesting to see which these were. One would like to know whether the attainment of particular types of goals or resolution of particular types of problems is consistently associated with clients' overall satisfaction with counseling.

In short, a brief client satisfaction questionnaire might be included as a part of the termination phase of assessing counseling outcome. One such questionnaire is presented below.

## EVALUATION

Please answer the following questions as frankly and honestly as possible. Your counselor will <u>not</u> see your responses.

1. The reception you received in our waiting room was:
   Disappointing _____ Satisfactory _____ Pleasing _____

2. How long were you kept waiting to see a counselor?
   _____ minutes

3. If kept waiting, did your counselor explain the delay?
   Yes _____ No _____

4. In general, do you feel you received the assistance you came
   to the Counseling Center for? Not at all _____ Not sure _____
   Only slightly _____ Somewhat _____ Very much so _____

5. How much progress did you make in resolving your concerns?
   Worse off _____ None _____ Not sure _____ Slight
   progress _____ Moderate progress _____ Considerable
   progress _____

6. Do you feel that your counselor was interested in you as a
   person? Not at all _____ Not sure _____ Slightly _____
   Moderately _____ Strongly _____

7. Did you and your counselor determine that another department
   or agency could serve you better? Yes _____ No _____
   If yes, where? _____

8. Would you return to the Counseling Center? Yes _____
   Not sure _____ No _____

9. Would you recommend the Counseling Center to a friend?
   Yes _____ Not sure _____ No _____

10. <u>Comments</u> (briefly describe)
    What were the most positive aspects of your experience at the
    Counseling Center? What would you commend?

    What were the most serious shortcomings or limitations of
    your experience at the Counseling Center? What would you
    criticize?

## SUMMARY

It has been the purpose of this chapter to acquaint the reader
with some of the complexities involved in carrying out the evaluation

of university counseling programs, especially in the areas of needs assessment and outcome measurement. Since singular solutions are not easily found in the field of evaluation, it seemed appropriate to present a range of alternative strategies, the relative utility of which will vary with the resources and objectives of different counseling programs.

In conclusion, it is important to mention one other dimension of program evaluation that was not dealt with in this chapter—the assessment of a program's efficiency. Generally speaking, program efficiency involves the following question: "What is our capacity to produce favorable results in proportion to efforts expended?" That is, it represents the ratio of effort (in terms of time, money, personnel, and public convenience) to performance or output. Probably the most important dimension of a program's efficiency is its capacity to monitor both the activities of counselors and the progress of clients from intake to termination. In the program evaluation literature, considerable attention is given to the development of optimally efficient monitoring systems, frequently called management information systems (MIS). The interested reader may find further discussion of this important dimension of evaluation in several places (Chapman 1976; Miller and Willer 1977; Mitchell 1977).

## REFERENCES

Auerbach, A. H., and L. Luborsky. 1968. Accuracy of judgments of psychotherapy and the nature of the "good hour." In J. Shlien, H. F. Hunt, J. P. Matarazzo, and C. Savage, eds., Research in psychotherapy. Vol. 3. Washington, D.C.: American Psychological Association.

Battle, C. C., S. D. Imber, R. Hoehn-Saric, A. R. Stone, E. R. Nash, and J. D. Frank. 1966. Target complaints as criteria of improvement. American Journal of Psychotherapy, 20: 184–192.

Bell, R. A., G. J. Warheit, and J. J. Schwab. 1977. Needs assessment: A strategy for structuring change. In R. D. Coursey, ed., Program evaluation for mental health. New York: Grune and Stratton.

Blaine, G. B., Jr., C. C. McArthur, et al. 1961. Emotional problems of the student. New York: Appleton-Century-Crofts.

Blum, H. L. 1974. Planning for health. New York: Human Sciences Press.

Buck, C. 1979. Survey of CSUF student need priorities. Fullerton: California State University. Unpublished report.

Campbell, D. T. 1972. Critical problems in the evaluation of social programs. Paper presented at the annual meeting of the Division of Behavioral Sciences, National Academy of Sciences.

_____. 1963. A counseling evaluation with a "better" control group. Journal of Counseling Psychology, 10: 334–338.

Campbell, D. T., and D. W. Fiske. 1959. Convergent and discriminant validation by the multitrait-multimethod matrix. Psychological Bulletin, 56: 81–105.

Carney, C. G., and A. Barak. 1976. A survey of student needs and student services. Journal of College Student Personnel, 17: 280–284.

Carney, C. G., C. G. Savitz, and G. N. Weiskott. 1979. Students' evaluations of a university counseling center and their intentions to use its programs. Journal of Counseling Psychology, 26: 242–249.

Cartwright, D. S., W. L. Kirtner, and D. W. Fiske. 1963. Method factors in changes associated with psychotherapy. Journal of Abnormal and Social Psychology, 66: 164–175.

Chapman, R. L. 1976. The design of management information systems for mental health organizations: A primer. Rockville, Md.: National Institute of Mental Health.

Ciarlo, J. A., and J. Reihman. 1977. The Denver Community Mental Health Questionnaire: Development of a multidimensional program evaluation instrument. In R. D. Coursey, ed., Program evaluation for mental health. New York: Grune and Stratton.

Coursey, R. D., ed. 1977. Program evaluation for mental health. New York: Grune and Stratton.

Cowan, E. L. 1978. Some problems in community program evaluation research. Journal of Consulting and Clinical Psychology, 46: 792–805.

Cronbach, L., and L. Furby. 1970. How should we measure "change"—or should we? Psychological Bulletin, 74: 68–80.

Davidshofer, C. O., A. Borman, and R. G. Weigel. 1977. The Counseling Services Assessment Blank: Is it reliable? Journal of College Student Personnel, 18: 215–218.

Fiske, D. W. 1974. The limits for the conventional science of personality. Journal of Personality, 42: 1–10.

——. 1971. Measuring the concepts of personality. Chicago: Aldine.

Fiske, D. W., H. F. Hunt, L. Luborsky, M. Orne, M. Parloff, M. Reiser, and A. H. Tuma. 1970. Planning of research on effectiveness of psychotherapy. American Psychologist, 25: 727–737.

Fox, P. D., and M. Rappaport. 1972. Some approaches to evaluating community mental health services. Archives of General Psychiatry, 26: 172–178.

Friedlander, J. 1978. Student ratings of co–curricular services and their intent to use them. Journal of College Student Personnel, 19: 195–201.

Fullerton, J. S., and C. R. Potkay. 1973. Student perceptions of pressures, helps, and psychological services. Journal of College Student Personnel, 14: 355–361.

Gabbert, K. H., A. E. Ivey, and C. D. Miller. 1967. Counselor assignment and client attitude. Journal of Counseling Psychology, 14: 131–136.

Gallagher, R. P., and S. Scheuring. 1978. Survey of student needs at the University of Pittsburgh. Pittsburgh, Penn.: University Counseling and Placement Services, University of Pittsburgh.

Garfield, S., R. Prager, and A. Bergin. 1971. Evaluation of outcome in psychotherapy. Journal of Consulting and Clinical Psychology, 37: 307–313.

Gelso, C. J., and N. J. Karl. 1974. Perceptions of counselors and other help givers: What's in a label? Journal of Counseling Psychology, 21: 243–247.

Getsinger, S. H., and N. J. Garfield. 1976. Male student perceptions of counselors, guidance counselors and counseling psychologists. Journal of College Student Personnel, 17: 7-10.

Giordano, P. C. 1977. The client's perspective in agency evaluation. Social Work, 22: 34-38.

Glaser, E. M., and T. E. Becker. 1972. A clinical approach to program evaluation. Evaluation, 1: 54-55.

Glass, G. V. 1976. Evaluation studies review annual. Vol. I. Beverly Hills, Calif.: Sage Publications.

Green, B. L., G. C. Gleser, W. M. Stone, and R. F. Seifert. 1975. Relationships among diverse measures of psychotherapy outcome. Journal of Consulting and Clinical Psychology, 43: 689-699.

Grigg, A. E., and L. D. Goodstein. 1957. The use of clients as judges of the counselor's performance. Journal of Counseling Psychology, 4: 31-36.

Guttentag, M., and E. L. Struening. 1975. Handbook of evaluation research. Vol. II. Beverly Hills, Calif.: Sage Publications.

Haase, R. F., and C. D. Miller. 1968. Comparison of factor analytic studies of the Counseling Evaluation Inventory. Journal of Counseling Psychology, 15: 363-367.

Hadley, S. W., and H. H. Strupp. 1977. Evaluations of treatment in psychotherapy: Naivete or necessity? Professional Psychology, 8: 478-490.

Hargreaves, W. A., C. C. Attkisson, and J. E. Sorensen. 1977. Resource materials for community mental health program evaluation. 2nd ed. DHEW Publication no. (ADM) 77-328. Washington, D.C.: U.S. Government Printing Office.

Harman, R. L. 1971. Client assessment of a university counseling service. Journal of Counseling Psychology, 18: 496-497.

Hathaway, S. R. 1948. Some considerations relative to nondirective counseling as therapy. Journal of Clinical Psychology, 4: 226-231.

Hill, A. H., and L. Grieneeks. 1966. Criteria in the evaluation of educational and vocational counseling in college. Journal of Counseling Psychology, 13: 198-201.

Hitchcock, J. 1963. The new vocationalism. Change, 4, April: 46-50.

Hurst, J. C., and R. G. Weigel. 1968. Counseling Services Assessment Blank. Ft. Collins, Colo.: Rocky Mountain Behavioral Sciences Institute.

Hurst, J. C., R. G. Weigel, R. Thatcher, and A. J. Nyman. 1969. Counselor-client diagnostic agreement and perceived outcomes of counseling. Journal of Counseling Psychology, 16: 421-426.

Isaac, S., and W. B. Michael. 1971. Handbook in research and evaluation. San Diego: Robert R. Knapp.

Ivey, A. E., C. D. Miller, and K. Gabbert. 1968. Counselor assignment and client attitude: A systematic replication. Journal of Counseling Psychology, 15: 194-195.

Jahoda, M. 1958. Current conceptions of positive mental health. New York: Basic Books.

Katz, M. M. 1977. On evaluating treatment outcome: Clinical, ethnic, and sociologic issues. In W. Neigher, R. J. Hammer, and G. Landsberg, eds., Emerging developments in mental health program evaluation. New York: Argold Press.

Keenan, B. 1975. Essentials of methodology for mental health evaluation. Hospital and Community Psychiatry, 26: 730-733.

Kiesler, D. J. 1966. Some myths of psychotherapy research and the search for a paradigm. Psychological Bulletin, 65: 110-136.

King, P. T., F. Newton, B. Osterlund, and B. Baber. 1973. A counseling center studies itself. Journal of College Student Personnel, 14: 338-344.

Kiresuk, T., and R. Sherman. 1968. Goal Attainment Scaling: A general method for evaluating comprehensive community mental health programs. Community Mental Health Journal, 4: 443-453.

Krumboltz, J. D. 1966. Behavioral goals for counseling. Journal of Counseling Psychology, 13: 153-159.

Leavitt, A., J. Cary, and J. Swartz. 1971. Developing a mental health program at an urban community college. Journal of the American College Health Association, 19: 289-292.

Levin, H. 1975. Cost-effectiveness analysis in evaluation research. In M. Guttentag and E. Struening, eds., Handbook of evaluation research. Vol. 2. Beverly Hills, Calif.: Sage Publications.

Linden, J. D., S. C. Stone, and B. Shertzer. 1965. Development and evaluation of an inventory for rating counseling. Personnel and Guidance Journal, 44: 267-276.

Liptzin, B., J. W. Stockdill, and B. S. Brown. 1977. A federal view of mental health program evaluation. Professional Psychology, 8: 543-552.

Littlepage, G. E. 1976. The problem of early outpatient terminations from community mental health centers: A problem for whom? Journal of Community Psychology, 4: 164-167.

Lord, F. M. 1963. Elementary models for measuring change. In C. W. Harris, ed., Problems in measuring change. Madison: University of Wisconsin Press.

Luborsky, L. 1971. Perennial mystery of poor agreement among criteria for psychotherapy outcome. Journal of Consulting and Clinical Psychology, 37: 316-319.

Luborsky, L., M. Chandler, A. H. Auerbach, J. Cohen, and H. M. Bachrach. 1971. Factors influencing the outcome of psychotherapy: A review of quantitative research. Psychological Bulletin, 75: 145-185.

McIntyre, M. H., C. C. Attkisson, and T. W. Keller. 1977. Components of program evaluation capability in community mental health centers. In W. A. Hargreaves, C. C. Attkisson, and J. E. Sorensen, eds., Resource materials for community mental health program evaluation. 2nd ed. DHEW Publication no. (ADM) 77-328. Washington, D.C.: U.S. Government Printing Office.

Margolis, R. B., J. L. Sorensen, and J. Galano. 1977. Consumer satisfaction in mental health delivery services. Professional Psychology, 8: 11-16.

Miller, A., and A. Thompson. 1973. Factor structure of a goal checklist for clients. Psychological Reports, 32: 497-498.

Miller, G. H., and B. Willer. 1977. An information system for clinical recording, administrative decision making, evaluation, and research. Community Mental Health Journal, 13: 194-204.

Mintz, J. 1972. What is "success" in psychotherapy? Journal of Abnormal Psychology, 80: 11-19.

Mischel, W. 1968. Personality and assessment. New York: Wiley.

Mitchell, R. 1977. The dimensions of an evaluation system for community mental health centers. In R. D. Coursey, ed., Program evaluation for mental health. New York: Grune and Stratton.

Moursand, J. P. 1973. Evaluation: An introduction to research design. Monterey, Calif.: Brooks/Cole.

Neigher, W., R. J. Hammer, and G. Landsberg, eds. 1977. Emerging developments in mental health program evaluation. New York: Argold Press.

Nunnally, J. 1975. The study of change in evaluation research: Principles concerning measurement, experimental design, and analysis. In E. L. Struening and M. Guttentag, eds., Handbook of evaluation research. Vol. I. Beverly Hills, Calif.: Sage Publications.

Perloff, R., E. Perloff, and E. Sussna. 1976. Program evaluation. Annual Review of Psychology, 27: 569-594.

Riecken, H. W. 1977. Principal components of the evaluation process. Professional Psychology, 8: 392-410.

Riedel, D. C., G. L. Tischler, and J. K. Myers, eds. 1974. Patient care evaluation in mental health programs. Cambridge, Mass.: Ballinger.

Roen, S. 1971. Evaluative research and community mental health. In A. Bergin and S. Garfield, eds., Handbook of psychotherapy and behavior change. New York: Wiley.

Rosen, D., and D. G. Zytowski. 1977. An individualized, problem-oriented self-report of change as a follow-up of a university counseling service. Journal of Counseling Psychology, 24: 437-439.

Schulberg, H. C. 1977. Issues in the evaluation of community mental health programs. Professional Psychology, 8: 560-572.

Schulberg, H. C., A. Sheldon, and F. Baker. 1969. Program evaluation in the health fields. New York: Behavioral Publications.

Sells, S. B. 1975. Techniques of outcome evaluation in alcohol, drug abuse, and mental health programs. In J. Zusman and C. R. Worster, eds., Program evaluation. Lexington, Mass.: Lexington Books.

Sherman, R. 1977. Will goal attainment scaling solve the problems of program evaluation in the mental health field? In R. D. Coursey, ed., Program evaluation for mental health. New York: Grune and Stratton.

Siegel, L. M., C. C. Attkisson, and A. H. Cohn. 1977. Mental health needs assessment: Strategies and techniques. In W. A. Hargreaves, C. C. Attkisson, and J. E. Sorensen, eds., Resource materials for community mental health program evaluation. 2nd ed. DHEW Publication no. (ADM) 77-328. Washington, D.C.: U.S. Government Printing Office.

Smith, M. L., and G. V. Glass. 1977. Meta-analysis of psychotherapy outcome studies. American Psychologist, 32: 752-760.

Speer, D. C. 1977. An evaluation of the Denver Community Mental Health Questionnaire as a measure of outpatient treatment effectiveness. Evaluation Quarterly, 1: 475-492.

Spitzer, R. L., M. Gibbon, and J. Endicott. 1977. Global Assessment Scale. In W. A. Hargreaves, C. C. Attkisson, and J. E. Sorensen, eds., Resource materials for community mental health program evaluation. 2nd ed. DHEW Publication no. (ADM) 77-328. Washington, D.C.: U.S. Government Printing Office.

Stockdill, J. W. 1977. The future role of evaluation in mental health. In W. Neigher, R. J. Hammer, and G. Landsberg, eds., Emerging developments in mental health program evaluation. New York: Argold Press.

Struening, E. L., and M. Guttentag, eds. 1975. Handbook of evaluation research. Vol. I. Beverly Hills, Calif.: Sage Publications.

Suchman, E. A. 1967. Evaluative research. New York: Russell Sage Foundation.

Sue, D. W., and B. Kirk. 1975. Asian-Americans: Use of counseling and psychiatric services on a college campus. Journal of Counseling Psychology, 22: 84-86.

Sue, S., and D. W. Sue. 1974. MMPI comparisons between Asian-American and non-American students utilizing a student psychiatric clinic. Journal of Counseling Psychology, 21: 423-427.

Tarial, M. 1977. New trends in mental health services—What are we evaluating? In W. Neigher, R. J. Hammer, and G. Landsberg, eds., Emerging developments in mental health program evaluation. New York: Argold Press.

Thompson, A., and A. Miller. 1973. A criterion system for measuring outcomes of counseling. Journal of College Student Personnel, 14: 483-489.

Thompson, A., and W. Wise. 1976. Steps toward outcome criteria. Journal of Counseling Psychology, 23: 202-208.

Thompson, A., and R. Zimmerman. 1969. Goals of counseling: Whose? When? Journal of Counseling Psychology, 16: 121-125.

Thorndike, E. L. 1920. A constant error in psychological rating. Journal of Applied Psychology, 4: 25-29.

Tripodi, T., P. Fellin, and I. Epstein. 1971. Social program evaluation. Itasca, Ill.: F. E. Peacock.

Truitt, E. I., and P. R. Binner. 1969. The Fort Logan Mental Health Center. In C. A. Taube, ed., Community mental health center data systems: A description of existing programs. USPHS Publication no. 1990. Washington, D.C.: U.S. Government Printing Office.

Twain, D. 1975. Developing and implementing a research strategy. In E. Struening and M. Guttentag, eds. Handbook of evaluation research. Vol. I. Beverly Hills, Calif.: Sage Publications.

Warheit, G. J., R. A. Bell, and J. J. Schwab. 1974. Planning for change: Needs assessment approaches. Rockville, Md.: National Institute of Mental Health.

Webster, D. W., and B. R. Fretz. 1978. Asian American, Black, and White college students' preferences for help-giving sources. Journal of Counseling Psychology, 25: 124-130.

Weiss, C. H. 1972. Evaluation research: Methods of assessing program effectiveness. Englewood Cliffs, N.J.: Prentice-Hall.

Westbrook, F. D., J. Moyares, and J. H. Roberts. 1978. Perceived problem areas by black and white students and hints about comparative counseling needs. Journal of Counseling Psychology, 25: 119-123.

Williamson, E. G., and E. S. Bordin. 1940. Evaluating counseling by means of a control group experiment. School and Society, 52: 434-440.

Wilson, N. C. 1977. The automated tri-informant goal-oriented note: One approach to program evaluation. In R. D. Coursey, ed., Program evaluation for mental health. New York: Grune and Stratton.

Wilson, N. C., and J. L. Mumpower. 1975. Automated evaluation of goal-attainment ratings. Hospital and Community Psychiatry, 26: 163-164.

Wortman, P. M. 1975. Evaluation research: A psychological perspective. American Psychologist, 30: 562-575.

# 5

## DSM-III AND THE
## COLLEGE COUNSELING CENTERS:
## NEW PAINT BUT AN OLD CHASSIS?
### *Lawrence Onoda*

In general, psychologists* in college counseling centers have viewed psychiatric diagnosis with disdain and suspicion. Rogers (1951) was a leading critic of medically based psychiatric diagnosis that labeled people as "sick." He felt that psychiatric diagnosis was palliative, superficial, and detrimental to the client-therapist relationship, as well as to the client's ability to understand himself/herself.

Rogers' (1951) negative view of psychiatric diagnosis was reinforced by other prominent counseling theorists. Carkhuff and Berenson (1967) saw psychiatric diagnosis as "not only intellectually repugnant, but usually meaningless for purposes of differential treatment" (p. 234). Arbuckle (1975), a proponent of the existential-humanistic orientation, viewed psychiatric diagnosis as irrelevant because it was an external labeling process that missed the inner reality of the person.

Even among the ranks of clinicians there has been strong criticism of the disease-based medical model that permeates psychiatric diagnosis—for instance, by Laing (1967), Albee (1969), and Szasz (1961). Kanfer and Saslow (1965) and Phillips and Draguns (1971) have stressed the importance of understanding the individual's interaction with the environment, rather than subscribing to a hypothetical disease model. Zubin (1967) concluded that the medical model of psychiatric diagnosis was in chaos.

---

*"Psychologist" is used in a general sense, and includes any professionals in the college counseling center, such as psychiatrists, social workers, and counselors.

Regardless of the psychologist's view of the philosophical foundations of the psychiatric diagnostic model, the categories of previous diagnostic manuals have not been especially relevant to counseling center professionals. Although the counseling psychologist may be exposed to a wide variety of psychiatric and developmental problems, he/she primarily delivers services to students who are "normal" but are experiencing developmental problems. In the DSM-II (1968) developmental problems were indirectly alluded to in the sections on conditions without manifest psychiatric disorder and nonspecific conditions (for instance, marital, social, and occupational maladjustment). However, these categories for nonmental disorders were so limited and vague that they were basically useless for psychologists in counseling centers.

The American Psychiatric Association has released the third edition of the Diagnostic and Statistical Manual of Mental Disorders (DSM-III; 1980). From preliminary drafts of the revised DSM, clinical psychologists have cautiously and skeptically begun to evaluate the new innovations listed in DSM-III (McReynolds 1979; Schacht and Nathan 1977). Likewise, college counseling psychologists need to begin evaluating the relevance of DSM-III for college counseling services. Before the DSM-III receives wide acceptance and utilization by psychologists in college counseling centers, several previous criticisms and concerns need to be resolved. First, has the philosophical foundation (medical model) of the DSM-III changed radically from its predecessors? Or does its philosophical premise allow for the counseling (normal) model? Second, is the DSM-III beneficial for planning counseling? Or does it provide the appropriate type and quantity of information needed to conceptualize the counseling process? Third, does the DSM-III effectively conceptualize the type of psychological conflicts seen in a college counseling setting? Or does it provide the counseling psychologist with a wide range of well-defined categories that are applicable to college counseling? Fourth, despite one's philosophical opposition to any type of psychiatric diagnosis, is it important to learn about DSM-III in order to communicate reliably with fellow mental health professionals? In addition to discussing these questions, the innovations and categories in DSM-III that are pertinent to college counseling services are discussed and critiqued.

CURRENT CHANGES IN DSM-III THAT
APPLY TO COUNSELORS

DSM-I (1952) consisted of 8 categories and 100 diagnoses. DSM-II (1968) consisted of 10 categories and 159 diagnoses.

DSM-III (1980) has 19 categories and 228 diagnoses. This increase represents about a 60 percent increase over DSM-II. If this trend continues, DSM-IV will likely have an even greater number of diagnoses.

Spitzer, Sheehy, and Endicott (1977) indicate that DSM-III has several purposes. First, it is a vehicle by which professionals can communicate clearly with each other about different recognizable conditions. Second, the classification system can be used as a means of determining the applicability of different treatment strategies. Third, diagnostic information can be used as an indicator of prognosis or outcome. Fourth, the classification should be consistent with current knowledge of etiological processes. The degree to which DSM-III meets these goals will determine how meaningful it will be for use in college counseling centers.

DSM-III was meant as a tool that all members of the professional community—clinicians, educators, and researchers—could use. Thus it would have to be comprehensive and include a range of psychiatric disorders and "normal" problems. The authors of DSM-III are not proposing that the disorders listed in it reflect scientifically validated disorders, but they have tried, briefly and clearly, to establish some agreement among professionals about the terms used. It is obvious that increased reliability of communication among professionals will significantly enhance clinical practice, research, and training.

In DSM-II the diagnoses were unreliable because of the modal-matching approach to diagnosis. For example, schizophrenia was described as a disturbance of thinking, mood, and behavior. The clinician was required to match the symptom of his/her patient to the descriptions in order to determine if it applied. The professional had to use his/her own judgment about how closely the patient matched the description of the disorder. Many aspects of the decision-making process in selecting the appropriate diagnosis were not directly listed: organic factors, duration of symptoms, and number of symptoms present.

Although DSM-III represents some innovations, it is still a matching system of diagnosis. One innovation is that a more specific but somewhat arbitrary criterion has been implemented. For example, "dysthmic" (depressive neurosis) is defined as having three of the following symptoms or signs: insomnia/hypersomnia; low energy; feelings of inadequacy; decreased effectiveness, attention, and concentration; social withdrawal; loss of pleasure; irritability; negative attitude; tearfulness; recurrent thoughts of death— these must occur for a period of two years. The depressive syndrome must be relatively persistent, but there can be periods of normal mood lasting a few days to a few weeks, but no more than a few months.

Decision-making branching trees for differential diagnosis outline the serial order of the decision-making process for determining a specific disorder. These trees are attempts at helping the clinician to consider the same issues when diagnosing. There are decision-making trees for psychotic features; irrational anxiety; mood disturbances; antisocial, aggressive, defiant, or oppositional behavior; physical complaints; academic or learning difficulties; and organic brain syndromes.

## DSM-III IS DESCRIPTIVE BUT ATHEORETICAL

The authors of DSM-III realized that it must be applicable to a wide variety of professionals having different theoretical orientations: behavioral, humanistic-existential, analytic. Since mental health professionals have no universal consensus on the etiology of various mental disorders, the DSM-III is atheoretical. In essence, it attempts to be descriptive and avoid implications of etiology. To the descriptive summarization of the symptoms and signs, the clinician must apply his/her own theoretical meaning.

Descriptions of the mental disorders tend to be primarily identifiable behaviors that require low inference on the part of the diagnostician, such as dyspnea, shaking, and hallucinations. Behavioral descriptions are more desirable than abstract ones because there is a greater probability of reliability among the observers.

However, the DSM-III does include descriptions that require the diagnostician to identify vague cognitive states that are referred to as high-order inferences. For example, the criteria for the borderline personality disorder are partially described in the following way:

> Identity disturbance manifested by uncertainty about
> several issues relating to identity, such as self-image,
> gender identity, long-term goals or career choice,
> friendship patterns, values, and loyalties, e.g., "Who
> am I?" "I feel like I am my sister when I am good."
> (p. 323)

This type of descriptive inference is highly subjective, and thus open to more criticism for being vague and abstract rather than concrete and objective. For example, there is a greater probability that clinicians will disagree about what constitutes an "identity disturbance" than about what constitutes specifically defined, observable behaviors. High-order inferences are plagued by problems of defining the quantitative and qualitative aspects of the symptoms or signs—for instance, how much uncertainty about one's gender constitutes an "identity crisis" or how many years is meant by "long-term." It seems that high-order inferences proliferate the descriptions of the personality disorders, and thus the reliability is lower than for disorders using more behavioral descriptions (Spitzer and Forman 1979; Spitzer, Forman, and Nee 1979).

## WHAT HAPPENED TO NEUROSIS

In the DSM-III the category of neurosis has been deleted. However, it is reassuring for some to know that disorders such as depressive neurosis have reappeared as dysthmic disorder in the affective disorder category. Anxiety, obsessive-compulsive, and phobic disorders were formed into a separate category identified as anxiety disorders. Hysterical and hypochondriacal neurosis were placed in somatoform disorders.

Why was neurosis eliminated? Although counseling and psychiatric-oriented professionals have used the term "neurosis," its roots are based in Freudian psychoanalytic theory. Freud used the term "psychoneurosis" descriptively and to imply unconscious conflicts that lead to the maladaptive defense mechanisms. Since there is no universal consensus on the etiology of neurotic behaviors, it was eliminated.

While it may be somewhat confusing and/or contradictory, the term "neurotic" is still used in the DSM-III. Nonetheless, neurotic disorders are used only in a descriptive sense, and etiological implications are still avoided. "Neurotic process" can be used by the clinician who wishes to indicate a specific etiological process such as unconscious conflicts.

## NEW PAINT, OLD CAR

Despite the innovations, the DSM-III, like its predecessors, is conceptualized within the context of the medical model. Spitzer, Sheehy, and Endicott (1977) stated: "We regard the medical model as a working hypothesis that there are organismic dysfunctions which are relatively distinct with regard to clinical features, etiology, and course" (p. 5). The inherent problems that have been associated with the disease/medical model are still applicable in the DSM-III (Laing 1967; Szasz 1961; Zubin 1967). Discussing the DSM-III specifically, Schacht and Nathan (1977) have criticized the medical model because it fails to adequately explain the environmental factors that contribute to or cause a mental disorder, such as alcoholism. Likewise, McReynolds (1979) feels that the medical model of psychiatric diagnosis is no longer heuristic for the social sciences. He believes the social sciences have outgrown the medical model, continuance of which only retards our understanding of behavioral processes.

There have been proponents of methods of defining mental disorders other than the medical/disease model. McLemore and Benjamin (1979) describe an interpersonal model as an alternative to the DSM-III. McReynolds (1979) has proposed a sociobehavioral classification of behavioral disturbances that views people seeking psychiatric care as those experiencing conflicts of a behavioral nature that affect the self or others. Maslow (1962) and Schacht and Nathan (1977) have suggested that a model defining mental health rather than mental illness would solve much of the confusion about psychiatric diagnosis.

MULTIAXIAL DIAGNOSIS

One of the innovations of DSM-III is the multiaxial diagnosis that replaces the singular decision analysis of DSM-II. The clinician is currently required to complete five different axes when formulating a diagnosis; however, he/she may elect to complete the first three axes only, since the last two pertain to prognosis.

Axis I consists of all psychological disorders except personality and developmental childhood disorders. Axis II consists of long-term or chronic maladaptive styles of interacting with the environment. Axis III is used to indicate any current physical disorder or condition that is relevant to understanding and management of the disorder. This category is not used for diagnosing organic mental disorders, since it refers to conditions outside the spectrum of mental disorders, such as tachycardia and diabetes. Axis IV (severity of psychosocial stressors) pertains to the clinician's evaluation of the overall severity of a stressor that may be contributing to the development or exacerbation of a psychological disorder. The focus of Axis IV seems to reflect the current interest in the relationship of stress to psychological and physical disorders. This axis is primarily used as an indicator of prognosis.

The clinician is required to rate what he/she considers an "average" reaction to a psychosocial stressor for a person in similar circumstances and having similar sociocultural values. The criterion for judgment is based on the amount of change incurred by the person from the stressor, the degree to which the stressor is perceived as desirable and under the control of the client, and the number of stressors.

Generally, the psychosocial stressor will have appeared within a year prior to the current disorder. However, a psychosocial stressor may be future-oriented. For example, the person may experience an intense stress in anticipation of retirement. In the DSM-III the stressor can be assigned a rating that ranges from 1 (no apparent stressor) to 7 (catastrophic stressor).

Schacht and Nathan (1977) have criticized Axis IV because the clinician is expected to know what constitutes an "average" stress reaction. This criticism appears to be valid, because the reliability correlation for Axis IV is between .60 and .66 (Spitzer and Forman 1979; Spitzer, Forman, and Nee 1979). Although the clinician is supposed to consider the client's perception of the stressor, Axis IV is still housed within the concept that the clinician "knows best."

Axis V (the highest level of adaptive functioning) is an indicator of the general stability of the patient's personality functioning one year prior to the onset of the disorder. This category is likewise used as a prognosticator of the patient's recovery from the disorder. If the patient has had a high level of adaptive functioning—such as good social relationships, stable occupational functioning, and appropriate use of leisure time—then there is an increased probability that the patient has the psychological ego strength to cope with and recover from the disorder. The clinician is required to make a rating from 1 (superior functioning) to 7 (grossly impaired).

For the most part, I feel that counseling psychologists will find this category relevant for determining the appropriateness of short-term developmental counseling. In essence, it can be used to determine the probability that a client will benefit from developmental counseling. The following case is an example:

A 28-year-old male Caucasian who has had a variety of different majors is currently seeking counseling because he cannot select a major or career. Vocational testing and career counseling have been previously completed, but were not found to be beneficial. He is a "loner" and does not have any close friends, since peers see him as "strange" and "odd." He has had numerous part-time jobs, but he was either fired or quit because he was unable to perform the job duties. A chronic history of depression, unexpressed anger, passivity, and dependence exists.

The type of prospective client described above would be a poor candidate for short-term personal counseling, since he has a chronic history of poor adaptive functioning. Perhaps some type of group counseling or a referral to a community mental health center for long-term psychotherapy would be more appropriate. I am not suggesting that if a client appears to have long-term personality problems, he/she must be immediately referred, but understanding adaptive functioning can be helpful in planning the course of short-term counseling.

## DSM-III AND THE COUNSELING INTERVIEW

It should be apparent that diagnosis, in terms of the DSM-III, requires more extensive history-taking than traditionally occurs in the counseling interview. Although the counseling interview is not devoid of background data collection, extensive history-taking (case study) is more common in psychiatric interviews (Wolberg 1954). Blocher (1966) has emphasized that counseling tends to place more emphasis on the "present" or "here and now" than on a detailed reconstruction of the person's past.

Psychiatric and counseling interviews vary regarding the amount and extent of history-taking because each emphasizes different goals. In the psychiatric interview more emphasis is placed on making a diagnosis than in the counseling interview. On the other hand, the most important goal in the counseling interview is laying a foundation for the relationship, rather than reconstructing the person's life history (Hansen, Stevic, and Warner 1977; Tyler 1969). Hansen, Stevic, and Warner (1977) have stated that counseling professionals find formal history-taking unnecessary, and they believe it may increase the client's resistance to self-disclosure.

Although lengthy and detailed case material may not be gathered by counseling psychologists, history-taking is necessary if a psychiatric diagnosis is going to be made. It is my opinion that most counseling professionals tend to gather historical information as an ongoing process of counseling, rather than as a formal process prior to starting treatment.

## DSM-III AND TREATMENT

The authors of DSM-III have attempted to make the new manual a viable document for planning treatment. Does it provide the type of information needed to begin treatment? Karasu and Skodol (1980) have questioned the value of Axis IV of DSM-III for planning treatment in psychodynamic therapy. They have demonstrated that three patients with the same diagnosis of dysthymia (depressive neurosis) were quite different regarding unconscious conflicts, coping styles, and ego functioning. The diagnostic information was insufficient for planning treatment.

A similar criticism can be made from the counseling perspective. The following exemplifies the limitation of DSM-III in planning counseling for a particular diagnosis: Axis I = dysthymic disorder; Axis II = no personality disorder but avoidant personality traits, such as hypersensitivity to rejection and unwillingness to enter relationships, and Axis III = no current medical problems.

> Case: 21-year-old female who is majoring in English. Presenting complaints were insomnia, depression, irritability, feelings of inadequacy, lack of concentration, and difficulties fulfilling work obligations. Symptoms have been present for eight years, with some periods of relief.
>
> Supplementary Data: She has feelings of inferiority because she has never felt attractive or desirable. She recounts her life history of being hurt by people (especially men). She desperately wants their approval, but she intensely fears rejection. Thus, she feels hostility toward men for being so dependent on them. Her friends consider her two-faced because she never states her feelings honestly. She wants to be more direct and honest with people, but she fears rejection.

One can readily see that the information needed to make a diagnosis is incomplete for planning treatment. Whether the counseling psychologist believes that the depression is due to incongruence with self, overdependency on environmental support rather than on self, or maladaptive conditioning, he/she will need to gather further information to plan counseling. Even though the authors of DSM-III designed the manual to be atheoretical, the professional must still gather information and conceptualize it within some theoretical orientation.

NEW OR ADAPTED CATEGORIES
RELEVANT TO COUNSELORS

It is not the purpose of this discussion to review every change in the DSM-III. For example, college counseling staffs rarely work with children, and thus childhood disorders are not relevant to the present discussion. I will outline some of the pertinent changes in the DSM-III and discuss how common types of cases seen in a college counseling center relate to it.

## Psychosis and Schizophrenia

Although schizophrenia and psychosis are not extremely common presenting problems at college counseling centers, these types of psychopathology are present, and require speedy and accurate diagnosis. There are several new definitions of schizophrenia and psychosis with which the counseling psychologist should be acquainted. Previously, counseling professionals tended to use the terms "psychosis" and "schizophrenia" interchangeably, but in the DSM-III they are defined differently. While both psychosis and schizophrenia are identified by the appearance of symptoms and signs such as hallucinations, and delusions, psychosis is defined when the previously mentioned symptoms or signs appear within the time span of a few hours to two weeks. If the symptoms or signs persist for at least six months, the term "schizophrenia" is used.

The counseling psychologist may feel that the temporal definition is arbitrary, but utilization of the universal nomenclature is nonetheless necessary in order to communicate effectively with the referring community agency. Misuse of the correct term may hinder the client's obtaining the appropriate treatment.

## Personality Disorders: A Disorder Themselves

DSM-III defines personality disorders as chronic, long-standing, inflexible, and maladaptive personality traits that significantly impair social, occupational, and interpersonal functioning. Frances (1980) indicated that terms such as "inflexible" and "maladaptive" have not been operationally defined. Thus, each clinician is required to use his/her own judgment about what they mean. These types of vague terms proliferate the descriptions of personality disorder, so the reliability of diagnosis is much lower than that for categories such as schizophrenia (Spitzer, Forman, and Nee 1979).

Asthenic, inadequate, and explosive personality disorders were deleted from DSM-II. The new personality disorder diagnoses are schizotypal, borderline, and narcissitic. Spitzer, Endicott, and Gibbon (1979) described how they derived the diagnosis of borderline personality. The controversy surrounding the borderline diagnosis concerns its lack of a clear definition. Frances (1980) indicated that even what the borderline personality "borders" is unclear.

The counseling psychologist is likely to be counseling clients who may have personality disorders. The problem is how personality disorders vary from the other diagnoses. Of special interest is how the V Codes or life development problems differ from personality disorders.

V Codes: Normal But Not Well

The V Codes in DSM-III are of special interest to counseling psychologists because they deal with psychological conflicts that are the focus of treatment but are not attributable to a mental disorder. What is noteworthy about this category is that it includes problems related to life development, interpersonal, and academic areas. Since college counseling centers are primarily mandated to deliver services for developmental life problems, the counseling psychologist is more likely to see students who fall within this category rather than within the mentally disordered categories. The vital questions about the V Codes are the following: Are the various diagnoses clearly and concisely presented? How distinct are the diagnoses listed in the V Codes from other categories? Do the V Codes help the counselor conceptualize the counseling process?

The V Codes are vague, and contain primitive descriptions that are basically useless to counseling center staff. For example, the term "academic problem" is defined as an "academic problem that is apparently not due to a mental disorder. An example is the pattern of failing grades or of significant underachievement with adequate intellectual capacity" (p. 332). A Phase-of-life problem is defined as a "problem associated with a particular developmental phase or some other life circumstance. . . . Examples include problems associated with going to school, separating from parental control, starting a new career, marriage, divorce, and retirement" (p. 333). The diagnosis of interpersonal problem is defined as "an interpersonal problem" (p. 334). If one considers the elaborate, branching-tree, decision-making process that must be adhered to for other categories of DSM-III, the V Codes are pitifully primitive. In fact, they do not even approach the standards for disorders such as schizophrenia and phobia in DSM-II. In DSM-III the interpersonal diagnosis is defined as "an interpersonal problem." In essence, this is like saying schizophrenia is defined as schizophrenia.

The following case might be a typical case seen in a college counseling center.

Case: 19-year-old male psychology student. He reports feeling anxious about asking girls for dates
because he does not feel attractive. When he asks a
girl for a date, he experiences heart palpitations,
trembling, perspiration, and anxiety. He has had girl-
friends in the past, but basically he is considered shy
and reserved because he cannot stand to be rejected by
a girl. There are some indications that he's had conflicts with his mother because his mother appeared
critical and favored the more popular older brother,
who was socially self-confident. His inability to overcome this problem has resulted in moderate depression,
which has subsequently caused his grades to drop. In
turn, the poor grades have caused further depression
because his chances of being admitted to a graduate
school appear bleak.

The question of whether the diagnoses in the V Codes are sufficiently
distinct is clearly shown by the case above. Should the diagnosis
be academic, phase-of-life, or interpersonal problem? Dating
would be considered a developmental concern at his age, and thus
it might be considered a phase-of-life problem. On the other hand,
this student is having interpersonal conflicts with girls. Also, he
is having academic problems that are contributing to his depression.
Since the V Codes are vaguely defined, the clinician cannot reasonably distinguish the various diagnoses in this category. It should
be noted that there are no branching-tree decision-making charts
for the V Codes.

The distinction between the V Codes and personality disorders
is especially confusing and vague. Even among clinicians the definitions of personality disorders are abstract. For example,
Masterson (1976) describes a case that he diagnosed as a borderline
adult. He called the case "The Perpetual Student." She is a 22-
year-old female who has trouble making decisions about herself or
her life. She has difficulty being at home and separating from it.
In addition, her insecurity tends to suffocate relationships. Historically, she has no sexual attraction to men who try to establish
a nurturing and intimate relationship, but is sexually attracted to
men who do not seek this. Her father was perceived as a maze of
subtle, conflicting messages that reinforced dependence and confusion about relationships.

Although Masterson (1976) describes this case as an example
of the borderline syndrome, it could be conceptualized as a developmental problem rather than a personality disorder. Perhaps counseling psychologists are failing to identify serious personality

pathology or clinicians are tending to "overdiagnose" life-phase problems. This controversy cannot be settled unless there is a clearer definition of the personality disorders and V Codes.

In terms of how meaningful the V Codes are for treatment planning in the counseling center, the answer is that they are not especially helpful. The V Codes are so vague that they do not provide the counseling psychologist with the type of descriptive information needed to plan counseling. In the case of the student with the dating anxiety, the counseling psychologist needed to gather more information about the level of the anxiety, interpersonal conflicts, and self-image before counseling could begin. The V Codes could have important relevance to counseling psychologists, but they have been sadly disappointing.

Who is to blame? It is easy to blame traditional targets such as the clinicians. However, I would rather consider the counseling professionals' responsibility for the disappointing V Codes. The weak and vague definition of life development is partially attributable to the unclear definition of what is "normal" life development. Counseling professionals have used the term "developmental counseling" to describe counseling techniques rather than a theoretical discussion of what constitutes "normal life development." Rogers (1961); Blocher (1966); Pietrofesa, Hoffman, Splete, and Pinto (1978); and Shertzer and Stone (1978) have defined developmental counseling as a process that facilitates a person's awareness and potential at different stages of "normal" development. More attention has been given to defining the goals and techniques of counseling than to the theoretical definition of what constitutes "normal" development.

Counseling professionals have clung tenaciously to theories such as Maslow's (1962) self-actualization and Roger's (1961) human potential. Although Maslow (1962) was a pioneer in trying to define effective human functioning rather than illness, his model does not explain stages of development. When reading Maslow's theory, one must ask: How does one evolve to become self-actualized? Can everyone attain self-actualization? If not, what is "normal" development rather than ideal functioning? Likewise, Rogers (1961) describes the factors for human development, but he does not explain the stages of development. A plant needs water, air, soil, and sunlight to grow, but these factors do not explain the process and stages of a plant's development.

There have been models proposed to describe the healthy person (Jahoda 1950; Rogers 1961; Shoben 1957). However, these are not developmental theories, but descriptions of the healthy person's personality. In an attempt to define normal development, counseling professionals have looked to theorists such as Havighurst

(1953), Erikson (1968), Piaget (1952), and Kohlberg (1969), all of whom discuss stages of an individual's development. Erikson's (1968) stages of development cover birth to age 26. Although meaningful and potentially applicable, Erikson's model is limited by not extending the life development past age 26. Despite its psychoanalytic approach, Erikson's outline of psychosexual development could be used to describe and explain different aspects of a student's identity formation. Havighurst (1953) defines development as a series of tasks that the individual faces at certain stages of development. His theory, too, covers only infancy to early adulthood. While it is true that theories have been proposed, it seems that counseling psychologists have not actively developed theories to explain the "normal" stages of development.

Anxiety Won't Make You Too Nervous

A common complaint by clients seeking counseling services is anxiety. In the DSM-II anxiety was found under major affective, neurotic, or adjustment disorders. In the DSM-III anxiety has become a separate category (although mania is still under affective disorders). Disorders such as agoraphobia, panic, generalized anxiety, and chronic or delayed anxiety are listed in this section.

A common form of anxiety for which students seek help is the phobia (such as test, speech, and social phobias). It is relatively uncomplicated to diagnose and differentiate a phobia from other mental disorders, but in the DSM-III the organization of the phobic diagnoses is contradictory and redundant. For example, agoraphobia is listed as a separate phobic reaction, but DSM-III does not list all the possible types of phobias. Perhaps the phobic diagnosis should describe the course of the reaction rather than list specific objects or ideas that persons are phobic about. The course of a phobia is identified by a persistent, irrational fear that produces an avoidant reaction. If this description was utilized rather than there being a focus on the object of the phobia, there would be no need to list every possible type of phobic reaction.

Another common anxiety reaction that has recently been receiving considerable attention from counseling psychologists relates to stress management. The anxiety associated with stress management tends to be lower than the anxiety associated with a diagnosis of generalized anxiety. Many students who experience stress feel pressured, tense, irritable, and somewhat depressed. The following is a typical example.

Case: 35-year-old male majoring in engineering. Presenting complaints were tension, worry, fatigue, and irritability. Although maintaining a B grade average, he worries constantly about his grades because engineering is a demanding curriculum. In addition, he is working 30 hours a week, and he is having serious financial pressures. Also, he is having some interpersonal conflicts with his roommate because his roommate likes to play his stereo loudly, which disturbs his sleep and studying. His girlfriend has been dating another man because she claims he is always too busy. Within the last six months he has noticed that he gets about one headache a week. There are no indications of personality problems, severe depression, or major psychiatric disorders.

This case represents a typical conflict that might be seen in a college counseling center. Although this student has somatic complaints, the frequency and severity do not seem to warrant a diagnosis of a psychosomatic disorder. Also, many of his stress reactions are due to situational factors: grades, finances, and interpersonal relationships. This type of case parallels the adjustment reaction, but there is no severe maladaptive social or occupational functioning. An alternative to a diagnosis of adjustment or generalized anxiety disorder would be to develop another diagnosis, perhaps called "developmental stress reaction" under the V Codes. This diagnosis would facilitate identification of the anxiety reaction without categorizing the person as having a disorder. In addition, it would recognize that an individual can have anxiety due to situational factors, but not necessarily be considered psychopathologic. Once again, the definition of this diagnosis would depend on what constitutes "normal" levels of anxiety.

The Meeting of Mind and Body

Another type of anxiety reaction is the psychosomatic symptom. Since the 1960s increasingly greater attention has been directed toward understanding the mind–body interaction. As a result of this increased awareness, counseling psychologists have been offering more counseling programs to help students alleviate psychosomatic complaints, such as headaches, colitis, and hypertension. One might ask whether the DSM-III is more effective than the DSM-II in categorizing psychosomatic problems.

Lipp, Looney, and Spitzer (1977) have discussed the limitations of DSM-II in classifying psychophysical problems. Their primary criticisms were that the classifications were rarely used,

that the mind-body interaction was not accurately portrayed, and
that the description of psychological factors affecting a physical
condition could not be indicated. Thus, in DSM-II the categories
called psychophysiologic disorders were deleted. In DSM-III the
psychosomatic disorders were rearranged and expanded. "Somatoform disorder" is a new category that reflects disorders in which
physical symptoms or signs are present, but there is a clearly
demonstrable psychological cause. Listed in the somatoform
category are disorders such as conversion, psychogenic pain, and
hypochondriasis. The other new addition is the category identified
as psychological factors affecting a physical disorder. This category allows the clinician to indicate the psychological factors that
initiate or exacerbate a physical condition, such as tension headache, angina pectoris, asthma, and gastric ulcer.

How relevant are the diagnostic categories for identifying the
types of problems seen in a college counseling center? Although
there are no empirical data on the types of psychosomatic problems
that are seen at college counseling centers, I would tend to estimate that the somatoform category is basically irrelevant (although
the category "psychological factors affecting a physical disorder"
is relevant). If the counseling center has a biofeedback program,
it is more likely that clients with psychosomatic problems, such as
headaches, hypertension, colitis, and gastric ulcers, will be treated.


Psychosexual Diagnosis: Somewhat Arousing

The new developments in the psychosexual category are of
interest to counseling psychologists because increasingly more
students are seeking counseling for sexual difficulties. In DSM-II
sexual problems were not listed unless they related to sexual
deviation—for instance, fetishes, pedophilia, and voyeurism. However, there were no diagnostic categories for persons experiencing
sexual dysfunctions, such as inhibited sexual desire, impotence,
premature ejaculation, and vaginismus. The advantage of the
DSM-III is that disorders related to sexual dysfunctioning are listed.

In general, the diagnoses of psychosexual dysfunctioning are
more relevant to the type of conflicts that students experience, but
there is a type of sexual counseling that the DSM-III does not include. Many counseling centers are offering services that appear
more developmental than remedial. In essence, many centers are
offering sex education groups that enhance "normal" functioning.
In addition, couples' groups may be offered that include discussion
of sexual values, attitudes, and the biological aspects of sexual
functioning, rather than sexual dysfunction. Once again, there is

a need for a new diagnosis under the V Codes that could be entitled "sexual enhancement."

Another new diagnosis in DSM-III is "ego-dystonic." This diagnosis is made when homosexuals have persistent conflicts because they desire to become heterosexuals. Homosexuals who have conflicts but prefer to be homosexuals are not given this diagnosis. Homosexuality was deleted from DSM-II as a mental disorder, and it remains deleted in DSM-III.


SUMMARY

Counseling psychologists in counseling centers have been disenchanted with DSM-II because of its philosophical orientation and its lack of relevance to the typical counseling client. The type of client seen in a college counseling center would be categorized as "normal," but nonetheless he/she may be experiencing life developmental problems. Thus, the medical/illness model of psychiatric diagnosis was not especially relevant. DSM-II had only limited categories for identifying developmental conflicts.

Before the DSM-III can be widely used by college counseling personnel, the basic limitation of DSM-II will have to be corrected or overcome. Basically, the DSM-III reflects many new innovations, but it has not overcome the previous criticisms by college counseling personnel. DSM-III is still predicated on the ineffectual medical model. Although there are more options to identify "normal" developmental problems, the descriptions of these diagnoses are vague. This vagueness makes it difficult to distinguish the different diagnoses in the "normal"category, as well as to distinguish them from the "mental disorders" diagnoses. In addition, the DSM-III category for defining "normal" developmental problems is ineffective for planning treatment or counseling.

Nevertheless, there are many innovations that are pertinent to clinicians and counseling psychologists. The multiaxial diagnosis is a prominent change that should help professionals using the DSM-III to increase consistency of diagnoses. The innovations that are relevant to college counselors, and the limitations, have been discussed. The prime advantage of learning to use DSM-III is to enhance communication with fellow mental health professionals. Thus, it is important that counselors learn about the manual and be capable of using it when necessary, even though it may not have extensive application in college counseling services.

REFERENCES

Albee, G. W. 1969. Emerging concepts of mental illness and models of treatment: The psychological point of view. American Journal of Psychiatry, 125: 870-876.

American Psychiatric Association. 1968. Diagnostic and statistical manual of mental disorders. 2nd ed. Washington, D.C.: American Psychiatric Association.

_____. 1980. Diagnostic and statistical manual of mental disorders. 3rd ed. Washington, D.C.: American Psychiatric Association.

Arbuckle, D. 1975. Counseling and psychotherapy: An existential-humanistic view. 3rd ed. Boston: Allyn and Bacon.

Blocher, D. H. 1966. Developmental counseling. New York: Ronald Press.

Carkhuff, R., and B. Berenson. 1967. Beyond counseling and therapy. New York: Holt, Rinehart and Winston.

Erikson, E. H. 1968. Identity, youth and crisis. New York: W. W. Norton.

Frances, A. 1980. The DSM-III personality disorders section: A commentary. American Journal of Psychiatry, 137: 1050-1054.

Hansen, J. C., R. R. Stevic, and R. W. Warner. 1977. Counseling theory and process. 2nd ed. Boston: Allyn and Bacon.

Havighurst, R. J. 1953. Human development and education. New York: David McKay.

Jahoda, M. 1950. Toward a social psychology of mental health. In M. F. C. Senn, ed., Symposium on the healthy personality. New York: Josiah Macy.

Kanfer, F. H., and G. Saslow. 1965. Behavioral analysis: An alternative to diagnostic classification. Archives of General Psychiatry, 12: 529-538.

Karasu, T. B., and A. E. Skodol. 1980. VIth for DSM-III: Psychodynamic evaluation. American Journal of Psychiatry, 137: 607-610.

Kohlberg, L. 1969. Stages in the development of moral thought and action. New York: Holt, Rinehart and Winston.

Laing, R. D. 1967. The politics of experience. New York: Ballantine.

Lipp, M. R., J. G. Looney, and R. C. Spitzer. 1977. Classifying psychophysiologic disorders: A new idea. Psychosomatic Medicine, 39: 285-287.

Maslow, A. H. 1962. Toward a psychology of being. New York: Van Nostrand.

Masterson, J. F. 1976. Psychotherapy of the borderline adult: A developmental approach. New York: Brunner/Mazel.

McLemore, C. W., and L. S. Benjamin. 1979. What happened to interpersonal diagnosis? A psychosocial alternative to DSM-III. American Psychologist, 34: 17-34.

McReynolds, W. T. 1979. DSM-III and the future of applied social sciences. Professional Psychology, 10: 123-132.

Piaget, J. 1952. The origins of intelligence in children. New York: International Universities Press.

Pietrofesa, J. J., A. Hoffman, H. H. Splete, and D. V. Pinto. 1978. Counseling: Theory, research and practice. Chicago: Rand McNally College Publishing.

Phillips, L., and J. G. Draguns. 1971. Classification of behavior disorders. Annual Review of Psychology, 22: 447-482.

Rogers, C. R. 1961. On becoming a person. A therapist's view of psychotherapy. Boston: Houghton Mifflin.

_____. 1951. Client-centered therapy. Boston: Houghton Mifflin.

Schacht, T., and P. E. Nathan. 1977. But is it good for the psychologists? Appraisal and status of DSM-III. American Psychologist, 32: 1017-1025.

Shertzer, B., and S. C. Stone. 1978. Fundamentals of Counseling. Boston: Houghton Mifflin.

Shoben, E. J. 1957. Toward a concept of the normal personality. Psychologist, 12: 183-189.

Spitzer, R., J. Endicott, and M. Gibbon. 1979. Crossing the border into borderline personality and borderline schizophrenia: The development of criteria. Archives of General Psychiatry, 36: 17-24.

Spitzer, R. L., and J. B. W. Forman. 1979. DSM-III field trials: II. Initial experience with multiaxial system. American Journal of Psychiatry, 136: 818-820.

Spitzer, R. L., J. B. W. Forman, and J. Nee. 1979. DSM-III field trials: I. Initial interrater diagnostic reliability. American Journal of Psychiatry, 136: 815-817.

Spitzer, R. L., M. Sheehy, and J. Endicott. 1977. DSM-III: Guiding principles. In V. M. Rakoff, H. C. Stancer, and H. B. Kedward, eds., Psychiatric diagnosis. New York: Brunner/ Mazel.

Szasz, T. 1961. The myth of mental illness. New York: Harper and Row.

Tyler, L. 1969. The work of the counselor. 3rd ed. New York: Appleton-Century-Crofts.

Wolberg, L. 1954. The technique of psychotherapy. New York: Grune and Stratton.

Zubin, J. 1967. Classification of the behavior disorders. Annual Review of Psychology, 18: 373-406.

# 6

# CONFIDENTIALITY AND RECORDS MANAGEMENT IN THE UNIVERSITY COUNSELING CENTER

## *Steven Katz*
## *Dee Leach*

> Psychologists respect the dignity and worth of the indi-
> vidual and strive for the preservation and protection of
> fundamental human rights.  They are committed to in-
> creasing knowledge of human behavior and of people's
> understanding of themselves and others and to the utili-
> zation of such knowledge for the promotion of human
> welfare.  While pursuing these objectives, they make
> every effort to protect participants that may be the
> object of study.  They use their skills only for purposes
> consistent with these values and do not knowingly permit
> their misuse by others.  While demanding for themselves
> freedom of inquiry and communication, psychologists ac-
> cept the responsibility this freedom requires: compe-
> tence, objectivity in the application of skills, and con-
> cern for the best interests of clients, colleagues,
> students, research participants, and society.

This affirmation of general values and beliefs begins the preamble
to the American Psychological Association's Ethical Standards of
Psychologists, and is followed by ten specific principles that stem
from this emphasis on the dignity and worth of the individual human
being.  A footnote informs us that these principles apply equally to
students of psychology and to others who do work of a psychological
nature under the supervision of a psychologist.  Principle 5, confidentiality, and the laws that protect it will be the focus of this
chapter.

The APA Code of Ethics was copyrighted in the early 1960s.
Since then, an unprecedented explosion of information and commu-

nications technology has taken place. The ensuing proliferation of computerized records has given rise to increasing concern, not only within the profession but also on the part of the public, for the the rights of privacy and confidentiality. Everstine et al. (1980) have pointed out that "Breach of confidentiality is properly conceived as only one of many kinds of invasion of privacy, and thus the issue of confidentiality is seen as a subset of the privacy issue."

That the American people are greatly concerned by threats to personal privacy is apparent in the findings of a national opinion survey report entitled The Dimensions of Privacy (Westin 1979), in which three out of four Americans believe that privacy is another "inalienable" right, like liberty. In December 1978, 64 percent of those surveyed were greatly concerned about this matter, and 92 percent of them felt that all employers should have a specific policy designed to safeguard information contained in personnel and medical files. The medical profession, and by extension those psychological professions that have privileged communication, enjoy a larger measure of public confidence. Of the 18 organizations and individual agents included in the survey, doctors are the least criticized for their efforts to keep patient information confidential. Only 17 percent of the public feels that doctors should do more in this regard (Westin 1979).

Concerns for confidentiality raise a number of issues: the nature of the information that may be revealed, the specific purpose of or need for information, the forms and terms of transmitting this information, the particular person or entity identified as receiving the information.

Statutory protection for information about people has been evolving rapidly in recent years. Many of the laws overlap, and also leave significant voids in protection for individual interests. There is great variation in the statutes of the several states, but these various classes of statutes, privacy acts, freedom of information acts, and agency regulations will be discussed primarily with reference to California. Further, we hope to provide some direction for the handling of the more routine decisions that are required to be made by the university counseling center practitioner.

This chapter is not an attempt to substitute for the individual and competent advice of an attorney, nor to present a summary of every law that may pertain, nor to present in their entirety those laws or actions that may be applicable to any given specific situation. It has been pointed out that specific state and local directives and laws, as well as internal operating procedures within the district or institution, also vary widely. Only when one has actually been involved in the day-to-day transactions of record-keeping at a large university can the multitude of variations in the circumstances that may arise be fully appreciated. Of primary importance is that each case calls for reasoned, good-faith, and professional judgment based on the best information available or obtainable.

As a common focal point, one should always balance the rights of the client's privacy, so essential to the effective counseling process (and in many instances compelled by law), against the need or purpose motivating disclosure of the particular record or portion of information. As a practical matter, the authors have found that it is helpful to remember that in most circumstances such disclosure decisions do not require instantaneous judgment. As a rule of thumb, once the record or information is disclosed, any opportunity to prevent damage by disclosure or release is lost. If, however, the records should have been disclosed, and were not, subsequent release will, in most instances, rectify the problem. (Possible areas of exception are court orders and emergency situations, subsequently addressed.)

As a professional psychotherapist,[1] or individual performing or assisting such personnel in their counseling functions, one either makes notes concerning matters discussed with the patient,[2] or receives memoranda, letters, or objects that pertain to the often confidential and sensitive matters disclosed in the psychotherapist/ patient relationship. Additionally, there will be personal sensory observations (such as clothes, mannerisms, objects), of which the psychotherapist will be cognizant, that may or may not be privileged, depending on the circumstances.

Questions that may arise cover a broad range of complexity and importance. Has the student the right to see the counselor's notes? What if the student requests that a copy of your notes be sent to an off-campus psychologist? Or priest? What are the student's rights if he/she disagrees with something, such as test results, in his/her counseling folder? Or the life of another is in imminent peril from your client, as disclosed in your counseling session with the client? Or you desire to discuss the notes of your session with your adviser or supervisor? Or you are served with a subpoena for your client's files?

A counseling center should have a formalized statement of its policies with regard to protecting the privacy of students. A custodian of records should be appointed in each operating unit, with the designated responsibilities of overseeing the general procedures for maintaining records in a confidential manner, and safeguarding the consistent treatment of requests for information that come to that unit.

The counseling center must have developed clear guidelines as to what information can be released, under what circumstances, for what purposes, and to whom. In addition to these safeguards, there are important questions of the regular maintenance and ultimate disposition of the student's (or client's) records. Additionally, the "records" that are to come under the jurisdiction of the custodian should be defined. A appointment book or daily schedule of a counselor that contains student names is a confidential record as much as is a file with test scores or counselor notes. Since personal notes of a counselor are not subject to subpoena, it may be preferred practice that each counselor maintain his/her personal notes concerning students locked in his/her own desk, and not submit them to a central file, however secure.

There are three major bodies of laws or regulations that may serve to assist the counselor/practitioner in the maintenance and access[3] requirements of counseling records at a higher education counseling center: constitutional and statutory law (municipal, state, and federal), the professional code of conduct, and administrative policy of the university.

At the federal level a primary directive concerning the maintenance and disclosure of student records on a university campus is the Family Educational Rights and Privacy Act (FERPA), as amended (20 U.S.C. 1232[g] [P.L. 93-380]). This act provides directions for disclosure of "educational records" maintained by a public or private college or university. The directives apply to those colleges and universities receiving funds under federal programs administered by the secretary of education, and failure to treat the records as specified under law may result in loss of some federal funds by the university. (This applies where voluntary compliance with the FERPA directives cannot later be obtained from the university.)

For purposes of the act, "educational records" means, with specific exceptions, those records, files, documents, and other materials that contain information directly related to a student who has been or is currently in attendance at the university, and are maintained by the university or a person acting for the university.[4]

There is a list of express exceptions that define categories of records not to be included under "educational records." Those exceptions most germane and most often in question for purposes of the university-level counseling center are enumerated in FERPA. These include records of institutional, supervisory, and administrative personnel and their assistants that are not accessible or revealed to any other person except a substitute.[5] Additional exceptions are personal notes and records retained by the counselor to serve as memory aids and not included in the student's central file folder maintained by the counseling center. Also excluded are records of students that are made or maintained by a physician, psychologist, psychiatrist, or other recognized professional or paraprofessional acting in his/her professional or paraprofessional capacity, and that are made, maintained, or used only in connection with the provision of treatment to the student, and are not available to any one other than persons providing such treatment. ("Treatment" does not include remedial education activities or activities that are a part of the program of instruction at the university.)

The privilege to inquire may overcome any asserted right to privacy whenever the inquiry is essential to the performance of a legitimate responsibility. The privilege to withhold information is directly connected to the import of confidentiality to the relationship. Both privileges are qualified by overriding concerns of public health, safety, and welfare. A great many of the inquiries made within an educational institution are legitimate, and the information is needed for the performance of someone's duty; but confidentiality must be maintained even in these delicate situations, unless there exists a clear threat to personal safety (as discussed in more detail later in this chapter). Also important to bear in mind is that records that are not personal notes, but are a part of the counseling center's central files pertaining to an individual client, may be personally reviewed by a "physician or other appropriate professional of the student's choice," consonant with proper record release procedures.

In addition, there are certain privileges in evidence codes attached to the psychotherapist/patient relationship that protect disclosure of communications obtained in the course of such relationships. (Both general requirements for release of records, and further discussion concerning the evidentiary privileges, appear below.) For the moment it should be noted that the psychotherapist/client privilege is controlled by the client, not the therapist, and must be breached by the therapist only under certain legal conditions, when criminal action or the courts are involved in certain circumstances, or when the client is believed to be a danger to self or others (Everstine et al. 1980). Ordinarily, access to information revealed in therapy is provided only upon application by the client acting in his/her own interest.

States may adopt constitutional or statutory provisions in areas where the U.S. Congress has not acted, or where the state regulations are more protective of individual privacy and not inconsistent with congressional provision where Congress has spoken. One such example is the California Constitution, section I, article 1, which states: "All people are by nature free and independent and have inalienable rights. Among these are enjoying and defending life and liberty, acquiring, possessing and protecting property, and pursuing and obtaining safety, happiness and privacy."

California has further adopted the California Public Records Act. Here the legislature restates that it is mindful of the right of the individual to privacy, then goes on to declare that access to information concerning the conduct of the people's business is a fundamental and necessary right of every person in the state. Recognizing the inherent conflict, specific exceptions to disclosure were incorporated; most notably "personnel, medical, or similar files, the disclosure of which would constitute an unwarranted invasion of privacy . . ." are exempt, as are records the disclosure of which is exempted or prohibited pursuant to provisions of federal or state law, including but not limited to the evidence code related to privilege (California Govt. Code secs. 6250ff.).

The act contains a further provision that serves as a general exemption: "The agency shall justify withholding any record by demonstrating that the record in question is exempt under express provisions of this chapter, or that on the facts of the particular case a public interest served by not making the record public clearly outweighs a public interest served by disclosure of the records."

These provisions of the California Public Records Act are set forth to give the reader a "flavor" for the privacy of records and the depth of concern the legislatures have displayed, and for which the practitioner is ultimately responsible. It is noted that there may be ambiguity or conflict among applicable laws. For example, chapter 13, article 1, section 67100 ff. was added to the California Education Code for the specific and stated purpose of resolving potential conflicts between California law and the federal provisions of FERPA, and to provide general revision and update of laws relating to such records. Where a conflict among laws is discovered by the practitioner, he/she would be well advised to consult with the university's legal adviser for resolution and the proper course of conduct.

Although thus far the focus has been on nondisclosure of records and information, the reader should note that there are circumstances that allow or even demand access. The reader will recall that under the parameters of FERPA a student may request that records be personally reviewed by a physician or "other appropriate professional" of the student's choice. The meaning of "other appropriate professional" is apparently left to the practitioner's reasoned discretion. There is no formula for such a determination, and perhaps that is why the legislature failed to define the term. It is suggested that the person to whom it is requested that the records be released, be examined to determine educational background, credentials, business or professional licenses, and whether these parallel those of the traditional "professionals," such as physicians and psychologists. To assist in making the decision, ask yourself, "Would the person to whom records would be provided be in a position to understand the disclosed information; to interpret it; and then perhaps to redisclose it to the client in a professional and meaningful manner, consistent with the best interest of all parties concerned?" Such decisions must necessarily be made on a case-by-case basis.

As a further condition for access or release of student counseling records to third persons, there must be written consent from the student specifying the particular records to be released, the reason for such release, and the party or class of parties to whom such records may be released. The recipient of the information must be notified that he/she must not permit any other party to have access to the information without the written consent of the student. A record of those to whom information is released pursuant to the request should be maintained, and the records of those obtaining access made available only to the student, the custodian of the records, and generally to specified parties for audit purpose.[7]

There should be a mechanism provided for the student to challenge material in the central files that he/she deems to be inaccurate, misleading, inappropriate, or an unsubstantiated personal conclusion not supported by the facts. There should also be a mechanism provided for questions concerning the student's right of access to the material in the files. The suggested procedure is for the initial review to take place between the records custodian and the student, in an informal attempt to resolve the issue where the counselor and the student are unable to do so. A further procedure would be developed in the event the matter cannot be resolved informally, such as a more formal hearing procedure that includes a decision by an unbiased party—for instance, an administrative law judge. Possible means of resolution include removing the challenged material from the file altogether; striking the challenged portion only; returning the material to the sender (where, for example, a letter is the document in question); or allowing the student to append an explanation of his/her position to the challenged material, such explanation to accompany the challenged material whenever released or used as the basis for making decisions.

Another situation that may require disclosure of the file is issuance of a court order for the student's records. This will often come in the form of a subpoena duces tecum (bring the records). Generally, the order will be directed to the president of the university, the records custodian of the unit holding such records, or the director of counseling, although it may be directed to a specific individual counselor. Many states provide that a copy of the records may be submitted to the court or issuing agency, accompanied by a certification of authenticity by the state agency; where permitted, this alleviates the necessity for a personal appearance to produce such records. However, because of the evidentiary privilege that the counselor may be required to assert on behalf of his/her client, legal counsel should be consulted prior to release of such records. Additionally, where a court order is received, the university should make a reasonable effort to notify the student of the order or subpoena in advance of compliance, since the student may desire to seek a court order quashing or modifying the original order for records. With the student's records, a record should be maintained of the attempt to notify, and the filing and ruling regarding modifying orders if there are any.

A further situation that may require disclosure, but only in the rarest of instances, is in connection with an "emergency." Major factors for the counselor to consider are the degree to which time is of the essence, the degree of harm or potential harm to the health or safety of the client or others, the degree to which the disclosure of the information is necessary to control the emergency, and the degree to which the person to whom the information is disclosed is in a position to control the emergency. Each situation requires a reasoned judgment but, again, the need for disclosure of confidential information during an emergency must, on balance, outweigh the primary rights of privacy stemming from the psychotherapist/client relationship. [8]

During the course of the psychotherapist/client relationship there exists a special privilege to ensure the free flow of communication. [9] This communication is then protected by law, and thus is made a "confidential communication." The parameters of these relationships are defined by statute and case law. There are, further, guidelines for the practitioner in the codes of ethics for the respective professions that enjoy such privileged communications; psychology and psychiatry are generally recognized as being among these professions.

However, not every communication between a patient and a psychologist is privileged as a confidential communication. Wigmore, in his famous treatise on evidence, summarized the four criteria that must be met for the confidential communication to exist:

The communication must originate in a confidence that it will not be disclosed.

The element of confidentiality must be essential to the full and satisfactory maintenance of the relationship between the parties.

The relationship must be one that, in the opinion of the community, ought to be assiduously fostered.

The injury that would occur to the relationship by the disclosure of
the communication must be greater than the benefit thereby
gained for current disposal of the litigation.

California Evidence Code is typical of the statutes that define
the law relating to privilege. (See, for example, California Evidence Code, secs. 1010-26.) With the admonition that the law is
complex, exceptions to the basic rules abound, [10] and the fact that
decisions may turn on the smallest variations in fact, the authors
will present the provisions that one is most likely to encounter in
the psychotherapist/patient context. These provisions relate to
disclosure and nondisclosure of confidential communications, and
records of the practitioner in the higher education environments.

Where one is the "holder" of the privilege, [11] he/she may
generally refuse to disclose, and prevent another from disclosing,
a confidential communication between the patient and the psychotherapist. This also applies to one authorized to claim the privilege
on behalf of the holder, or the person who was the psychtherapist
at the time of the confidential communication.

In addition to the privilege of nondisclosure of confidential
communications applying to the psychotherapist himself/herself,
there may be occasions where a third person—an assistant, or a
physician, or other person necessary for the effective performance
of the psychotherapist's duties—is also present. Should the holder
of the privilege voluntarily disclose a portion of the communication
that is substantial, or if he/she has provided approval for another
in possession of the communication's content to disclose it, then the
right to the privilege is waived. Where the information is conveyed
to another who is bound by the privileged relationship, the privilege
is not lost. For example, if a counselor seeks advice from a supervisor or an associate or an attorney, the supervisor or attorney
is one who is furthering the business of the confidential psychotherapist/client relationship, and is also ethically and legally bound
to retain the client's confidentiality. The exceptions, of course,
may be in the rare instances constituting an "emergency" as previously discussed.

The importance of adherence to the professional mandates of
confidentiality cannot be overemphasized. In addition to the university's liability for improper or illegal disclosure, the Laws,
Rules and Regulations Relating to the Practice of Psychology, which
are issued by the Board of Medical Quality Assurance Psychology
Examining Committee (California 1979) state in section 2960: "The
committee may order the denial of an application for, an issue with
terms and conditions, or the suspension for a period not exceeding
one year, or the revocation of, or the imposition of probationary

conditions upon, a license or registration for any of the following causes: . . . (h) Willful unauthorized communications of information received in professional confidence, and . . . (j) Being grossly negligent in the practice of his profession." Also included is a reference to confidentiality, which states that the confidential relations and communications between the psychologist and client shall be privileged, as provided by the appropriate provisions of the California Evidence Code.

In addition to the legal safeguards to confidentiality, there are ethical decisions to be made concerning protection of records and communications. There is a responsibility to advise the client about the possible effect on his/her own interests by the release of the requested material. There is a determination to be made as to whether the technical level of the information to be released (such as certain test protocols) is transmitted to professionally trained persons who can be expected to interpret it knowledgeably and, in their turn, maintain the necessary confidentiality.

Educational institutions are responsible for protecting confidentiality, both as an ethical obligation and a means of implementing the myriad laws that may overlap or be in contradiction.

Consideration must be given not only to security of files and systematic procedures for transmission of confidential material, but also to the security of this material when it is being handled in the course of daily work. For example, mailboxes or secretaries' desks, or even counselors' desks, may be visually accessible to numbers of people. Therefore, confidential material should never be in these places uncovered. When records are designated for disposal (usually conducted on a fixed schedule), they should be stored in a locked facility until they are shredded. In addition, other materials that are confidential should be clearly marked "Confidential," "Personal," or in some other appropriate manner, to assist in avoiding improper duplication or dissemination.

Observation of a student in a public setting (such as a classroom or waiting room) does not constitute privileged information. Privileged information is that given by the student within the context of established trust in the counselor. A counselor may ethically serve as a consultant about specific student behavior (if faculty or administration should ask an opinion or seek advice) without having seen the student as a client. In fact, it is safer to perform this consultative role with reference to a student who has not been a client. Schroedel (1979) advises that such consultation be done without stating whether the student is a client at the counseling center. "In most instances it would prove difficult for the counselor involved with a student in question to function as consultant to the administration while maintaining the integrity of the therapeutic relationship. The privacy of this relationship must remain intact; therefore the counseling center and administration should define channels of communication when a consultation on a specific student is requested" (Schroedel 1979, p. 422).

An institution should formalize its policy regarding confidentiality in statements that should include the following (Schroedel 1979, p. 423):

Recognition of the dual role of the counseling center—therapy and consultation

Recognition of the necessity for complete confidentiality in the therapeutic relationship

Recognition of the requirement to break confidentiality when there is a clear and present danger to life

Definition of the consultant role and procedures for requesting consultation

Responsibility for educating the college community with regard to these policy positions.

In closing, there can be no substitute for experience. Only professional experience, a solid educational background, and practical knowledge and reasoning will make one proficient in the areas of recordkeeping and confidentiality in a university counseling center. It is hoped that this chapter will stimulate thinking concerning the importance and sensitivity of records, and the professional relationships and confidences in the university counseling center, and that some direction has been provided for resolving the questions raised here and those encountered in everyday practice.

NOTES

1. A "psychotherapist" is "(a) a person authorized, or reasonably believed by the patient to be authorized, to practice medicine in any state or nation who devotes, or [is] reasonably believed by the patient to devote, a substantial portion of his time to the practice of psychiatry; or (b) a person licensed as a psychologist" (under the laws of the state). California Evidence Code, sec. 1010.

2. A "patient" is "a person who consults a psychotherapist or submits to an examination by a psychotherapist for the purpose of securing a diagnosis or preventive, palliative, or curative treatment of his mental or emotional condition or who submits to an examination of his mental or emotional condition for the purpose

of scientific research or mental or emotional problems." California Evidence Code, sec. 1011.

3. California Education Code, sec. 67110 (d), defines "access" as "a personal inspection and review of a record or an accurate copy of a record, and a request to release a copy of any record." Where a record may be seen, or the information from the record read to the client, the client is sometimes permitted to obtain copies of such record (for instance, if not a psychological test question booklet). A reasonable charge may be made for copies, not to exceed the actual cost of furnishing the copies of the student's record (such as $.10 per copy). However, no charge may be made to search for or retrieve any student record. See California Education Code, sec. 67123.

4. A person not yet attending the university—for instance, an applicant for admission—does not fall within this category. The exceptions to "educational records" are further delineated in note 6.

5. A "substitute" shall mean "a person who performs the duties of the individual who made the notes, on a temporary basis, and does not refer to a person who permanently succeeds the maker of the notes in his or her position." California Education Code, sec. 67110.

6. Other exceptions include, in a broad sense, law enforcement records complying with restricted access and use for law enforcement purposes; records relating exclusively to a person's employment capacity; information provided by parents in relation to applications for financial aid or scholarships; confidential letters or statements of recommendation filed on or before January 1, 1975; and alumni records that contain information relating to a person after that person was no longer a student.

7. For example, the comptroller general of the United States, state educational authorities, and accrediting organizations. However, care must be taken not to violate confidentiality. The implication is that only information that will not permit the personal identification of the student, where personal counseling records are maintained in the course of the psychotherapist/client relationship, should be revealed.

8. A well-known case involving failure to disclose information is Tarasoff v. Board of Regents of the University of California (13 Cal. 3d 177, 118; Cal. Rptr. 129, 529 p. 2d 553). The case involves an outpatient at a hospital on the Berkeley campus. The patient informed the psychologist that he was planning to kill a woman. In this case it was not the failure of the psychologist or his supervisor to predict violence that made the case a viable one, but the failure of the psychologist to provide an adequate warning of violence to the intended victim or her parents. The case is a leading case and well worth reading in its entirety.

9. The Senate Judiciary Committee noted in a comment that "Psychoanalysis and Psychotherapy are dependent upon the fullest revelation of the most intimate and embarrassing details of the patient's life. Unless a patient . . . is assured that such information can and will be held in utmost confidence, he will be reluctant to make the full disclosure upon which diagnosis and treatment . . . depends" (California Evidence Code, comment to sec. 1014).

10. For example, there are 11 major exceptions in the California Evidence Code as to when the psychotherapist is required to claim the privilege.

11. The patient when he/she has no guardian or conservator, or the guardian or conservator of the patient when the patient has a guardian or conservator, or the personal representative of the patient if the patient is dead.

## REFERENCES

California Board of Medical Quality Assurance, Psychology Examining Committee. 1979. Laws, rules and regulations relating to the practice of psychology. Sacramento.

Everstine, L., D. S. Everstine, G. M. Heymann, R. H. True, D. H. Frey, H. G. Johnson, and R. H. Seiden. 1980. Privacy and confidentiality in psychotherapy. American Psychologist, 35, no. 9: 828-840.

Powledge, Fred. 1977. The therapist as double agent. Psychology Today, July, pp. 44-47.

Schroedel, David L. 1979. Confidentiality and the role of the college counselor. Journal of College Student Personnel, 20, no. 5: 418-423.

Stevens, George E. 1980. Invasion of student privacy. Journal of Law and Education, 3: 343-351.

Taylor, Alton L., ed. 1977. Protecting individual rights to privacy in higher education. New Directions for Institutional Research, 4, no. 2.

Van Hoose, William H., and Louis V. Paradise. 1979. Ethics in counseling and psychotherapy. Cranston, R.I.: Carroll Press.

Westin, Alan F. 1979. The dimensions of privacy: A national opinion research survey of attitudes toward privacy. Stevens Point, Wis.: Sentry Insurance.

# 7

# PSYCHOLOGICAL ASSESSMENT SERVICES

## *Van Roussos*

This chapter will deal primarily with psychological assessment of college counselees through the use of psychological tests. This service is normally provided through the cooperation of the testing office by referral from the college or university counseling center. Broadly speaking, the testing office provides information of two kinds: educational and psychological. Educational information is typically provided to the instructional areas through such programs as admission and placement testing, equivalence testing, proficiency testing, test scoring services to faculty, and the student-faculty evaluation program.

Admission tests (also known as entrance tests) are tests of scholastic aptitude, and are used to determine a student's eligibility for admission. Typical undergraduate admission tests, the scores of which serve as one criterion for admission, are the Scholastic Aptitude Test (SAT) of the College Entrance Examination Board and the American College Testing (ACT) Program. The other common, and the most weighted, criterion is the high school grade point average. Placement tests determine the appropriate course placement of students once they are admitted to a program. Proficiency examinations are tests through which students demonstrate competency required for entering special programs or for completing a degree objective. The testing office also assists faculty in scoring objective tests constructed by faculty for the purpose of measuring student progress. Equivalence tests are customarily advanced placement tests that are administered to determine whether students should be granted credit for advanced course work in high school. Through the student-faculty evaluation program, students rate classes and faculty classroom performance so that faculty, departments, and schools may receive feedback from student input.

With this brief information on the educational services that the testing office provides to the instructional area and the student population at large, the remaining sections will be devoted to the area of psychological assessment. The term "psychological assessment" is preferred to other terms such as "psychometric testing" or "psychological testing." Assessment implies the use of psychological tests or other techniques to evaluate individuals, with an emphasis on assisting these individuals to investigate their potentials, their strengths, and their weaknesses as they engage in self-exploration, striving to solidify their concepts of the self and seeking help in achieving self-understanding and making accurate and well-informed personal decisions. Matarazzo (1972) describes assessors as being application-oriented practitioners, in contrast with psychometric-oriented theorists; the former develop and administer instruments for individual assessment, and the latter are involved, through research and writing, with the nature of what it is to be assessed. McReynolds (1968, p. 2) defines psychological assessment thus:

> . . . the systematic use of a variety of special techniques to better understand a given individual, group or psychological ecology.

Maloney and Ward (1976) view psychometric testing as being oriented toward describing and studying groups of people in terms of individual differences, but demanding little if any expertise on the part of the examiner. By contrast, psychological assessment focuses on solving problems of a particular individual. The process of assessment requires the assessor to define the problem, possess a broad psychological knowledge, and know what techniques to use and how to collect, evaluate, and integrate data so that a model or a map of the person being assessed is developed. The person of the assessor is crucial in the process, and the assessor must be aware not only of the context of the individual being assessed but also of the assessor's role in the assessment process.

In addition to being knowledgeable in the field, a successful assessor must be dedicated, committed, intellectually inquisitive, and psychologically minded. He/she must be able to make use of past experience and want to understand fellow human beings, and at times must work with data in an almost compulsive manner. We understand others through empathy, introspection, and projection although these processes are often conducive to subjectivity, personal bias, and errors of omission and commission. Personal bias must be held in check or minimized, and subjectivity must be modulated as much as possible. A careful and methodical analysis of the test data and a prudent synthesis of data obtained from different sources—including different tests, the life situation of the examinee, observations, and information obtained in the counseling relationship and from interviewing—will help minimize these errors.

Assessors and counselors alike should take time to go through the various tests they use, in order to know what the examinee goes through when responding to the test items. In addition, these professionals should be familiar with all the relevant information that is readily available in test manuals and handbooks, and make it a habit to review these sources from time to time.

## PSYCHOLOGICAL TESTS AND PSYCHOTHERAPY

Counselors and psychotherapists represent a variety of attitudes and opinions on the use of tests in counseling and psychotherapy. At one extreme are those who espouse the medical point of view and consider psychological testing necessary for diagnosis and treatment. Rapaport (1954) and Schafer (1948) represent this point of view. These clinicians employed tests to arrive at personality descriptions and psychological functioning. At the other extreme, existentialists protest that psychodiagnosis and psychological testing have the effect of fractionating the individual, of dehumanizing and of depriving him/her of his/her uniqueness and individuality, and interfere with the establishment of a spontaneous and therapeutic relationship. In this camp are Bugental (1965), Buhler (1971), Buhler and Allen (1972), and Maslow (1962).

Breger (1968) argues that the use of psychological tests for diagnosis prior to treatment may obstruct the patient's initial efforts to do something about his/her difficulties if the initial contact is followed by referral for testing. He goes on to say that insofar as erroneous expectations are fostered by testing, psychological tests may be antitherapeutic. Frank et al. (1959) found that patients with the most accurate expectations exhibited the most favorable response to psychotherapy. Breger concedes that psychological testing may be appropriate for research and in cases where volunteers seek diagnostic help or when specific decisions have to be made.

Another criticism of psychodiagnosis is that the diagnostic instruments are poor predictors of behavior (Goldfried and D'Zurilla 1969; Greenspoon and Gersten 1967). Still another criticism is that psychodiagnostic measures involve levels of inference that increase errors of measurement. Weiner (1972) refutes both of these criticisms and that of the humanists. He declares that the purpose of psychodiagnosis is to appraise personality processes and not to predict behavior. The personality construct criticism depends on how many levels of inference lie between the test data and the conclusions to be drawn, and on the strength of the chains of evidence linking levels. The key to the potential accuracy of an assessment approach is not whether it involves intervening variables, but the nature of the levels of inferences required. As to humanistic criticisms, they have to do with abuses of assessment, and not with its aims and characteristics. As Palmer (1980, pp. 54-55) remarks:

> An assessment is not an evaluation or judgment but rather a broad survey of the client's life and the client's psychological functioning. Moreover such an assessment is designed merely to acquaint the therapist with the client's personality but even more important to introduce the client to the task of self-exploration.

A more specific criticism of psychological tests, and especially of intelligence tests, is that general population norms are not applicable to minority groups. A frequently proposed solution to this problem is the creation of multiple norms. Although the use of multiple norms may result in a more accurate description of minority students' standing in relation to their special group, the problem of identifying the student's problems and needs still remains. Diagnosing a student's strengths and weaknesses, and enabling the student to take advantage of educational opportunities, are of paramount importance.

A special issue of <u>American Psychologist</u> (Glaser and Bond 1981) is devoted to the area of testing and social issues. In the same issue Reschly (1981) examines the issues of bias and discrimination as they relate to psychological testing, educational placement, and classification, and concludes with the following recommendations:

1. Replacement of the concept of mild retardation by more descriptive and less misleading terms, such as "low academic aptitude" and "low classroom achievement"

2. Abandonment of the IQ concept in order to avoid negative connotations and unfounded implications for innate potential

3. Use of multifactored assessment techniques, including variables such as adaptive behavior, primary language, and sociocultural status

4. Emphasis on improving educational programs, and use of criterion-referenced tests and assessment techniques based on

behavioral and consultation technology, in order to identify target behaviors, collect relevant data in a natural environment,
and evaluate programs.

Furthermore, Reschly (1981) assetts that good tests by themselves do not contribute to bias and discrimination. It is the improper use of tests, the implications that people attribute to tests
or derive from them, and the social consequences that result in
real or perceived bias, stereotypes, and injustices. The crucial
issue is the special education need and improvement of educational
programs. IQ tests either have a neutral effect on overall propor-
tionality or reduce the overrepresentation of minority students that
might exist from teacher referral alone. Variables involved in
overrepresentation in special educational programs include race,
ethnic group, sex, and socioeconomic status. More students from
minority backgrounds, more male students, and more members of
the lower socioeconomic levels are represented in special classes.

Survey studies are found in the literature pertaining to the
usefulness of psychological reports to therapists and psychiatrists.
Adams (1972), in assessing the impact of psychological evaluations
upon psychiatric diagnosis, found that psychological reports had a
meaningful impact on more than 16 percent of the cases. Smyth
and Reznikoff (1971) asked 57 psychiatrists whether they considered
psychodiagnostic reports valuable in planning treatment. These
psychiatrists reported that they found psychodiagnosis valuable for
treatment planning. Thirty-seven percent of the sample indicated
that they would request testing for help with diagnosis, and an additional 21 percent for consultation on organicity. Affleck and Strider
(1971), in a follow-up study of 340 psychological test reports two
months after each report was prepared, found that in 22 percent the
report was felt by the referring person to have had no effect on
management of the patient. In 24 percent of the cases the report
was considered generally helpful, and in 52 percent the report
altered the treatment approach or assisted in some specific action
regarding the patient.

In a survey of members of the American Psychological Association, Division 17, Fee, Elkins, and Boyd (1982) report that
counseling psychologists devote considerable time to testing activities in order to obtain information regarding the following five
areas (listed in descending order from the most frequent to the
least frequent): career-vocational, diagnosis of psychopathology,
intellectual assessment, determination of academic status, and
determination of organicity. The responders reported that they use
objective tests for an average of 36 percent of their counselees and
projective tests for 11 percent. In responding to a question referring

to the specific psychological tests that they would advise counseling psychology students to learn to use, this group listed the following tests in order of preference: MMPI, WAIS, Strong-Campbell Interest Inventory, WISC-R, TAT, Bender, Rorschach, and Stanford-Binet. It is apparent that counseling psychologists in general recommend the use of a combination of tests including personality, general ability, interest, and (to some extent) projective tests.

The APA members who responded to this survey were engaged primarily in counseling/therapy, teaching, and administration. Although these professional activities are similar to activities of counselors in settings of higher education, the preferred tests of higher education counselors may be different from those mentioned above. From many years of working with counselors in higher education, I can assert that they use a wide variety of tests and that they vary in the number and kinds of tests they employ. Typically, they generally prefer one or two interest tests, a personality test, an ability test, and other tests as needed.

Another aspect of the study mentioned above (Fee, Elkins, and Boyd 1982) concerned the reasons why counselors would advise counseling psychology students to learn to use psychological tests. Of the ten reasons that had to be rank-ordered, the top five were information about personality structure, employability, satisfaction of legal requirements, provision of a specialty, and saving therapist time. The reasons that were rated low included satisfaction of institutional demands, enabling accurate prediction, obtaining intrinsic motivation, increasing of client-therapist rapport, and enhancement of therapist prestige.

It appears reasonable that whether tests are useful depends to a large extent on how the counselor or psychotherapist prepares the counselee prior to testing and what the counselor does with the test results. Telling the counselee about the nature of the tests and their use will enable him/her to tolerate the tests and to develop realistic expectations. Following testing, the referring person has an obligation to communicate the findings to the counselee in language that the counselee can understand. It is assumed that it is the primary responsibility of the counselor or psychotherapist to offer some help and to attempt to establish a growth-facilitating relationship by using appropriate tools that will aid in self-exploration, help clarify issues, generate alternatives, and facilitate decision making. The assessor has a responsibility to aid the counselor-counselee endeavors. The new model for assessment practice offered by Richard H. Dana (1980, p. 1043) includes these aspects:

(1) Assessor confers with referral source person in
order to define problems and the assessor role during
feedback or communication of findings; (2) assessment
procedures and rationale for consultation are discussed
with the client by the referral source person with emphasis on the roles of all participants during feedback
and the potential usages of findings; (3) assessor sees
client, describes procedures and administers tests;
(4) assessor describes and discusses findings with
client and referral source person simultaneously;
(5) assessor provides copies of written report to referral source person and to client; (6) assessor and referral source person maintain communication in order
to provide feedback for assessor regarding subsequent
utilization of findings. . . .

This model of assessment is based on humanistic values and
is admittedly an ideal to be pursued by the busy counselor and the
busy assessor, but it clearly recognizes that the assessment process involves the interaction of all three participants—counselor,
counselee, and assessor—and makes explicit the responsibility of
both the counselor and the assessor to involve the counselee in
most of the aspects of the process and to communicate the findings
to the counselee. This model is included in this chapter because it
is thought-provoking and because assessment need not be contrary
to humanistic values.

THE TEST REFERRAL FORM

To facilitate referrals of college counselees to the psychological assessor who frequently works in the testing office, a test
referral form listing the tests available is initially developed by the
assessor and other professional members of the testing office and
the counseling center. The test referral form has spaces for identifying information such as name, address, and telephone number
of the counselee, date the form is received, date of completion of
the tests, and the name of the counselor. Below this information
tests from which the counselor and the counselee choose are listed
by category: interest tests, objective personality tests, general
ability tests, differential aptitude tests, achievement tests, and
general clinical tests. Following the clinical tests there is an open
category for "other" tests, additional tests that are available but
are not listed for lack of space or because of infrequency of use.
Periodically tests may be dropped because they are no longer requested by counselors or are obsolete.

The interest and objective personality tests are self-explanatory. Tests listed under the category of general ability include tests of intelligence and scholastic ability, such as the Wechsler Adult Intelligence Scale (WAIS) and its revision WAIS-R, the Otis-Lennon Mental Ability Test, and the Ohio State Psychological Test. An example of a differential aptitude test is the Guilford-Zimmerman Aptitude Survey, which consists of seven parts: verbal comprehension, general reasoning, numerical operations, perceptual speed, spatial orientation, spatial visualization, and mechanical knowledge. Counselors may refer students for the whole series of this survey or may select parts of it, depending on the needs of the counselee. Differential aptitude tests are multifactorial tests providing information relevant to a number of specific aptitudes. Examples of special aptitude tests are the Graves Design Judgment Test, the Meier Art Judgment Test, the Knauber Art Ability Test, and the Seashore Tests of Musical Talents. There are also special aptitude tests for specific academic areas such as mathematics, chemistry, and physics. Examples of achievement tests are the Cooperative English Mechanics Test and the Cooperative Reading Comprehension Test.

Aptitude tests quite frequently overlap with achievement tests because there are no pure aptitude tests and, to some extent, achievement tests require some aptitude. Both types of tests are based on prior experience, but differ in terms of the breadth or narrowness of their content and in terms of their specific use. Typically, aptitude tests have a more general pool of item content. In contrast, the pool of item content of achievement tests is narrower and more precise. Additionally, aptitude tests are used to predict future behavior, while achievement tests are used to determine mastery of specific areas of instruction.

Returning to the test referral form, the category of special tests includes the Bender, the Rorschach, the TAT, sentence completions, and other projective tests. Because psychological assessment is viewed as part of the counseling process, students requesting psychological testing are advised to make an appointment with a counselor at the counseling center. With the counselor, and the assessor if necessary, the tests to be administered are selected. The test referral is then presented to the testing office for the appointments required to complete the indicated tests. Upon completion and processing of the tests, the results are reported to the counselor and the student is advised to make an appointment for discussion of the test findings.

In addition to helping with the test selection and administering and evaluating the tests requested, the assessor may assist counselors and their counselees by providing technical information from test sources and aiding in test interpretation. Examples of such

aid include clarification of discrepancies between tests or within
tests and providing information dealing with special tests or special
scales of particular tests.  Discrepancies between tests may be due
to differences in test items constituting the scales, the format of
the test questions (whether forced-choice or open-ended), and differences in the normative groups.  Occasionally discrepancies may
reflect intrapersonal contradictions suggesting the presence of
ambivalence or endopsychic conflict within the counselee.  An
alternative reason may be a change in the mental set assumed by
the counselee while responding during the examination.

Over the years I have learned to appreciate the importance of
examining the test items that make up a scale.  If a discrepancy
within a test is apparent, the assessor and the counselor should
check the counselee's responses to examine the kinds of items
that were endorsed or rejected by the examinee.  I can recall the
Guilford-Zimmerman Temperament Survey of a female counselee
that showed an extremely high masculinity score.  Rechecking the
scoring and seeing no clerical error, my original hypothesis was
that this young woman was projecting the image of a tough individual
who was denying fears and emotional sensitivity.  Upon examining
the test items, both the counselor and the assessor were satisfied
that my hypothesis was correct.  The counselee accepted the interpretation, and explained that through most of her life she had had
to fend for herself and learn to survive.  This example also reminds
me of the importance of interpreting test results within the context
of the counselee's life situation.

FURTHER COMMENTS ON TEST INTERPRETATION

Test interpretation is complex and requires knowledge of the
particular techniques, experience in applying the techniques, and
skill in reporting the test findings to the counselee in language that
is easily understood and in ways that allow the counselee to be part
of the process and to consider the meanings and implications of the
results, how these results relate to the counselee's life situation,
and how they can be implemented in terms of decision making and
choices.

At the lowest level, test interpretation begins with the particular scales and their definitions, which are provided in the test
manual.  A good test manual has a wealth of information regarding
test characteristics and ways to use the test.  Every assessor and
counselor should periodically review the manuals and technical
reports for the tests they use, in order to refamiliarize themselves
with the available information.  As counseling interns and counselors

become more familiar with particular tests, their interpretations should become more complex and sophisticated, taking into account interrelationships with other variables, as well as congruencies and contradictions and implications about the relationships of the test variables with other behavioral or psychological constructs.

Generally, test interpretation should proceed from the general to the specific. If there are validity scales on a test or scales that infer mental sets or test-taking attitudes, interpretation should begin with these scales in order to shed light on the motivation of the counselee. It is also preferable to give positive feedback before proceeding to weaknesses and negative feedback. A test report should also be balanced, including both strengths and weaknesses. It should also be remembered that behavior is multiply determined, and that there may be a number of alternative explanations that must be entertained or examined.

I recall a specific instance that occurred while I was writing a report on the Rorschach of a young woman. On card V one of her responses was "chicks squeaking for food." Usually such a response implies oral-dependency needs, and I mentioned this possible interpretation, but then it came to my mind that in addition to these needs on the part of the counselee, the response also referred to possible guilt feelings for her children, who had been far away from her. This interpretation was added, so that the counselor and counselee would be aware of it.

The counselee should be encouraged to look for reasons for the results, to see whether they make sense as expressing the areas of agreement and disagreement. We should also remember that psychological tests have errors of measurement. Psychological tests, and especially personality tests, vary in terms of the level of the self-concept they tap. Klopfer (1968), using concepts of Timothy Leary, conceives of personality tests as measuring four levels of the self-concept. Level I is that of public communication and its variant, public image, and taps the way significant others perceive an individual and the level of public image perceived by the counselee. Level II is the level of conscious self-concept, and level III is the level of private symbolizations, which is usually measured by projective techniques. Level IV is that of the unexpressed and unaware, representing material that is systematically excluded from all other levels.

Because of the complexity of human behavior, the different levels of the self-concept, and the many factors involved in psychological functioning, a battery of tests is preferable to single tests. An efficient battery of tests should avoid redundancy and include tests that have convergent and discriminant validity. Variables are convergent to the extent that they correlate with variables measuring aspects of a similar construct. In nontechnical terms, the concept of discriminant validity means that a test should provide some additional, independent information supplementing that obtained from other tests.

Among the assessment services provided by the assessor are screening for organicity and determining learning disabilities. In order to achieve these objectives, a complete test battery is required. The usual tests administered for this purpose include the WAIS or WAIS-R, the Shipley Institute of Living Scale, a scale providing an index of conceptual thinking by relating a task of abstract thinking to the level of vocabulary; the Wide Range Achievement Test, the Wechsler Memory Scale, the Trail Making Test, Bender, Rotter Incomplete Sentences Blank, and a structured neuropsychological interview. These techniques may be supplemented by additional tests such as the MMPI, the Draw a Person Test, the Rorschach, and the Purdue Pegboard.

## WORKING WITH THE MMPI

In this concluding section, a step-by-step description of my personal examination of the MMPI is offered to show the way at least one assessor strives to understand the examinee through the use of this technique.

1. After the test is completed by the examinee, the standard scales are scored and profiled by me or by a test technician who has been properly instructed in performing this function.

2. The profile code is noted, and if the K scale is high, the clinical scales are profiled both with and without the K correction factor.

3. Following the initial profiling, I spend about one hour scoring special scales and examining items. Routinely I score Barron's Ego-Strength Scale (1953), the Welsh Anxiety and Repression Scales and Internalization Ratio (1952), the MacAndrew Alcoholism Scale (1965), the Goldberg Index (1965), and the Overcontrolled Hostility Scale (Megargee and Cook 1967). The raw scores at this point are converted into standard scores, using available tables.

4. Other experimental scales reflecting such traits as dominance, dependency, control, responsibility, and rigidity of thinking are similarly scored.

5. The F items that are endorsed by the examinee and other critical items are examined.

6.  Depending on the elevation of the clinical scales, subscale analysis of scales 4, 5, 6, 8, and 9 may be undertaken.

7.  Item examination for fears and poor physical health is next.

8.  Once the above steps are completed, test interpretation begins, proceeding from the validity scales and the other special scales to the clinical scales and their subscales and ending with item analysis. The final product is a report of one to three type-written pages.

It is my considered opinion, gained over the years of working with the MMPI and other instruments, that accurate information is obtained by supplementing that from the scales with that from actual test items. Without this thorough examination one is left with statistical guesses that are generally correct for groups but only partly correct for the particular examinee.

REFERENCES

Adams, J. 1972. The contribution of psychological evaluation to psychiatric diagnosis. Journal of Personality Assessment, 36: 561–566.

Affleck, D. C., and F. D. Strider. 1971. Contributions of psychological reports to patient management. Journal of Consulting and Clinical Psychology, 37: 177–179.

Barron, F. 1953. An ego strength scale which predicts response to psychotherapy. Journal of Consulting Psychology, 17: 327–333.

Breger, L. 1968. Psychological testing: Treatment and research implications. Journal of Consulting and Clinical Psychology, 32: 176–181.

Bugental, J. F. T. 1965. The search for authenticity. New York: Holt, Rinehart, and Winston.

Buhler, C. 1971. Basic theoretical concepts of humanistic psychology. American Psychologist, 26: 378–386.

Buhler, C., and M. Allen. 1971. Introduction into humanistic psychology. Belmont, Calif.: Brooks-Cole.

Dana, R. H. 1980. Receptivity of clinical interpretation. In
R. H. Woody, ed., Encyclopedia of clinical assessment. Vol. II,
pp. 1042-1049. San Francisco: Jossey-Bass.

Fee, A. F., G. R. Elkins, and L. Boyd. 1982. Testing and counseling psychologists: Current practices and implications for
training. Journal of Personality Assessment, 46: 116-118.

Frank, J. D., L. H. Gliedman, S. D. Imber, A. R. Stone, and
E. H. Nash. 1959. Patient's expectancies and relearning as
factors determining improvement in psychotherapy. American
Journal of Psychiatry, 115: 961-968.

Glaser, R., and L. Bond, eds. 1981. Testing: Concepts, policy
and research. American Psychologist, 36, whole no. 10.

Goldberg, L. R. 1965. Diagnosticians vs. diagnostic signs: The
diagnosis of psychosis vs. neurosis from the MMPI. Psychological Monographs, 79, whole no. 602: 1-28.

Goldfried, M. R., and T. J. D'Zurilla. 1969. A behavioral-
analytic model for assessing competence. In C. D. Spielberger,
ed., Current topics in clinical and community psychology.
Vol. I, pp. 151-196. New York: Academic Press.

Greenspoon, J., and C. C. Gersten. 1967. A new look at psychological testing from the standpoint of a behaviorist. American Psychologist, 22: 848-853.

Klopfer, W. G. 1968. Integration of projective techniques in the
clinical case study. In A. I. Rabin, ed., Projective techniques
in personality assessment. Pp. 523-552. New York: Springer.

MacAndrew, C. 1965. The differentiation of male alcoholic out-
patients from non-alcoholic patients by means of the MMPI.
Quarterly Journal of Studies on Alcohol, 26: 238-246.

Maloney, M. P., and M. P. Ward. 1976. Psychological assessment: A conceptual approach. New York: Oxford University
Press.

Maslow, A. H. 1962. Toward a psychology of being. Princeton:
Van Nostrand.

Matarazzo, J. D. 1972. Wechsler's measurement and appraisal of intelligence. Baltimore: Williams and Wilkins.

McReynolds, P., ed. 1968. Advances in psychological assessment. Vol. I. Palo Alto, Calif.: Science and Behavior Books.

Megargee, E. I., and P. E. Cook. 1967. Development and validation of an MMPI scale of assaultiveness in overcontrolled individuals. Journal of Abnormal Psychology, 72: 519-528.

Palmer, J. O. 1980. A primer of eclectic psychotherapy. Monterey, Calif.: Brooks-Cole.

Rapaport, D. 1954. The theoretical implications of diagnostic testing procedures. In R. P. Knight and C. R. Friedman, eds., Psychoanalytic psychiatry and psychology. New York: International Universities Press.

Reschly, D. J. 1981. Psychological testing in educational classification and placement. American Psychologist, 36: 1094-1102.

Schafer, R. 1948. The clinical application of psychological tests. New York: International Universities Press.

Smyth, R., and M. Reznikoff. 1971. Attitudes of psychiatrists toward the usefulness of psychodiagnostic reports. Professional Psychology, 2: 283-288.

Weiner, I. B. 1972. Does psychodiagnosis have a future? Journal of Personality Assessment, 36: 534-546.

Welsh, G. S. 1952. An anxiety index and an internalization ratio for the MMPI. Journal of Consulting Psychology, 16: 65-72.

# 8

# ACADEMIC ADVISING CENTERS
## *Margaret E. Gerlach*

In a college student personnel text, a chapter on academic advising centers serves a dual purpose. The first is the description (the organization, functions, and staffing of academic advising centers) for those interested in improving academic advising on their own campuses. The second could be of greater significance to the college student personnel field. If readers will use this chapter as a case history of university administrators' response to change, both internal and external, they may be encouraged to apply strategic analysis and planning to their own programs, as administrators do to the university as a whole. For through strategic analysis of the ever-changing university environment, college student personnel will be able to respond at the leading edge of change, rather than after the fact. Changes in function and structure of services as a response to the changing environment then percolate up to administrators rather than down from them, giving college student personnel the satisfaction of being in charge of change.

## WHY ACADEMIC ADVISING CENTERS WERE CREATED IN THE 1970S

The function of "academic advising has been a companion to instruction from the beginning of the formal university, and at today's university the major portion of academic advising is handled by faculty members. Academic advising centers were created not to replace faculty advising but to supplement and improve the function of advising in response to four major changes in university environments: projected declining enrollment; the addition of new types of student populations, the largest of which was reentering adults; the strengthening of the student consumer movement; and the general reform of education. In all of these changes, administrators felt that improved academic advising would allow the university to adjust in the most beneficial way.

Declining Enrollment

The specter of declining student enrollment haunted colleges and universities throughout the 1970s, and reduced attrition was seen as one way to halt the decline. Academic advising had been proven by limited research before the 1970s to reduce attrition rates among freshmen and undeclared majors, and to improve retention, particularly of students in academic difficulty. Kapraun and Coldren (n.d.) of Pennsylvania State University identified seven components of an academic advising program that facilitates student retention, the first of which was institutional commitment to academic advising. Further limited research conducted in the 1970s supports the positive correlation between good advising and improved retention (Edington and Gilliard 1978). As a result, academic advising centers often add to their regular services the special advising of students either on probation or already disqualified.

As of 1982 declining enrollment is seen to be more of a specter than a reality. Carol Francis, chief economist for the American Council on Education, quoted by Nielsen (1981, p. 4), says: "We have been talking about enrollment declines for virtually the entire decade of the 1970's. Yet, over this period full-time equivalent enrollments increased 25 percent." And, according to National Council on Education data, there were 12,087,200 students enrolled in the fall of 1980, up from 11,707,126 in 1979 (an increase of 3.2 percent). Total enrollment actually increased by 40 percent between 1970 and 1980 (Nielsen 1981, p. 4).

Various reasons are given for this increase, including higher unemployment and the considerable "marketing" effort of colleges and universities to attract new students. How this change will affect administrative support of advising centers remains to be seen.

New Populations: Returning Adults

If it were not already apparent to those involved in post-secondary education, recent Census Bureau figures have confirmed it: more than a third of today's college students are 25 years of age or older. (Cross 1978, preface)

The influx of this new population, the reentry or returning adults, offers university administrators both "promises and problems," according to Cross (1978, p. 1). On one hand, the influx of reentry adults may be a partial answer to declining enrollment. On the other hand, higher education must begin "the strenuous process of adaptation, innovation or reorganization because of this new population." As Cross (1978) reminds us, "Many educators are not yet reconciled with the possibility that these adult learners may, in the future, constitute a significant proportion of the student population of higher education" (p. 1). (Adults have been involved in continuing education through high schools, community colleges, and other educational settings for many years. It is their enrollment at baccalaureate, masters, and doctoral degree-granting institutions that has mushroomed.)

According to Loring (1978, p. 1) there are six major adaptations to which traditional four-year colleges and universities have resorted in trying to accommodate the adult learner: flexible scheduling; different learning environments, such as a model United Nations; special admission and retention policies; development of interdisciplinary degrees and programs; use of mass media for delivery of knowledge; and special-funded programs. In addition to these adaptations, universities must adjust to specific educational objectives, which are often nonvocational.

The present vocational orientation at American universities will soon need to give way to other objectives, according to Stonier (1979, p. 34). "At least as important" in the new education order will be "education for life," "education for the world," "education for self-development," and "education for pleasure." Adults already seek these nonvocational objectives, and academic advising plays a significant role in helping reentry adults attain them. Through description of opportunities for self-development or for pleasure within the curriculum, adults who otherwise might not return to campus may be encouraged to do so. Forward-looking administrators are supportive of this possible role of academic advising centers.

The Student Consumer Movement

The student consumer movement is a part of the greater consumer movement in which consumers reacting to devious practices

in the marketplace challenge the old practice of "let the buyer
beware."

Students have not always been thought of as "consumers,"
nor have educational institutions been thought of as "merchants"
selling education. Certain poor practices, particularly misleading
advertising by colleges and vocational schools, caused the Federal
Interagency Committee on Education to label the postsecondary
student a consumer. When this occurred in 1975, "The federal
government moved rapidly . . . to protect students . . . from
misleading advertising" (Stark and Terenzini 1978, p. 2).

Students and parents demanded better and more accurate
information about colleges and universities. Not only was better
information demanded, but when information was not accurate or
was misleading, the student consumer went to court.

In two separate court cases academic advising is seen as a
method of providing information on the contractual agreements between colleges and students. In Bower v. O'Reilly (1971), quoted
in Berilacqua (1976, p. 490), the New York State Supreme Court
implied that "academic regulations should be explicit and stated."
In Healy v. Larson (1971), the same court pointed out the existence
of a contractual relationship between a college and a student,
"wherein the institution may not exceed its stated degree requirements by arbitrary judgment."

Such decisions make the information sector of the advising
process subject to legal suits and make academic advising a matter
of legal importance to the university.


General Education Reform

In the spring of 1978, Henry Rosovsky, Harvard's dean of
the Faculty of Arts and Sciences, presented his curriculum reform
proposal, four years in preparation, to the Harvard faculty
(Schiefelbein 1978, p. 12). At Cornell a committee on general
education called for more interdisciplinary courses. In the fall
of 1981 the California State University and Colleges implemented a
new general education curriculum including courses that meet a
requirement for critical thinking as well as interdisciplinary courses.
At Stanford seven separate task forces tried to determine "what is
fundamental to undergraduate education." And the president of
Johns Hopkins urged a return to general education because, he said,
"we're turning out highly-technical and highly-skilled people who
are literally barbarians" (Schiefelbein 1978, p. 12).

Most American colleges and universities have instituted some
reforms in general education or are in the process of doing so. At

the same time, more support for advising on the general education part of the curriculum is being given to academic advising centers. Before the new emphasis on general education, students were able to graduate without knowing why there was such a requirement. Now academic advising centers are expected to do more to make the rationale for general education more explicit, while universities are still struggling with the question of what a modern education should be. This ambiguous position is one of the most frustrating problems facing academic advising centers today—frustrating because the reform movement is still in a fluid state, while students must continue to complete general education requirements that seem to change yearly.

The four environmental changes (declining enrollment, new populations, student consumer movement, and general education reform) are primarily responsible for the support given to academic advising centers by administrators as of 1982. But each of these changes is in the process of change. Enrollments are increasing, particularly in some segments of the curriculum. New populations include the Indochinese, who present other problems to administrators. The student consumer movement is quiescent at the moment, and general education reforms are being solidified. At universities, change is the constant.

## ORGANIZATION, FUNCTIONS, AND STAFFING OF ACADEMIC ADVISING CENTERS

The organizational structure, functions, and staffing of centralized academic advising centers vary from campus to campus. One reason for this variation, as Tully (1978, p. 7) states, is that "There is no clear agreement about what academic advising means." Eppinger (1979, p. 1.2) agrees with Tully:

> The definition of academic advising varies widely. For some schools, academic advising has been simply scheduling for classes. For other schools, advising is given the broadest possible definition and includes scheduling, tutoring, career counseling, job placement, and a host of other support activities.

Tully (1978, p. 8) identifies academic advising processes that have a "direct bearing upon the success or failure of the student's academic career." They include

. . . entry and re-entry, academic program development, academic consultation, career choice and development, access to general information, identifying aspects which may be interfering with the student's academic progress and identification of possible academic failures.

As is apparent, a very simple definition of academic advising confines the help given students to scheduling of classes. The more complex definition of academic advising, with which most centralized centers agree, is that academic advising is the help and support given to students from the time they explore choice of college and enter to the time they attain their educational objectives and leave. This diversity of definition creates a diversity in organization, functions, and staffing of academic advising centers.

Organization

Because the more complex definition may encompass so many departments, the coordinator or director and the services of advising centers have been located under a variety of offices, including student affairs/services, academic affairs, or a combination of both. At Brigham Young University the office is under admissions and records (Eliason 1978, p. 3.15). Sometimes the central advising office has a coordinator using faculty on released time, as at Aurora College (Reuland 1979, p. 1.2). Or there may be an autonomous advising center for each school in a university (Potter 1979, p. 1.243).

Functions

Functions of academic advising centers vary from campus to campus in the same way organizational structure varies. A popular model places the emphasis of the central office on coordinating the advising done by individual faculty members (Titley 1978, p. 3.37). Another popular model confines the functions of the central advising office to specific groups of students, most often freshmen and undeclared majors (Patton 1978, p. 3.176). And there is an "all-inclusive" model similar to the academic advisement center at the University of Utah, Salt Lake City, whose functions include conferences for new students; advising on registration, general education/liberal education, scholastic standards (students in academic difficulty), guided studies, and veterans and military affairs; tutoring of ethnic minorities; informing about learning and educational alternatives; and staffing satellite advising centers (Pappas 1978, p. 3.228).

Other models combine academic advising and career advising (Baker and Dubois 1979, p. 1.161; Gordon 1979, p. 1.127) or see only freshmen (Mahon 1979, p. 1.76) or undeclared majors (Goldenberg 1979, p. 1.38).

### Staffing

Staffing of central advising centers includes peer advisers at SUNY, Fredonia (Anderson 1978, p. 3.162); faculty advisers on released time at Aquinas College and Aurora College (Keller 1979, p. 1.12; Reuland 1979, p. 1.34); paraprofessionals at Orange County College (King 1979, p. 1.119); and counseling center staff at Memphis State University (Heitzmann 1979, p. 1.104).

In general the organization, functions, and staffing of central advising centers reflect the needs and profile of specific colleges and universities. These comparatively new units are experiencing the same flow of changing circumstances that created them. For instance, computer-assisted advising is now available at some centers—for instance, at Brigham Young University (Eliason 1978, p. 3.15)—and is under consideration at other campuses. Academic advising centers are subject to technology and other influences of the changing world.

### IMPLICATIONS FOR COLLEGE STUDENT PERSONNEL

As Magoon says (1973, p. 176), "The collegiate work setting reflects . . . a very non-static state of affairs." The first lesson to be learned from the establishment of academic advising centers is the influence of change on student services. College student personnel who are aware of future trends in higher education, who use the same kind of information as administrators do to adjust and adapt to change, are able to suggest changes in programs or services rather than have change mandated from above.

The second lesson to be learned is a question of identity. In 1950 the American Council on Education (p. 6) identified 12 future needs in student personnel work, the second of which was to "achieve a higher degree of integration between student personnel services and instructional programs." In 1973 Magoon (p. 176) emphasized the "renewed concern for the reintegration of student affairs into the mainstream of institutional affairs." In 1981 the most pressing priority for college student personnel services was to remember their prime reason for existence: to help college students attain their educational objectives. If college student personnel kept this objective in mind, the chasm that often exists between academic affairs and student affairs would disappear.

The third lesson concerns evaluation. Magoon (1973, p. 178) identifies a major weakness when he says, "To begin with in all candor, counselors and counseling centers (as well as student personnel workers generally) have invested precious little time in identifying the outcomes or consequences of their professional work."

Academic advising centers, although a relatively new method of delivering a student service, are much concerned with evaluation. Hardee and Mayhew (1970, p. 25) identify the major focus of evaluating advising as a change in the behavior of the advisee: "How much better does the student . . . perform as a result of the advising process than he would without it?"

These three lessons—awareness of change, integration with instruction, and evaluation—if pursued by college student personnel, will help to keep student services in the mainstream instead of in the minor tributaries, where funding tends to evaporate during fiscal dry spells.

REFERENCES

American Council on Education. 1950. Annual report. Washington, D.C.: the Council.

Berilacqua, Joseph P. 1976. The changing relationship between the university and the student: Implications for the classroom and student personnel work. Journal of College Student Personnel, 17, no. 6: 489-494.

Crockett, David S., ed. 1978. Academic advising: A resource document. Iowa City: American College Testing Program. Includes the following:

Anderson, David L., S. C. Looney, and N. L. Lord. Use of peer advisors at SUNY, Fredonia. Pp. 3.162-3.169.

Eliason, LeGrand O. Academic advisement at Brigham Young University, Provo, Utah. Pp. 3.15-3.36.

Pappas, James P. The academic advisement center: A model at the University of Utah, Salt Lake City. Pp. 3.228-3.235.

Patton, Carol R. Centralized advisement at Texas Christian University, Fort Worth, Texas. Pp. 3.176-3.181.

Titley, Bonnie. Academic advising at Colorado State University. Pp. 3.37-3.42.

_____. 1979. Academic advising: A resource document, 1979 supplement. Iowa City: American College Testing Program. Includes the following:

Baker, Donald D., and W. D. Dubois. Careers and academic advising: Students can assume responsibilities. Pp. 1.161-1.175.

Eppinger, Richard. The basic advising program: An approach to freshman advising in the residential liberal arts college. Pp. 1.1-1.11.

Goldenberg, David H., and K. Poindexter. The academic exploration program: A comprehensive administrative and academic advising program for "undecided" students. Pp. 1.38-1.59.

Gordon, Virginia H. Integrating the academic and career advising process for exploratory college students. Pp. 1.127-1.139.

Heitzmann, Dennis. Integrating academic counseling into the center for student development. Pp. 1.104-1.119.

Keller, Michael C. A centralized academic advising delivery system for small liberal arts colleges. Pp. 1.12-1.34.

King, Margaret C. Utilizing part-time paraprofessionals as academic advisors: A model. Pp. 1.119-1.127.

Mahon, Ellenor. Academic advising at the College of Charleston. Pp. 1.76-1.87.

Potter, E. Bruce. On developing an effective decentralized advisement system. Pp. 1.243-1.258.

Reuland, Wilma F. A centralized advising model for the small liberal arts college. Pp. 1.34-1.37.

Cross, K. Patricia. 1978. The adult learner. Washington, D.C.: American Association of Higher Education.

Edington, Robert V., and F. Gilliard. 1978. RAP, a retention advising program. Journal of College Student Personnel, 19, no. 5: 472-473.

Hardee, Melvene, and L. B. Mayhew. 1970. Faculty advising in colleges and universities. Washington, D.C.: American College Personnel Association.

Kapraun, E. Daniel, and D. W. Coldren. N.d. Abstracts of readings on academic advising. Uniontown, Pa.: Pennsylvania State University. (Unpublished.)

Loring, Rosalind K. 1978. Strategies of adaptation. In Adapting institutions to the adult learner: Experiments in progress. Washington, D.C.: American Association of Higher Education.

Magoon, Thomas. 1973. Outlook in higher education: Changing functions. Personnel and Guidance Journal, 52, no. 3: 175-179.

Nielsen, Robert. 1981. The illusion of declining enrollment. In On campus. American Teacher supplement. Washington, D.C.: American Federation of Teachers. (Reprint of February 1981 issue of American Teacher.)

Shiefelbein, Susan. 1978. Confusion at Harvard: What makes an educated man. Saturday Review, April 1, pp. 12-20.

Stark, Joan S., and P. T. Terenzini. 1978. Alternatives to federal leadership in student consumer information. Paper presented at national conference, American Association of Higher Education. Chicago, March 21.

Stonier, Tom. 1979. Changes in western society: Educational implications. World yearbook of education: Recurrent education and lifelong learning. New York: Kogan Page Co.

Tully, Toni H., ed. 1978. Report of a survey of the status of academic advising in the California State Universities and Colleges. Long Beach, Calif.: Office of the Chancellor, CSUC.

# 9

# THE COUNSELING NEEDS
# OF MINORITY STUDENTS

## Vicente N. Noble
## Louis Preston
## Henry Reyna

INTRODUCTION

Astin (1980) published a survey describing the characteristics
of entering college freshmen indicating that 14 percent of them
(26,000) were nonwhite. This reflects national statistics, and thus
it could reasonably be expected that this percentage could be higher
or lower in urban or rural areas. In a few urban colleges the nonwhite college enrollment exceeds the majority enrollment.

Prior to the civil rights movement of the 1960s, minority
group members who earned a college degree had few, if any, more
job opportunities than those without one. Consequently, the general
attitude of many potential minority college students was that higher
education, if available, was pointless if postgraduate opportunities
at appropriate levels were perceptibly denied. The effects of almost two decades of civil rights legislation, affirmative action programs, and age-sex discrimination acts have produced an increased
awareness by many minority group members that higher education
is feasible, and the concomitant opportunities are viable. Many institutions are experiencing an increase in the number of minority
students seeking higher education. The impact of minority college
graduates has become much more visible in all facets of American
society. The effects of this "modeling" have served to readjust
minority perceptions that appropriate college-level opportunities
are realistically available.

However, there is still a pressing need to recruit and retain
a larger percentage of the pool of potential college students present
in minority communities. Astin (1980) indicated that of 187,000
freshmen, only 9.2 percent were black, 0.8 percent were American

COUNSELING MINORITIES / 191

Indian, 1.4 percent were Oriental, 2.1 percent were Mexican American/Chicano, 0.9 percent were Puerto Rican American, and 1.7 percent were "other." As the subfigures illustrate, the percentages per group are almost negligible in comparison with the dominant population (86.0 percent white). In view of this, institutions should be more active in developing programs for the growing minority student population. Academic, personal, and vocational/career counseling and advising programs specifically designed for these populations can be of great importance in retaining and helping these students.

A major problem in a discussion of the counseling needs of minority students is one of overgeneralization of the needs of specific groups and individuals. The nonwhite minority populations reflect the same diversity that is present in the dominant population with respect to individual-family motivations, social class, parental education aspirations, and income. However, because the opportunities for higher education for minorities and the subsequent socioeconomic opportunities have, in comparison, been actively promoted since the 1970s, most of the minority students pursuing higher education still tend to come from families whose educational attainment has been the high school level or less (Astin 1980). Although a significant number of these families have had members with college potential, the effects of past educational-job discrimination have provided little incentive or "inside" knowledge of campus life, curriculum planning, and institutional differences.

Moreover, many minority students, like many other students from noncollege backgrounds, view higher education as little more than a sophisticated form of apprenticeship to a higher form of trade. It has often been said by high school seniors and college freshmen that they are seeking an undergraduate degree in a particular major in order to be immediately employed in that field (as a psychologist or historian, for example). This concept of higher education indicates a misunderstanding by a significant portion of the public in terms of appreciating the goals and perspective higher education espouses for the individual in personal-social as well as economic development.

This discussion does not ignore the fact that among minority college students there are those who have sufficient family or personal awareness of higher education to fully advance their particular needs. It does, however, acknowledge a premise that, because of past discriminatory societal-educational practices and parental socioeconomic status, minority student attainment and retention in higher education can be significantly enhanced by providing counseling services specifically designed for these students.

It is from this premise that the following pages will discuss and identify obstacles that commonly affect minority students but can be alleviated through specifically designed counseling services. The format will present specific concerns and will suggest ways in which institutions can advocate constructive changes. The outline of the format, as well as many suggestions, is adapted from a paper by Loribeth Weinstein (1980) on counseling reentry women. Women and minorities have a great deal in common with regard to discriminatory practices, stereotypes, historical-economic injustices, and personal-social concerns. Thus, it is readily acknowledged that many of the recommendations will overlap and be similar.

In each institution the use of particular suggestions (institutional advocacy) will obviously depend on the characteristics of the institution and those of the minority population(s). Nonetheless, a range of possible responses is suggested whereby an institution can promote the most appropriate course of action in its particular situation.


MINORITY STUDENTS AND COUNSELING

Minority students, like all groups of students, have particular problems and concerns that require special services during their academic careers. These services can support the academic process and also can assist in the retention of the students. However, these services (and helpers dealing with minority students) must be based on a fairly comprehensive study of who minority students are, how they differ from traditional, dominant-group students, and what their specific needs are with regard to academic, vocational-career, and personal counseling.

Minority students, for purposes of this discussion, are distinguished as members of the nonwhite segment of American society. These students have traditionally included black Americans, Native Americans (American Indians), and other-than-English-speaking reference groups (Hispanic and Asian Americans). Conceptually the concerns addressed could also be applied to other groups, such as ethnic whites, women, and the handicapped.

As noted previously, there exists within each minority student group a wide range of achievement, marital status, maturity, background, experiences, responsibilties, work experiences, and objectives. In every institution there usually is a greater number of one or several groups than of others.

Age

Minority students can be anywhere between the ages of 17 and over 60. The majority may fall in the typical college age group. However, a significant number of minority men and women delay college entry. These students had to work immediately after high school to help their families or to support themselves. A sizable percentage of minority men enlist in the armed forces immediately after high school. In many instances academic self-doubts or "older" age consciousness occurs, affecting the students' studies and relationships with other students.


Race-Ethnicity

The race or ethnic awareness of many minority students may vary considerably at a given institution. For some Hispanic or Asian American groups, lack of written or oral English fluency may create an uncertainty in academic activities, as well as make them unable to fully appreciate academic-career advice. Sibatani (1980, pp. 25-26) reported that "The logical thinking and emotional responses of Japanese are not partitioned into separate hemispheres as Westerners but are tucked into one and the same verbal hemisphere. This may cause the Japanese [and perhaps bilingual minorities] to depend more on intuition and emotional reactions than on logical trains of thought."

In addition to language, minority students may be distinguished by their racial or ethnic awareness in a sociopsychological context. Cabrera (1967) described four phases of acculturation that can occur in an individual or may occur throughout successive generations. The first phase describes the kaleidoscopic experiences of a newly arrived immigrant (like our own first sensory experiences upon arriving in the midst of confusing and confounding new stimuli). The second phase is an individual who has discarded all vestiges of past heritage (language, name—perhaps through name change—mannerisms, values) to become "110 percent" Anglo American. In some instances these individuals deride their origins or overemphasize aspects of Anglo Americans that they feel will elicit societal approval and promotion. The third phase describes an individual who, for some reason, was not accorded societal approval (employment, social entry, residence) or did not seek it. This individual subsequently rejects majority approval and culture, and seeks to reestablish identity with the original, "back home" culture. The fourth phase is an individual who has examined, selected, and rationally accepted certain values of both cultures. This individual is described as a true bicultural person.

Vontress (1971) has described a similar theory regarding black Americans, which the author of this chapter feels may be applied to other groups (Asian Americans, Chicanos/Hispanics, and so on). Individuals who describe themselves as "blacks" or "black Americans" typically are not ashamed of their skin color or hair, and cease to deny traits that previously caused anxiety. They appear to be more prevalent among young people, live in urban areas, have more education or political awareness, possess a more positive self-concept, and be intolerant of people who demonstrate adverse racial postures.

"Negroes" are described as possessing ambivalent values, being willing to give whites a chance to prove their goodwill, being integrationists, being representatives of middle-class values, and using language that does not cause anxiety to white listeners. They are the group most whites have known, do not wear extreme styles, and are found easy to relate to by white counselors.

"Coloreds" are described as perceiving themselves as whites have perceived them, and often refer to themselves as "colored." They are also described as possessing a symbiotic relationship with whites who determine, as well as label, their behavior. Coloreds find the civil rights movement incomprehensible, are used by white employers to validate their comparisons of radicals, and show a respect for the judgment of whites or authorities. Vontress remarked that these perceptions of intragroup differences and generalizations must be observed with caution for individual differences.

The minority student can be conceptually described from a number of perspectives. The range and complexity of each individual is as great as that of individuals in the larger society or within families. It is not the purpose of this discussion to fully describe all minority students. As mentioned earlier, each institution should address itself to serious, formal study of its preponderant minority populations, in order to more effectively understand and articulate institutional services.

The language and sociopsychological descriptions may also be applied to other ethnic student groups. The theories describe a means for channeling the complexities of individuals and groups into a construct of testable hypotheses when working with the subjective (relationships, for example) aspects of people. These theories also serve as tentative frameworks for the "ordering of observations" in the counseling process.

## Class

Research studies prior to 1970 tended to view the minority college student as the ascended product of poverty. Recent figures indicate that the present-day minority college student reflects the wide social-class spectrum of the majority population. There is also emerging a sizable percentage of minority college students who come from middle-class, professional family backgrounds. However, the large portion of minority college students typically, as with the general population, comes from high school-educated, nonprofessional, working-class families.

## Education

The majority of the urban minority students enroll at two-year community colleges prior to transfer to a four-year baccalaureate institution. In some instances these students began their studies in one- or two-year terminal vocational programs (licensed vocational nurse or medical assistant, for instance). During these programs, and often in completing general education requirements, they find that they can succeed in four-year-college general education courses. This is often coupled with successful interactions with faculty and peers and the realization that they can keep up with their classmates. These situations often encourage these students to change to four-year transferable programs or to apply to four-year institutions.

## Work Experience

A number of minority college students come from large families in which many children help to support the family financially. In other instances the families are financially unable to help these students. These students often work full-time while taking part- or full-time college programs.

## MINORITY INTERPERSONAL-PSYCHOLOGICAL CONCERNS

The literature on counseling minority populations covers a wide range of ethnic groups that spans Jewish immigration from Russia to Vietnamese refugees. At the risk of overgeneralization, a number of features and psychological distinctions are presented that may be common to many minority students.

Minority students enrolling in higher education for the first time often are involved in the pursuit of higher education opportunities as well as in a search for personal and social integrity and identity development. Students from a barrio or ghetto in many instances have had to detach themselves from the interactions of their social milieu or sacrifice their college plans. This quest has often created an ambiguous or extreme identity, as characterized by Cabrera or Vontress (see "Race-Ethnicity," above). For example, the student may be presented as a "110 percent incognito Anglo" who disavows her/his ethnic heritage or as a person seeking to determine and integrate the convergences of the dualities of her/his existence.

## The Development of Bicultural Identity and Integrity

This development is often confounded by the superficial aspects of the dominant society. That everyone wears clothes, eats food, finds shelter, frowns, smiles, is a statement of commonality that often prevents the growth of individual development and individual distinctions sought by youth. This approach is particularly hazardous to a minority individual who is attempting to develop a personal identity that acknowledges the influences and effects of two cultures. The assimilative approach (versus pluralistic), which overemphasizes dominant society values, can hinder the effective integration of a minority individual's personality and self-esteem. The minority person, in this case, is hindered in the development of personal-social perspectives and self-approval/esteem, and in integrating the progress of social-academic aspirational development from her/his prior (singular) ethnic life. The readers might imagine their own reactions if they were in another country for an extended period of time. Gross as well as nuance behaviors (food-taste preferences, color, style, gestures, relationships, status, and attitudinal expectations) would be constantly at the forefront of one's thoughts in these circumstances. Moreover, there are also the emotional-interactive aspects and nuances of communicating ideas, feelings, and thoughts in another language. (Present-tense communication in any language is limited!)

## Historical Perspective

Many minorities distrust the formal or bureaucratic/institutional approach because of past injustices by such agencies. In many Hispanic and Asian cultures the initiation of relationships starts with the "person" first and the "business" role second. Because of these two factors, the more traditional minority persons will be more responsive to representatives of institutions who approach them as people first and who are concerned with them in another-adjunct relationship (teacher/adviser-student) second.

## Stereotypes

Many service personnel (such as counselors or faculty members) disavow racism per se but maintain generalized preconceptions about minorities. This is often expressed by " 'they' do" this or that. Minority groups are also said to have particular qualities. More often than not, service personnel possess misconceptions based on biased, outdated knowledge. A peripheral example is the average person's knowledge of the Neandertal man. This name usually connotes a stooped, inarticulate, unsocial type of person who is commonly thought of as moronic. Kurten (1980) and other scientists have dispelled this unfortunate image and replaced it with the following: the Neandertal stood straight, possessed a social organization, existed as far back as 100,000 years, utilized a ritual for burying the dead. In any event, popular and erroneous information-knowledge is extremely persistent. Many educated persons continue to refer to past, probably erroneous knowledge without examining its continued veracity. On many occasions this is coupled with a priori "common knowledge" as a basis for judging unorthodox or different behaviors. In clinical psychiatry or psychology, it has often been reported that the incidence of misdiagnosing minority patients is inordinately higher than that for the general white population.

## Socioeconomic Status

Minority students, like society, represent a cross section of many social classes. Students from middle-class backgrounds or having families with middle-class aspirations will more often be like the typical students of their age. In many instances, when they come from families whose native language is other than English, their parents did not teach or encourage the acquisition of the heritage language. This is the case with a great majority of Hispanic and Asian American students born in this country. This may create a predicament when students are confronted with their "assumed" bilingual status. Upon meeting native speakers or others who assume they speak the language, they may experience a self-consciousness of their identity and, in some instances, experience patronization or a sense of alienation.

Aside from language, many minority students often experience a uniformity of approach that deals with them only as units of a preconceived group (abject Indians, subjugated women, passive Asians). This is frequently decried as being "talked at" as opposed to being talked to and talking to others. This situation can frustrate the more middle-class-oriented minority person as a form of patronization. The minority student from a working-class background might also experience frustration in sensing a lack of opportunity to interact on an equal basis and in not being listened to attentively.

In all situations a minority student needs to be heard and recognized on an individual basis.

Socioeconomic status or the student's aspired status most often is a determinative factor in ascertaining how the person perceives her/his viability in a social-economic system. This perception and its concomitant expectations and behaviors indicate the degree of association with one's identity, aspiration, and fluency (mobility) in the school-career-social structure. Specifically, the closer the proximity of the values of the minority student to the aspiration, the greater the ease of transition and the perception of one's viability with its opportunities. However, many minority students come from working-class backgrounds and are frequently the first of their family to attend higher education institutions. In these cases their aspirations will be similar to those of their working-class peers. Both are often unaware of the "ramifications" of their academic-career choices and are sometimes perplexed by procedural issues. In this respect many of these students are more strongly influenced by social class attitudes and mores than by intragroup cultural values.

## Interpersonal-Social Behaviors

Many minority groups indicate a preference for more elaborate, sometimes flowery-circular, flamboyant, subjective (intuitive), lively, informal approaches to life and relationships. This is often in sharp contrast with institutional (and societal) preferences for formal, objective, understated, emotionless, detached, precise approaches. Cultural and ethnic traditional identity-proximity will probably influence the emotional emphasis or preference for a particular approach in various life situations. This is often manifested in introductory meetings, color-design choices, manner of speech, and involvement in relationships with persons and institutions.

As in many life stages, the minority student in college may experience an identity crisis. Interactions with college-level peers and teachers may exacerbate unresolved problems with identity and self-esteem. Facts and myths abound about the alleged inferiority of minority schools and minorities in general. Overall, many students experience some readjustment of self-esteem when they go from being at the top of the academic peak in high school to being one of a crowd of college students. The minority student who is undergoing cultural-psychological dual identity crisis while coping with these adjustments needs support and assistance. Programs designed to identify and assist these students contribute to one of the central goals of higher education by assisting in the development of self-growth and perspective, and the exercise of a rational approach to living, working, and relating. Successful assistance can produce individuals who may constructively integrate their identities and promote their potential to society and themselves. Supportive services can enable the minority students to discuss their situations and aspirations, relate to others who share their condition, and promote their growth.

In its provision of counseling to minority students, an institution of higher learning should do the following:

Increase counselors'-advisers' awareness of the needs and concerns of minority students by providing counselors-advisers with materials and training

Periodically assess the effectiveness of counseling-advising programs for minority students

Develop periodic outreach programs and materials about counseling and advising services for institutional and community circulation, so that minority students will be aware of a cordial reception

Provide and publicize counseling-advising services at a variety of times (evenings-weekends), so that potential minority applicants or working students can utilize these services

Include minority counselors-advisers on the staff when possible, particularly those who have been through outreach contact or delayed entry

Include in institutional and community newspapers stories about minority students and alumni that publicize counseling-advising services and the institution; also mention these individuals in brochures and other materials

Evaluate tests for appropriateness for minority students; many service personnel are unaware that the majority of intelligence-social-career tests and inventories did not include minorities (or the elderly or the handicapped) in the test norms, to avoid research and norming contamination.

## MINORITY STUDENT NEEDS: ENTRY AND RETENTION

Although minority students enroll in college for a variety of reasons, higher career opportunities are frequently the single most important reason. This is particularly true of the bright, academically able minority student from a working-class background. Attainment of college and/or graduate degrees is perceived, in the traditional manner, as a vehicle for obtaining jobs appropriate to her/his level of ability. Secondary reasons usually include a desire for self-improvement, extending horizons, and professional contacts.

A number of obstacles hinder the entry and retention process.

### Institutional Obstacles

Policies and procedures with regard to complex application forms, admissions, enrollment, transfer of credit, scheduling, campus advising, and program planning are among these obstacles. The minority student who is entering college often lacks familiarity with the multitude of bureaucratic-academic procedures and policies. When this unfamiliarity is coupled with nonsupportive, indifferent, or hostile attitudes of clerical staff, faculty, or administrators, these students may easily be discouraged from entry or continuance.

### Situational Obstacles

These include transportation, child care, financial constraints, and campus indifference (staff, faculty, students, organizations). Going to college involves a great deal of time beyond the classroom. Minority students often have family and/or job commitments, and the schedule of priorities is frequently disrupted by the myriad problems of existence (car breakdowns, family or financial crises).

### Personal Considerations/Obstacles

Among these obstacles are uncertainty with regard to skills, abilities, and goals; academic insecurity; unsupportive family or spouse; and feelings of guilt, frustration, and fear. Unclear academic or career goals, a prior history of inconsistent or poor grades, or a patchwork of earlier courses and schools may also cause many of these students to hesitate in their college pursuits.

Personal concerns may be an additional obstacle in entering college. Many minorities, because of past injustices and discriminatory practices, lack confidence in their ability to succeed in a higher-education environment. This feeling may be particularly acute for the minority veteran, the student who had to delay college to help a family, the working student, or the minority student interested in a traditional noncareer subject area (humanities, for example). Uncertainty about academic skills, such as report or essay writing, math-science, recall-recognition-retention, and keeping up with classmates, may serve to hinder, if not deter, a minority student's academic progress.

These obstacles—institutional, situational, personal—often make it difficult for minority students to enter or continue college. Minority students need services that are directly related to their unique circumstances. A good academic/personal/career counseling program(s) can be an important turning point for minority students who encounter difficulties with the above obstacles. In some institutions these services often overlap. In large institutions they are often separate, and the activities seldom converge. Providing information, preferably on a one-to-one personal basis, at the outset can often be a pivotal point in a minority student's decision to enter or continue college. This may be accomplished through several community-based approaches to reach a sizable portion of the potential minority college students in any area.

Some of these community-based outreach services are listed below.

Compile brief, attractive booklets or brochures that contain information about programs and services and are aimed at minority students. When permissible, cite the names of minority faculty and staff who have expressed interest in talking with and helping minority students. They need not be exclusively minority persons, as long as they have demonstrated compassion, a fairly comprehensive understanding of available services, and a willingness to work with minority students. These booklets should be distributed within the surrounding community: at libraries, supermarkets, churches, local service clubs (Kiwanis, Lions), ethnic group organizations, minority professional organizations, YWCA/YMCA, local union chapters, minority newspapers, boards of education, and local PTAs.

Conduct meetings at local schools or neighborhood centers with all interested representatives of the above groups to orient them on a personal basis, in order to establish an ongoing relationship with these outreach resources. This can also serve as their "personal" contact with the institution that will facilitate questions, concerns, and person-to-institution relations. Minority groups, like many people, prefer personal contact. Past history with bureaucracies has created a wariness of impersonal "papers" from institutions.

Provide free preadmission academic-career counseling on a periodic basis. This could be a once-a-month (weekend/one day) session to assist and advise minority persons in their decision to pursue higher education.

Offer "entry orientation" courses or workshops in the community. This program could range from one-time sessions to extended series of meetings to assist the potential student in academic-career advice and to help the student clarify needs, strengthen and develop academic skills, and broaden knowledge of the academic and institutional processes and services.

ACADEMIC ADVISING

Since many minority students are the first of their families and friends to attend college, they need help in getting information about and assistance with programs, courses, requirements, and entry. These students need counseling advice regarding their specific interests in programs, assistance in gaining an understanding of general education in relation to their life-career aspirations, and knowledge of the ramifications of this knowledge in their decisions.

Academic advice is generally provided by faculty. In many large institutions, counselors and advising centers often provide some campuswide information. Many minority students, particularly those undecided about their majors, need help in initial academic planning, encouragement to enter nontraditional fields of study (for example, Asians in drama-dance, Hispanics in science-engineering), and long-range planning for career or postgraduate pursuits.

Institutions can do the following to further academic counseling:

Assign minority students to interested academic advisers. Institutions should encourage, support, and train a cadre of faculty, counselors, and other staff as interim academic advisers who will aid a student until she/he has determined a major. An interested person is critical for two reasons. Research studies indicate that unselected, uninterested advisers do not relate effectively. Second, minority students, as a group, are more likely to respond well to someone who is warm, interested, and supportive of them as a "person" first rather than to someone who happens to relate to them as an academic entity (student) in an institutional unit. The adviser can be particularly helpful to the transfer student who has earned a substantial amount of exploratory units or to a student who plans to investigate academic interests through lower-division courses.

Have academic advisers meet with their minority students during the earliest stage of enrollment. Many institutions sponsor general academic orientation, preregistration sessions with incoming students. Special sessions, informal or formal, within the orientation schedule should be planned specifically for minority students with their newly assigned "interested" advisers. This would permit the student to become acquainted with the adviser(s), learn about the institution (procedures, services, programs, goals), and get immediate personal assistance in developing a program (first-semester schedules, for instance).

Have advisers continue to meet frequently during the student's first semester, to assist with course changes and personal-social perceptions of institutional activities (seemingly hostile or indifferent faculty or staff, institutional procedures/paperwork, campus activities, other services). Frequent informal group meetings (at lunch, for example) can be helpful in discussing and overcoming many of these concerns.

Develop liaison between the interested adviser (faculty, counselor, staff), the minority student, and a faculty member from the student's potential department(s) or one(s) in which the student has shown interest. This would give the student the broadest personal contact with faculty, developing a meaningful academic and perhaps social-helping relationship.

Communicate the institution's commitment and concern about minority students directly to academic advisers. This could be accomplished by policy statements or letters or certificates of recognition from deans or presidents.

Provide information specifically addressed to the concerns of academic advisers working with minority students. This should include information about the advisers' particular advisee group.

Conduct training and orientation sessions with informational materials about other campus services. Also important is listing interested faculty, staff, and administrative personnel, in order to facilitate more direct, effective referrals and assistance.

Periodically assess the academic adviser services. Each semester the advisers could submit oral or written comments describing positive as well as difficult experiences. Minority students should be assessed, to determine their views of the efficacy of services.

PERSONAL COUNSELING

College entry and continuation can frequently be difficult, overwhelming, and anxiety-producing. In many institutions a minority student is away from a "we" family-centered unit for the first time, the sole minority student in a particular program, and sometimes the only minority person in the dormitory. These students often need a time and place where they can examine, share, and discuss concerns that may be affecting their lives and academic progress.

College counseling, in its contemporary form, goes far beyond the traditionally defined individual "therapy" type of counseling. Counseling services within many institutions are usually diverse, and often include the following:

Traditional individual counseling

Group counseling

Peer advice-assistance

Support groups (peer or professionally assisted)

"Talk" groups (consciousness/awareness discussions)

Assertiveness training and value clarification

Stress management workshops

Special-interest lunch groups

Credit or noncredit courses that focus on career exploration, report writing, fear of math, study skills

Weekend seminars

Faculty "mentor-student relationship" programs

Preadmission sessions

These programs are frequently provided both formally and informally, in a variety of settings:

Counseling centers

Ethnic studies programs or departments

Advising centers

Learning assistance centers

Educational opportunity programs offices

Career planning offices

Academic departments

Financial aid offices

Specific minority affairs offices

Health centers

In many institutions minority faculty and staff are few in number. However, these individuals are often familiar with each other's services, and will frequently join to help coordinate assistance for minority students.

Because counseling and advising can occur in a number of places within the institution, the individuals providing these services may need help in dealing more effectively with minority students. To provide more effective services, an institution could do any or all of the following:

Provide materials about minority students to inform personnel throughout the institution who are most likely to give informal or formal counseling and advice

Assist personnel by providing materials to be given directly to minority students to inform them about special services and programs

Provide information to institutional personnel about campus services for minority students, so personnel can effectively refer these students to appropriate services

Provide formal or informal training to those who might provide advice or counseling to minority students

Construct an institutionwide committee made up of service personnel, to coordinate services, develop materials and resources, examine and evaluate services and trends, plan training, and develop ongoing policies.

CAREER COUNSELING

Because many minority people have not had higher educational opportunities in the past, a large number of minority students are unaware of the ramifications of higher education in relation to student development, as well as of the effects of their curriculum and career goals. Exploration of career options, choices, and ramifications is necessary to fully assist them in planning their education and postgraduate pursuits.

Because many low-income minority students enroll in higher education with job preparation as their central goal, their career counseling needs are often different from those of the typical white student. Minorities and women college graduates still earn less than the equivalently trained white male graduate. There is also a continued broad pool of resistance to hiring and, more important, promoting these individuals; discouraging stories are an ever-present concern.

Some of the problems minorities face with career development and vocational counseling include a lack of information on career choices and options, a lack of knowledge of the "ramifications/implications" and sociopolitical nuances of these career choices and options, feelings of insecurity and self-doubt about procuring employment, unfamiliarity with the process of seeking and applying for a job or graduate school, unfamiliarity with career counseling "in-house" terminology, and promoting the employment of particular minorities in or out of certain nontraditional fields.

An institution can promote career counseling through the following means:

Designate a specific location, time, and individual who will provide vocational-career counseling for minority students—some institutions, for example, publicize a particular afternoon or evening at the counseling center, conducted by a particular minority counselor for particular groups in specific fields

Initiate career planning/career counseling at the earliest stages of students' academic entry—this is sometimes done in conjunction with the admissions orientation sessions

Assess career materials for ethnic as well as age-sex bias, and develop new materials where needed

Conduct a variety of sessions or workshops on career planning and career information in a variety of locations and at various times for minority students—perhaps in the student union or community center on weekends or evenings, or in ethnic studies program classes

Bring in minority graduates who have experienced academic-career uncertainty and who have worked it through to a successful conclusion, to speak to classes and workshops

Develop a liaison with minority students, minority programs, organizations, and incoming job recruiters, to encourage contacts

Promote information about training programs (industrial or postgraduate) that are geared for recruiting minorities in nontraditional and/or underserved fields

Conduct workshops on résumé writing, job applications, interviewing procedures, as well as provide information about job-social-behavior expectations and postentry opportunities

Work closely with minority students to ensure that their academic, work, and other experiences are incorporated into their portfolios to adequately portray their strenghts.

## SUPPORT

The preponderant number of minority students, as with the general population, do not need traditional psychotherapy.  Most of them need support and encouragement.  Many counseling centers can, and do, provide support services.  In many institutions counseling centers provide advice and career-academic counseling, as well as long-term therapy and growth opportunities (self- or career exploration workshops, assertiveness training, time-management training).

Counseling centers and minority programs can provide a number of support services, which might include any of the following:

Develop a multicultural minority center—the multicultural aspect could be informative for the student body and also serve as a nonisolated unit for minority students

Utilize current or former minority students to talk with new applicants or continuing students

Conduct and promote brown-bag lunches for minority students at which they meet with each other, faculty, and student organization representatives to discuss issues of concern

Establish a formal association of minority students and alumni to develop opportunities to become acquainted and share their experiences, difficulties, and successes

Conduct special orientation sessions for minority students

Conduct meetings of campus, community, and business representatives, and minority students to acquaint them with their activities and people.

Develop a list of off-campus services and personnel who are willing to assist minority students (emergency home care, social services, affirmative action officers from business and industry).

## GENERAL INSTITUTIONAL CONSIDERATIONS

Many institutions use some form of computerized data-gathering from student applications. More often than not, this information is used only for institutional description or generalized statistics rather than to prompt institutional outreach. Some of the information could be used to delineate who (specifically, by group and name) the minority students are among the general student body. Then brochures, workshops, sessions, and services could be more effective in reaching every minority student.

In larger institutions a variety of services are available, but the minority student is often confused or unaware of whom to turn to. There should be a designated and publicized office (minority affairs), center, group, or program that offers information/advice/counseling. Some institutions have minority affairs officers and minority hot lines.

Finally, the institution should sponsor and conduct periodic conferences on issues relevant to the concerns of minorities. These conferences can provide an institutional-community forum and encourage a heightened awareness of minorities in the larger community.

## CONCLUSION

The current trends in higher education indicate that significant shifts in college populations are occurring. More minorities and women are enrolling in higher education, and as the social and economic fabric of society broadens, more of these graduates will influence—and perhaps change—the personnel expectations of the roles of traditional career-social areas.

Institutions today are enrolling a second "civil rights generation" of minority students who are aware of affirmative action efforts, grew up with the civil rights movement, are generally skeptical of formal testing, and compel services and programs that are specific to their concerns. The promotion of counseling services that address the complexities of minority identity development and academic and personal-social-career growth will significantly assist the determination and success of these students in society.

## REFERENCES

Astin, Alexander. 1980. The American freshman: National norms for fall, 1980. In The chronicle of higher education. Washington, D.C.: American Council on Education and UCLA.

Cabrera, Y. A. 1977. Schizophrenia in the Southwest: Mexican Americans in Angloland. In Claremont reading conference yearbook. XXXI. Claremont, Calif.: Claremont Graduate Schools and University Center.

Kurten, Bjorn. 1980. Dance of the tiger. New York: Pantheon.

Sibatani, Atuhiro. 1980. The Japanese brain. Science, 80, December: 23-26.

Vontress, Clemmont. 1971. Racial differences: Impediments to rapport. Journal of Counseling Psychology, 18: 1033-1041.

Weinstein, Loribeth. 1980. The counseling needs of re-entry women. Washington, D.C.: Association of American Colleges.

# 10

## CAREER PLANNING
## AND PLACEMENT

### *H. Edward Babbush*

One of the most dynamic and satisfying student personnel programs is career planning and placement. Because of changing student populations, economic conditions, and constantly evolving career areas, this program has grown tremendously since the early 1970s and offers increasing opportunities for the future. Surveys of entering freshmen have repeatedly indicated that students have a crying need for career planning assistance early in their academic careers, and placement assistance when they are about to graduate.

The career planning and placement function, with its emphasis on individual and group counseling assistance, may or may not be a part of the counseling center. On some campuses it is separate from personal counseling, and in other cases it is an integral part of the entire student counseling program. In either case there must be constant interchange between personal counselors and career planning and placement counselors, since it is often very difficult to separate personal, family, financial, and other types of counseling when attempting to provide career planning and placement counseling. The following will discuss the evolution of today's career planning and placement responsibilities.

HISTORY

Just as the counseling function has become more sophisticated and complex in the last few years, so has the career planning and placement function on the university campus. Career planning and placement offices often are a vital part of the entire educational and student development process; not only do they provide career planning and placement assistance to the students and graduates, but they also serve as a liaison in interpreting the university's programs and the attributes of their graduates to business, industry, and government, as well as in articulating business, industry, and government needs to the faculty, students, and administration.

But this wasn't always the case. Placement offices evolved out of the practice of faculty members preparing written evaluations and letters of referral for students in order to assist them in obtaining employment. This was a common practice early in this century, especially for students who intended to teach or to enter graduate school. When faculty members tired of writing numerous letters for the same students, placement offices or appointment bureaus were established as a depository for the letters, so that they could be duplicated and sent out at students' or employers' requests. The major role change of the placement offices occurred after World War II, when there was a large increase in college enrollments, spurred by the G.I. Bill, which provided federally funded educational opportunities for veterans. Many of the students who inundated the colleges were very job- and career-oriented, especially after their experiences in the service. Often they were from lower- or middle-class families, and were striving for upward mobility through a college education. After completing their education, they were eager to obtain a job that would offer them security and a good salary, and that would lead to a satisfying career.

Universities responded to this need of their graduates by expanding the role of the placement offices to expedite the process of getting graduates and business, industry, and government representatives together rather than relying on personal faculty contacts, a system that was often inefficient and unfair. Because business, industry, government, and education were booming in the postwar years and needed college-educated human resources, it was a simple matter, in many cases, of bringing students and employers together for interviews. Colleges and employers continually expanded their on-campus interview programs up through the 1960s. Often it didn't matter what an individual graduate's major was— it was sufficient that he/she was a college graduate in order to receive an offer of employment.

All of this changed drastically in the late 1960s, when the supply of college graduates began to exceed the demand for them. Employers no longer sought just a college graduate, but those with particular strengths, education, and experience. Frequently it was too late in the academic year, for some liberal arts students visiting a placement office for the first time as seniors, to meet the requirements of many employers with job openings. Consequently, many of the colleges added to their placement assistance programs the function of providing early, unbiased, and current career counseling for their undergraduates. Today there are a number of recognized functions of the career planning and placement office on the university campus.

## THE CAREER PLANNING AND PLACEMENT PROGRAM

The primary objective is to assist students in obtaining the greatest benefits possible from their college education through satisfying career placement upon graduation. All activities of the career planning and placement office are directed toward this goal.

To assist the office in reaching this objective, two fundamental services are provided:

1.  Career planning. A service designed primarily to assist undergraduate students in obtaining appropriate information that will enable them to determine career choices commensurate with their abilities, interests, and desired lifestyles. This service enables students to be better prepared for jobs when they graduate, and consequently enhances their ability to compete for available positions.

2.  Placement. A service designed to assist graduates in obtaining jobs appropriate to their academic achievement, experience, career objectives, and desires.

To fulfill these responsibilities, the career planning and placement offices are organized accordingly.

I.  To enable students to accomplish the required career planning, the following objectives are instituted:
    a.  In cooperation with faculty-academic advisers and psychological counselors, help students early in their academic program to relate aptitudes, experiences, attitudes, and resources to developing career goals and alternatives through group or individual career counseling, tests, workshops, seminars, career days, community outreach, and other information programs
    b.  Serve the unique career planning needs of special student populations such as women, minorities, the disabled, and older students through specialized academic programs in which a sense of identity, role models, and planning are vital

    c.   Provide information on, and interpretation of, the labor market, and disseminate such information to faculty, administration, and students

    d.   Conduct follow-up surveys to determine the employment status of recent graduates and provide the information to students, faculty, and administrators

    e.   Assist students in obtaining information on graduate and professional programs and their admission requirements

    f.   Inform faculty and administrators of employment trends related to the academic programs of the institution, in order to assist student program planning and advising

    g.   Maintain and constantly update a comprehensive collection of resource materials for the use of students and faculty.

II.   To assist in graduate placement, the following activities are provided:

    a.   Develop and maintain effective relatioship with employers

    b.   Counsel and assist students and graduates in learning about specific clusters of occupations, employment data, position requirements, career alternatives, and related information

    c.   Assist graduating students and alumni (on a reimbursed basis) in locating suitable and rewarding full-time employment by utilizing appropriate job-search techniques—this includes providing information on job vacancies, administering employment tests, assisting in preparing résumés, cover letters, and applications, and teaching skills appropriate for interviewing and obtaining and keeping a job

    d.   Provide job vacancy notices and on-campus interview services

    e.   Enable students to obtain experience during college that will help them either to reach their career objectives or to defray educational expenses through temporary, part-time, or summer employment

    f.   Develop opportunities for jobs, volunteer work, cooperative education experiences, and internships for students that provide career-related experience during college.

ORGANIZATIONAL STRUCTURE OF CAREER
PLANNING AND PLACEMENT

A typical career planning and placement organizational structure will recognize the main services of the office and provide
recognition of the placement, career planning, and (often) experiential education, cooperative, and/or student employment functions (see Figure 10.1).

The trend in the organizational structure of career planning
and placement offices has been toward the strong, centralized program rather than individual departments or schools providing their
own career planning and placement services.  The centralized office
often provides greater economies of operation and efficiency of
available staff.  It also makes it easier for the college recruiter to
contact one office to obtain the services of graduates with a variety
of academic majors.  However, the centralized organization is not
universal.  Some colleges maintain separate graduate school of
business or separate engineering services, and some may have
three or four independently operating placement offices to meet
their individual needs.

Staffing

The staffing provided the career planning and placement offices is not standardized to any degree.  It ranges from one-half
position per thousand students enrolled to, in some cases, 2.0
professional, clerical, and administrative staff per thousand, with
the majority of schools falling somewhere in the range of one per
1,200 or 1,500 students enrolled.  In other words, some schools of
25,000 students may have 50 employees, and some of the same
size may have 15-25.  Naturally, the number of staff positions
available for this function will affect the services available.  The
professional members of the staff of the office of career planning
and placement typically will have a bachelor's or master s degree
and/or doctorate in a variety of fields, with the trend leaning
toward an advanced degree in counseling.  In addition, many of the
professional members will have a number of years of practical
work experience, in many cases in personnel offices in business
and industry.  The combination of counseling and practical work
experience enables these staffs to provide current, competent,
realistic career planning assistance and placement services to
students, as well as an understanding of the problems of employers.

FIGURE 10.1

Organization Chart

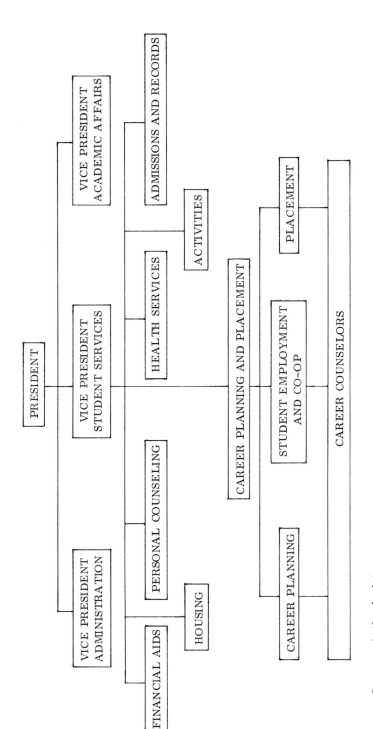

Source: Author's data.

Facilities

There is a wide variance in the facilities available at the various college campuses. Individual private offices are required for the professional career counselors because of the personal discussion that is often a part of career decision making. Interviewing rooms are provided for on-campus interviews. These will vary from cubicles in temporary buildings and trailers to bedrooms in houses and apartments to pleasant, carpeted offices with a reception area.

In addition to the individual interviewing cubicles, some campuses may have group interview facilities that are utilized before individual interview sessions to disseminate information regarding the company or agency and its needs for the next year. The campus may also have various conference and seminar rooms available. These will allow the office of career planning and placement to present, for its students, a variety of workshops—in résumé writing, job search techniques, skills identification—and seminars in which employers will be invited to participate, such as careers for liberal arts majors, careers in the aerospace industry, careers in the communications industry, careers in government. Some universities also have audiovisual studio services that enable them to tape the workshops and seminars, which can then be viewed by students. They encourage employers to make audio-video taped presentations about the aims and goals of their companies, their plans, opportunities for the future, and the types of expertise they seek. These video studios are often utilized to encourage the students to improve their interviewing techniques through videotaped sessions, which are played back and critiqued individually with counselors or personnel representatives.

Most colleges provide a career resource center, which in many cases is a multimedia library consisting of general career planning information, both written and audiovisual, such as the Occupational Exploration Kit, Dictionary of Occupational Titles, and the Occupational Outlook Handbook. This is also where the colleges typically store and index notebooks concerning the companies recruiting on their campus. These contain the literature provided by the employers on the benefits of working for their particular firm, their annual reports, their recruiting literature, and other pertinent information. They also have racks for the brochures that employers provide in quantity for the use of individual students.

ADDITIONAL SERVICES TO EMPLOYERS AND STUDENTS

Many colleges provide additional services to employers and students.

## Career Days

In order to encourage students to do career planning early in their academic lives, many colleges provide a general career day or days. Twenty-five to 100 or more employers may be situated at tables in the student union or common area, and students, without appointments, are given the opportunity to discuss with them what the companies and agencies are looking for, the career opportunities with them, the benefits of working for them, and the majors or courses that would be advantageous for students to take. Seniors and graduate students sometimes utilize these career days to leave résumés with interested employers.

## Speakers Bureaus

Some colleges, through the office of career planning and placement, establish a speakers' bureau. A brochure or publication, disseminated through the office of career planning and placement, contains information gathered from employers concerning the availability of speakers and the variety of topics for classroom presentations. Company representatives from personnel offices, engineering, accounting, administration, graphics, and other areas describe the presentations they are available to make. Individual faculty members can then contact those who are appropriate to their academic programs.

## Computer-Assisted Career Guidance

With the increasing applications of computer technology to higher education, several interactive career guidance programs have been made available. These serve as a valuable tool for the career counselor to utilize in helping students to make career decisions and in enabling students to obtain increasing amounts of sophisticated supply-and-demand and career information, including but not limited to, job descriptions, career ladders, how to qualify, what schools offer what programs, salary information, and chances of success. An office of career planning and placement typically will lease the software from firms or agencies that are constantly updating their information files; through a cathode ray tube and printer tied in with the campus' systems or microcomputer, students can use the information bank in a logical sequence that will develop their decision-making skills and lead to sophisticated career decisions.

### Workshops and Seminars

Career planning and placement offices attempt to provide as realistic a picture of the job market today and the career opportunities for the future as possible. To augment their expertise, they are continually seeking to provide workshops and seminars that will be of value to the students. These may be given in the office of career planning and placement or in various academic settings before student interest groups and organizations. These programs are extremely beneficial to the students, and pay off for the employers with increased rapport and improved recruitment efforts if they are represented by articulate, well-prepared, and interested participants. Topics of workshops and seminars include résumé writing, interviewing techniques, decision making, job search techniques, dual careers, museum and gallery careers, careers for liberal arts majors, government careers, jobs in banking, computer careers, and so on.

### Job Orders

In some cases, employers may not have sufficient openings to merit an on-campus visit, or additional jobs may come up after campus visits. Most campuses maintain a job-order or vacancy-notice type of service for their students. Jobs are categorized by appropriate academic majors, so that students may follow up on them by sending a résumé or making individual contact with the appropriate parties. Some offices provide a daily updated phone line and/or computer matching service to make students aware of current jobs.

### Alumni Services

Employers often seek to employ individuals with a number of years of appropriate job experience or particular types of expertise that are not normally found in a new college graduate. Many offices of career planning and placement maintain separate job listings for their alumni and experienced personnel. These are often extremely valuable to employers because a telephone job order or a written job description can be disseminated to the college office of career planning and placement, and thus obtain exposure to another valuable recruitment source. Alumni coming out of the armed services or deciding to change jobs or careers, will utilize the office of career planning and placement to find out the current labor market conditions and jobs available. Some alumni may be permitted to interview on campus if space is available, but most will apply directly to employers. At some universities alumni are charged a fee for career planning and placement services.

Part-Time and Summer Jobs

Offices of career planning and placement also provide a service to students that will enhance their financial ability to stay in school and to obtain valuable work experience. This is also a service to employers to aid them in obtaining part-time employees, and summer and vacation replacements. Part-time jobs and summer jobs often allow students to size employers up before they graduate. While the procedures to utilize this service vary, most campuses will take job orders either through the mail or via telephone, and will post the notices and refer students to employers, appropriate to the valid qualifications they establish under equal opportunity regulations.

Feedback

Many college and university offices of career planning and placement seek feedback from employers and graduates regarding the evaluations they have of the currency and applicability of the academic programs and services. This enables the offices to provide this information to curriculum committees and academic departments, in order to encourage modifications and improvements of existing programs. Additional information regarding the types of jobs and salaries that graduates have obtained is often valuable in providing career counseling to undergraduates.

Specialized Training and Career Planning for Employers

Some offices of career planning and placement have the facilities, equipment, and professional capabilities to assist employers in providing specialized training to their employees. They can provide individual or group sessions on interviewing techniques, often with videotaped mock interviewing sessions that can be critiqued. This can assist employers in the training of new recruiters or those hired on an intermittent basis for on-campus interviews. These group sessions are provided free or for a nominal charge, and include a day on campus for personnel to be acclimated ahead of time to the campus scene, what's expected of the interview process, the functioning of the office of career planning and placement, services available, and the current needs and demands of the students. Another service provided by some offices of career planning and placement is career planning or outplacement services for employers' staffs. On a contract basis or through continuing education, the expertise of the professional career planning counselors may be brought to a particular organization's facility to assist in providing career planning, skills identification, and job search and decision-making techniques for their employees. In many cases it will be cheaper and better accepted by employers to utilize these professionals from outside their organizations, rather than in-house personnel, in order to make the program of career planning for their employees most effective.

SUMMARY

This has been a brief discussion of the services of typical offices of career planning and placement. Those desiring more detailed information are referred to the publications of the College Placement Council, Bethlehem, Pennsylvania. It is well to remember that different colleges in various locales require different services. Individual programs should be tailored to meet the needs of the particular students being served. Career planning and placement is a recognized student service, and students, as consumers, have a right to information that they need to make educated career and academic choices. Students require unbiased counseling that is not self-serving, and is provided by well-educated, experienced professionals who are aware of the changing economic and labor conditions and their effect on old and new careers, as well as versed in the constantly changing legal ramifications of rights to privacy, equal opportunity, affirmative action, screening criteria, and test validation.

Universities, when establishing their career planning and placement programs, need to be constantly aware that the career planning and placement function not only has tremendous interface with a large number of students at the university but also is often the only exposure that the personnel recruiters from business, industry, government, and school districts have to the university. A professionally staffed, well-designed, and well-equipped facility not only will assist the university in marketing its graduates, and consequently in attracting students to the institution, but also will often be of assistance in increasing private donations for scholarships, fellowships, equipment, and other items. The publics that the university serves—the students, the community, and employers—will, in the long run, judge the impact of the institution not on how successful its football team or basketball team is, nor on the fancy architectural features, but on the graduates of the institution and their contributions to society.

# APPENDIX A
# STANDARDS FOR PROVIDERS OF PSYCHOLOGICAL SERVICES

In January 1975, the APA Council of Representatives created the original Committee on Standards for Providers of Psychological Services. The Committee was charged with updating and revising the Standards adopted in September 1974. Members of the Committee were Jacqueline C. Bouhoutsos, Leon Hall, Marian D. Hall, Mary Henle, Durand F. Jacobs (Chair), Abel Ossorio, and Wayne Sorenson. Task force liaison was Jerry H. Clark, and Central Office liaison was Arthur Centor.

In January 1976, Council further charged the Committee to review the Standards and recommend revisions needed to reflect the varying needs of only those psychologists engaged in the activities of clinical, counseling, industrial-organizational, and school psychology. The Committee was reconstituted with one member representing each of the four applied activities, plus one member representing institutional practice and one representing the public interest.

Members were Jules Barron, clinical; Barbara A. Kirk, counseling; Frank Friedlander, industrial-organizational (replacing Virginia Schein); Durand F. Jacobs (Chair), institutional practice; M. Brewster Smith, public interest; Marian D. Hall, school; Arthur Centor was Central Office liaison.

The Standards that follow are the first revision of the national Standards for Providers of Psychological Services originally adopted by the American Psychological Association (APA) on September 4, 1974.[1] [Note: Notes 1-24 appear at the end of the Standards.] The intent of these Standards is to improve the quality, effectiveness, and accessibility of psychological services to all who require them.[2]

These Standards represent the attainment of a goal for which the Association has striven for over 20 years, namely, to codify a uniform set of standards for psychological practice that would serve the respective needs of users, providers, and third-party purchasers and sanctioners of psychological services. In addition, the Association has established a standing committee charged with keeping the Standards responsive to the needs of these groups and with upgrading and extending them progressively as the profession and science of psychology continue to develop new knowledge, improved methods, and additional modes of psychological service. These Standards have been established by organized psychology as a means of self-regulation to protect the public interest.

While these revised Standards contain a number of important changes, they differ from the original Standards in two major respects:

1. They uniformly specify the minimally acceptable levels of quality assurance and performance that providers of those psychological services covered by the Standards must reach or exceed. Care has been taken to assure that each standard is clearly stated, readily measurable, realistic, and implementable.

2. The revised Standards apply to a more limited range of services than the original Standards. The present Standards have been restricted to applications in "human services" with the goal of facilitating more effective human functioning. The kinds of psychological services covered by the present Standards are those ordinarily involved in the practice of specialists in clinical, counseling, industrial-organizational, and school psychology. However, it is important to note that these Standards cover psychological functions and not classes of practitioners.

Any persons representing themselves as psychologists, when providing any of the covered psychological service functions at any time and in any setting, whether public or private, profit or nonprofit, are required to observe these standards of practice in order to promote the best interests and welfare of the users of such services. It is to be understood that fulfillment of the requirements to meet these Standards shall be judged by peers in relation to the capabilities for evaluation and the circumstances that prevail in the setting at the time the program or service is evaluated.

Standards covering other psychological service functions may be added from time to time to those already listed. However, functions and activities related to the teaching of psychology, the writing or editing of scholarly or scientific manuscripts, and the conduct of scientific research do not fall within the purview of the present Standards.

## HISTORICAL BACKGROUND

Early in 1970, acting at the direction of the Association's Council of Representatives, the Board of Professional Affairs appointed a Task Force composed of practicing psychologists with specialized knowledge in at least one of every major class of human service facility and with experience relevant to the setting of standards. Its charge was to develop a set of standards for psychological practice. Soon thereafter, partial support for this activity was obtained through a grant from the National Institute of Mental Health.[3]

First, the Task Force established liaison with national groups already active in standard setting and accreditation. It was therefore able to influence the adoption of certain basic principles and wording contained in standards for psychological services published by the Joint Commission on Accreditation of Hospitals (JCAH) Accreditation Council for Facilities for the Mentally Retarded (1971) and by the Accreditation Council for Psychiatric Facilities (JCAH 1972). It also contributed substantially to the "constitutionally required minimum standards for adequate treatment of the mentally ill" ordered by the U.S. District Court in Alabama (Wyatt v. Stickney, 1972). In concert with other APA committees, the Task Force also represented the Association in national-level deliberations with governmental groups and insurance carriers that defined the qualifications necessary for psychologists involved in providing health services.

These interim outcomes involved influence by the Association on actions by groups of nonpsychologists that directly affected the manner in which psychological services were employed, particularly in health and rehabilitation settings. However, these measures did not relieve the Association from exercising its responsibility to speak out directly and authoritatively on what standards for psychological practice should be throughout a broad range of human service settings. It was also the responsibility of the Association to determine how psychologists would be held accountable should their practice fail to meet quality standards.

In September 1974, after more than 4 years of study and broad consultations, the Task Force proposed a set of standards, which the Association's Council of Representatives adopted and voted to publish in order to meet urgent needs of the public and the profession. Members of Council had various reservations about the scope and wording of the Standards as initially adopted. By establishing a continuing Committee on Standards, Council took the first step in what would be an ongoing process of review and revision.

The task of collecting, analyzing, and synthesizing reactions to the original Standards fell to two successive committees. They were charged similarly to review and revise the Standards and to suggest means to implement them, including their acceptance by relevant governmental and private accreditation groups. The dedicated work of the psychologists who served on both those committees is gratefully acknowledged. Also recognized with thanks are the several hundred comments received from scores of interested persons representing professional, academic, and scientific psychology, consumer groups, administrators of facilities, and others. This input from those directly affected by the original Standards provided the major stimulus and much of the content for the changes that appear in this revision.

## PRINCIPLES AND IMPLICATIONS
## OF STANDARDS

A few basic principles have guided the development of these Standards.

1. There should be a single set of standards that governs psychological service functions offered by psychologists, regardless of their specialty, setting, or form of remuneration. All psychologists in professional practice should be guided by a uniform set of standards just as they are guided by a common code of ethics.

2. Standards should clearly establish minimally acceptable levels of quality for covered psychological service functions, regardless of the character of the users, purchasers, or sanctioners of such covered services.

3. All persons providing psychological services shall meet minimally acceptable levels of training and experience, which are consistent and appropriate with the functions they perform. However, final responsibility and accountability for services provided must rest with psychologists who have earned a doctoral degree in a program that is primarily psychological at a regionally accredited university or professional school. Those providing psychological services who have lesser (or other) levels of training shall be supervised by a psychologist with the above training. This level of qualification is necessary to assure that the public receives services of high quality.

4. There should be a uniform set of standards governing the quality of services to all users of psychological services in both the private and public sectors. There is no justification for maintaining the double standard presently embedded in most state legislation whereby providers of private fee-based psychological services are subject to statutory regulation, while those providing similar psycho-

logical services under governmental auspices are usually exempt from such regulations. This circumstance tends to afford greater protection under the law for those receiving privately delivered psychological services. On the other hand, those receiving privately delivered psychological services currently lack many of the safeguards that are available in governmental settings; these include peer review, consultation, record review, and staff supervision.

5. While assuring the user of the psychologist's accountability for the nature and quality of services rendered, standards must not constrain the psychologist from employing new methods or making use of support personnel in staffing the delivery of services.

The Standards here presented have broad implications both for the public who use psychological services and for providers of such services:

1. Standards provide a firmer basis for a mutual understanding between provider and user and facilitate more effective evaluation of services provided and outcomes achieved.

2. Standards are an important step toward greater uniformity in legislative and regulatory actions involving providers of psychological services, and Standards provide the basis for the development of accreditation procedures for service facilities.

3. Standards give specific content to the profession's concept of ethical practice.

4. Standards have significant impact on tomorrow's training models for both professional and support personnel in psychology.

5. Standards for the provision of psychological services in human service facilities influence what is considered acceptable structure, budgeting, and staffing patterns in these facilities.

6. Standards are living documents that require continual review and revision.

The Standards illuminate weaknesses in the delivery of psychological services and point to their correction. Some settings are known to require additional and/or higher standards for specific areas of service delivery than those herein proposed. There is no intent to diminish the scope or quality of psychological services that exceed these Standards.

Systematically applied, these Standards serve to establish uniformly the minimally acceptable levels of psychological services. They serve to establish a more effective and consistent basis for evaluating the performance of individual service providers, and they serve to guide the organizing of psychological service units in human service settings.

DEFINITIONS

"Providers of psychological services" refers to the following persons:

A. Professional psychologists.[4] Professional psychologists have a doctoral degree from a regionally accredited university or professional school in a program that is primarily psychological[5] and appropriate training and experience in the area of service offered.[6]

B. All other persons who offer psychological services under the supervision of a professional psychologist.

"Psychological services" refers to one or more of the following:[7]

A. Evaluation, diagnosis, and assessment of the functioning of individuals and groups in a variety of settings and activities.

B. Interventions to facilitate the functioning of individuals and groups. Such interventions may include psychological counseling, psychotherapy, and process consultation.

C. Consultation relating to A and B above.

D. Program development services in the areas of A, B, and C above.[8]

E. Supervision of psychological services.

A psychological service unit is the functional unit through which psychological services are provided:

A. A psychological service unit is a unit that provides predominantly psychological services and is composed of one or more professional psychologists and supporting staff.

B. A psychological service unit may operate as a professional service or as a functional or geographic component of a larger governmental, educational, correction, health, training, industrial, or commercial organizational unit.[9]

C. A psychologist providing professional services in a multi-occupational setting is regarded as a psychological service unit.

D. A psychological service unit also may be an individual or group of individuals in a private practice or a psychological consulting firm.

"User includes:

A. Direct users or recipients of psychological services.

B. Public and private institutions, facilities, or organizations receiving psychological services

C. Third-party purchasers—those who pay for the delivery of services but who are not the recipients of services.

"Sanctioners" refers to those users and nonusers who have a legitimate concern with the accessibility, timeliness, efficacy, and standards of quality attending the provision of psychological services. In addition to the users, sanctioners may include members of the user's family, the court, the probation officer, the school administrator, the employer, the union representative, the facility director. Another class of sanctioners is represented by various governmental, peer review, and accreditation bodies concerned with the assurance of quality.

## STANDARD 1. PROVIDERS

1.1 Each psychological service unit offering psychological services shall have available at least one professional psychologist and as many more professional psychologists as are necessary to assure the quality of services offered.

Interpretation: The intent of this Standard is that one or more providers of psychological services in any psychological service unit shall meet the levels of training and experience of the professional psychologist as specified in the preceding definitions. [10]

When a professional psychologist is not available on a full-time basis, the facility shall retain the services of one or more professional psychologists on a regular part-time basis to supervise the psychological services provided. The psychologist(s) so retained shall have authority and participate sufficiently to enable him or her to assess the needs for services, review the content of services provided, and assume professional responsibility and accountability for them.

1.2 Providers of psychological services who do not meet the requirements for the professional psychologist shall be supervised by a professional psychologist who shall assume professional responsibility and accountability for the services provided. The level and extent of supervision may vary from task to task so long as the supervising psychologist retains a sufficiently close supervisory relationship to meet this standard.

1.3 Wherever a psychological service unit exists, a professional psychologist shall be responsible for planning, directing, and reviewing the provision of psychological services.

Interpretation: This psychologist shall coordinate the activities of the psychological service unit with other professional, administrative and technical groups, both within and outside the facility. This psychologist, who may be the director, chief, or coordinator of the psychological service unit, has related responsibilities including, but not limited to, recruiting qualified staff, directing training and research activities of the service, maintaining a high level of professional and ethical practice, and assuring that staff members function only within the areas of their competency.

In order to facilitate the effectiveness of services by increasing the level of staff sensitivity and professional skills, the psychologist designated as director shall be responsible for participating in the selection of the staff and supporting personnel whose qualifications and skills (e.g., language, cultural and experiential background, race, and sex) are directly relevant to the needs and characteristics of the users served.

1.4    When functioning as part of an organizational setting, professional psychologists shall bring their background and skills to bear whenever appropriate upon the goals of the organization by participating in the planning and development of overall services. [11]

Interpretation: Professional psychologists shall participate in the maintenance of high professional standards by representation on committees concerned with service delivery.

As appropriate to the setting, these activities may include active participation, as voting and as office-holding members, on the facility's executive, planning, and evaluation boards and committees.

1.5    Psychologists shall maintain current knowledge of scientific and professional developments that are directly related to the services they render.

Interpretation: Methods through which knowledge of scientific and professional development may be gained include, but are not limited to, continuing education, attendance at workshops, participation in staff development, and reading scientific publications. [12]

The psychologist shall have ready access to reference material related to the provision of psychological services.

Psychologists must be prepared to show evidence periodically that they are staying abreast of current knowledge and practices through continuing education.

1.6    Psychologists shall limit their practice to their demonstrated areas of professional competence.

Interpretation: Psychological services will be offered in accordance with the provider's area of competence as defined by verifiable training and experience. When extending services beyond the range of their usual practice, psychologists shall obtain pertinent training or appropriate professional supervision.

1.7    Psychologists who wish to change their service specialty or to add an additional area of applied specialization must meet the same requirements with respect to subject matter and professional skills that apply to doctoral training in the new specialty. [13]

Interpretation: Training of doctoral-level psychologists to qualify them for change in specialty will be under the auspices of accredited university departments or professional schools that offer the doctoral degree in that specialty. Such training should be individualized, due credit being given for relevant coursework or requirements that have previously been satisfied. Merely taking an internship or acquiring experience in a practicum setting is not considered adequate preparation for becoming a clinical, counseling, industrial-organizational, or school psychologist when prior training has not been in the relevant area. Fulfillment of such an individualized training program is attested to by the award of a certificate by the supervising department or professional school indicating the successful completion of preparation in the particular specialty.

STANDARD 2.  PROGRAMS

2.1    Composition and organization of a psychological service unit

    2.1.1   The composition and programs of a psychological service unit shall be responsive to the needs of the persons or settings served.

Interpretation: A psychological service unit shall be so structured as to facilitate effective and economical delivery of services. For example, a psychological service unit serving a predominantly low-income, ethnic, or racial minority group should have a staffing pattern and service program that is adapted to the linguistic, experiential, and attitudinal characteristics of the users.

    2.1.2   A description of the organization of the psychological service unit and its lines of responsibility and accountability for the delivery of psychological services shall be available in written form to staff of the unit and to users and sanctioners upon request.

Interpretation: The workload and diversity of psychological services required and the specific goals and objectives of the setting will determine the numbers and qualifications of professional and support personnel in the psychological service unit. Where shortages in personnel exist so that psychological services cannot be rendered in a professional manner, the director of the psychological service unit shall initiate action to modify appropriately the specific goals and objectives of the service.

2.2   Policies

2.2.1   When the psychological service unit is composed of more than one person wherein a supervisory relationship exists or is a component of a larger organization, a written statement of its objectives and scope of services shall be developed and maintained.

Interpretation: The psychological service unit shall review its objectives and scope of services annually and revise them as necessary to insure that the psychological services offered are consistent with staff competencies and current psychological knowledge and practice. This statement should be distributed to staff and, where appropriate, to users and sanctioners upon request.

2.2.2   All providers within a psychological service unit shall support the legal and civil rights of the user. [14]

Interpretation: Providers of psychological services shall safeguard the interests of the user with regard to personal, legal, and civil rights. They shall continually be sensitive to the issue of confidentiality of information, the short-term and long-term impact of their decisions and recommendations, and other matters pertaining to individual, legal, and civil rights. Concerns regarding the safeguarding of individual rights of users include, but are not limited to, problems of self-incrimination in judicial proceedings, involuntary commitment to hospitals, protection of minors or legal incompetents, discriminatory practices in employment selection procedures, recommendations for special education provisions, information relative to adverse personnel actions in the armed services, and the adjudication of domestic relations disputes in divorce and custodial proceedings. Providers of psychological services should take affirmative action by making themselves available for local committees, review boards, and similar advisory groups established to safeguard the human, civil, and legal rights of service users.

2.2.3 All providers within a psychological service unit shall be familiar with and adhere to the American Psychological Association's <u>Ethical Standards of Psychologists</u>, <u>Psychology as a Profession</u>, <u>Standards for Educational and Psychological Tests</u>, and other official policy statements relevant to standards for professional services issued by the Association.

Interpretation: Providers of psychological services, users, and sanctioners may order copies of these documents from the American Psychological Association.

2.2.4 All providers within a psychological service unit shall conform to relevant statutes established by federal, state, and local governments.

Interpretation: All providers of psychological services shall be familiar with appropriate statutes regulating the practice of psychology. They shall also be informed about agency regulations that have the force of law and that relate to the delivery of psychological services (e.g., evaluation for disability, retirement, and special education placements). In addition, all providers shall be cognizant that federal agencies such as the Veterans Administration and the Department of Health, Education, and Welfare have policy statements regarding psychological services. Providers of psychological services shall be familiar with other statutes and regulations, including those addressed to the civil and legal rights of users (e.g., those promulgated by the federal Equal Employment Opportunity Commission) that are pertinent to their scope of practice.

It shall be the responsibility of the American Psychological Association to publish periodically those federal policies, statutes, and regulations relating to this section. The state psychological associations are similarly urged to publish and distribute periodically appropriate state statutes and regulations.

2.2.5 All providers within a psychological service unit shall, where appropriate, inform themselves about and use the network of human services in their communities in order to link users with relevant services and resources.

Interpretation: It is incumbent upon psychologists and supporting staff to be sensitive to the broader context of human needs. In recognizing the matrix of personal and societal problems, providers shall, where appropriate, make available information regarding human services such as legal aid societies, social services, employment agencies, health resources, and educational and recreational facilities. The provider of psychological services shall refer to such community resources and, when indicated, actively intervene on behalf of the user.

    2.2.6  In the delivery of psychological services, the providers shall maintain a continuing cooperative relationship with colleagues and co-workers whenever in the best interest of the user.[15]

Interpretation: It shall be the responsibility of the psychologist to recognize the areas of special competence of other psychologists and of other professionals for either consultation or referral purposes. Providers of psychological services shall make appropriate use of other professional, technical, and administrative resources whenever these serve the best interests of the user, and shall establish and maintain cooperative arrangements with such other resources as required to meet the needs of users.

2.3   Procedures

    2.3.1  Where appropriate, each psychological service unit shall be guided by a set of procedural guidelines for the delivery of psychological services. If appropriate to the setting, these guidelines shall be in written form.

Interpretation: Depending on the nature of the setting, and whenever feasible, providers should be prepared to provide a statement of procedural guidelines in either oral or written form that can be understood by users as well as sanctioners. This statement may describe the current methods, forms, procedures, and techniques being used to achieve the objectives and goals for psychological services.

This statement shall be communicated to staff and, when appropriate, to users and sanctioners. The psychological service unit shall provide for the annual review of its procedures for the delivery of psychological services.

    2.3.2  Providers shall develop a plan appropriate to the provider's professional strategy of practice and to the problems presented by the user.

Interpretation: Whenever appropriate or mandated in the setting, this plan shall be in written form as a means of providing a basis for establishing accountability, obtaining informed consent, and providing a mechanism for subsequent peer review. Regardless of the type of setting or users involved, it is desirable that a plan be developed that describes the psychological services indicated and the manner in which they will be provided.[16]

A psychologist who provides services as one member of a collaborative effort shall participate in the development and implementation of the overall service plan and provide for its periodic review.

2.3.3 There shall be a mutually acceptable understanding between the provider and user or responsible agent regarding the delivery of service.

Interpretation: Varying service settings call for understandings differing in explicitness and formality. For instance, a psychologist providing services within a user organization may operate within a broad framework of understanding with this organization as a condition of employment. As another example, psychologists providing professional services to individuals in clinical, counseling, or school settings require an open-ended agreement, which specifies procedures and their known risks (if any), costs, and respective responsibilities of provider and user for achieving the agreed-upon objectives.

2.3.4 Accurate, current, and pertinent documentation shall be made of essential psychological services provided.

Interpretation: Records kept of psychological services may include, but not be limited to, identifying data, dates of services, types of services, and significant actions taken. Providers of psychological services shall insure that essential information concerning services rendered is appropriately recorded within a reasonable time of their completion.

2.3.5 Providers of psychological services shall establish a system to protect confidentiality of their records.[17]

Interpretation: Psychologists are responsible for maintaining the confidentiality of information about users of services, whether obtained by themselves or by those they supervise. All persons supervised by psychologists, including nonprofessional personnel and students, who have access to records of psychological services shall be required to maintain this confidentiality as a condition of employment.

The psychologist shall not release confidential information, except with the written consent of the user directly involved or his or her legal representative. Even after the consent has been obtained for release, the psychologist should clearly identify such information as confidential to the recipient of the information.[18] If directed otherwise by statute or regulations with the force of law or by court order, the psychologist shall seek a resolution to the conflict that is both ethically and legally feasible and appropriate.

Users shall be informed in advance of any limits in the setting for maintenance of confidentiality of psychological information. For instance, psychologists in hospital settings shall inform their patients that psychological information in a patient's clinical record may be available without the patient's written consent to other members of the professional staff associated with the patient's treatment or rehabilitation. Similar limitations on confidentiality of psychological information may be present in certain school, industrial, or military settings, or in instances where the user has waived confidentiality for purposes of third-party payment.

When the user intends to waive confidentiality, the psychologist should discuss the implications of releasing psychological information, and assist the user in limiting disclosure only to information required by the present circumstance.

Raw psychological data (e.g., test protocols, therapy or interview notes, or questionnaire returns) in which a user is identified shall be released only with the written consent of the user or legal representative and released only to a person recognized by the psychologist as competent to use the data.

Any use made of psychological reports, records, or data for research or training purposes shall be consistent with this Standard. Additionally, providers of psychological services shall comply with statutory confidentiality requirements and those embodied in the American Psychological Association's Ethical Standards of Psychologists (APA 1977).

Providers of psychological services should remain sensitive to both the benefits and the possible misuse of information regarding individuals that is stored in large computerized data banks. Providers should use their influence to ensure that such information is used in a socially responsible manner.


STANDARD 3. ACCOUNTABILITY

3.1 Psychologists' professional activity shall be primarily guided by the principle of promoting human welfare.

Interpretation: Psychologists shall provide services to users in a manner that is considerate, effective, and economical.

Psychologists are responsible for making their services readily accessible to users in a manner that facilitates the user's freedom of choice.

Psychologists shall be mindful of their accountability to the sanctioners of psychological services and to the general public, provided that appropriate steps are taken to protect the confidentiality of the service relationship. In the pursuit of their professional activities they shall aid in the conservation of human, material, and financial resources.

The psychological service unit will not withhold services to a potential client on the basis of that user's race, color, religion, sex, age, or national origin. Recognition is given, however, to the following considerations: The professional right of psychologists to limit their practice to a specific category of user (e.g., children, adolescents, women); the right and responsibility of psychologists to withhold an assessment procedure when not validly applicable; the right and responsibility of psychologists to withhold evaluative, psychotherapeutic, counseling, or other services in specific instances where considerations of race, religion, color, sex, or any other difference between psychologist and client might impair the effectiveness of the relationship.[19]

Psychologists who find that psychological services are being provided in a manner that is discriminatory or exploitative to users and/or contrary to these Standards or to state or federal statutes shall take appropriate corrective action, which may include the refusal to provide services. When conflicts of interest arise, the psychologist shall be guided in the resolution of differences by the principles set forth in the Ethical Standards of Psychologists of the American Psychological Association and by the "Guidelines for Conditions of Employment of Psychologists" (1972).[20]

3.2  Psychologists shall pursue their activities as members of an independent, autonomous profession.[21]

Interpretation: Psychologists shall be aware of the implications of their activities for the profession as a whole. They shall seek to eliminate discriminatory practices instituted for self-serving purposes that are not in the interest of the user (e.g., arbitrary requirements for referral and supervision by another profession). They shall be cognizant of their responsibilities for the development of the profession, participate where possible in the training and career development of students and other providers, participate as appropriate in the training of paraprofessionals, and integrate and supervise their contributions within the structure established for delivering psychological services. Where appropriate, they shall facilitate the development of, and participate in, professional standards review mechanisms.[22]

Psychologists shall seek to work with other professionals in a cooperative manner for the good of the user and the benefit of the general public. Psychologists associated with multidisciplinary settings shall support the principle that members of each participating profession shall have equal rights and opportunities to share all privileges and responsibilities of full membership in the human service facility, and to administer service programs in their respective areas of competence.

3.3 There shall be periodic, systematic, and effective evaluations of psychological services.[23]

Interpretation: When the psychological service unit is a component of a larger organization, regular assessment of progress in achieving goals shall be provided in the service delivery plan, including consideration of the effectiveness of psychological services relative to costs in terms of time, money, and the availability of professional and support personnel.

Evaluation of the efficiency and effectiveness of the psychological service delivery system should be conducted internally and, when possible, under independent auspices.

It is highly desirable that there be a periodic reexamination of review mechanisms to ensure that these attempts at public safeguards are effective and cost efficient and do not place unnecessary encumbrances on the provider or unnecessary additional expense to users or sanctioners for services rendered.

3.4 Psychologists are accountable for all aspects of the services they provide and shall be responsive to those concerned with these services.[24]

Interpretation: In recognizing their responsibilities to users, sanctioners, third-party purchasers, and other providers, wherever appropriate and consistent with the user's legal rights and privileged communications, psychologists shall make available information about, and opportunity to participate in, decisions concerning such issues as initiation, termination, continuation, modification, and evaluation of psychological services. Additional copies of these "Standards for Providers of Psychological Services" can be ordered from the American Psychological Association.

Depending upon the settings, accurate and full information shall be made available to prospective individual or organization users regarding the qualifications of providers, the nature and extent of services offered, and, where appropriate, financial and social costs.

Where appropriate, psychologists shall inform users of their payment policies and their willingness to assist in obtaining reimbursement. Those who accept reimbursement from a third party should be acquainted with the appropriate statutes and regulations and should instruct their users on proper procedures for submitting claims and limits on confidentiality of claims information, in accordance with pertinent statutes.

STANDARD 4. ENVIRONMENT

4.1 Providers of psychological services shall promote the development in the service setting of a physical, organizational, and social environment that facilitates optimal human functioning.

Interpretation: Federal, state, and local requirements for safety, health, and sanitation must be observed. Attention shall be given to the comfort and, where relevant, to the privacy of providers and users.

As providers of services, psychologists have the responsibility to be concerned with the environment of their service unit, especially as it affects the quality of service, but also as it impinges on human functioning in the larger unit or organization when the service unit is included in such a larger context. Physical arrangements and organizational policies and procedures should be conducive to the human dignity, self-respect, and optimal functioning of users, and to the effective delivery of service. The atmosphere in which psychological services are rendered should be appropriate to the service and to the users, whether in office, clinic, school, or industrial organization.

NOTES

1. Members of the Task Force on Standards for Service Facilities that submitted the original Standards in September 1974 were Milton L. Blum, Jacqueline C. Bouhoutsos, Jerry H. Clark, Harold A. Edgerton, Marian D. Hall, Durand F. Jacobs (Chair, 1972-1974), Floyd H. Martinez, John E. Muthard, Asher R. Pacht, William D. Pierce, Sue A. Warren, and Alfred M. Wellner (Chair, 1970-1971). Staff liaisons from the APA Office of Professional Affairs were John J. McMillan (1970-1971), Gottlieb C. Simon (1971-1973), and Arthur Centor (1973-1974).

2. The notes appended to these Standards represent an attempt to provide a coherent context of other policy statements of the Association regarding professional practice. The Standards extend these previous policy statements where necessary to reflect current concerns of the public and the profession.

3. NIMH Grant MH 21696.

4. For the purpose of transition, persons who met the following criteria on or before the date of adoption of the original Standards on September 4, 1974, shall also be considered professional psychologists: (a) a master's degree from a program primarily psychological in content from a regionally accredited university or professional school; (b) appropriate education, training, and experience in the area of service offered; (c) a license or certificate in the state in which they practice, conferred by a state board of psychological examiners, or the endorsement of the state psychological association through voluntary certification, or, for practice in primary and secondary schools, a state department of education certificate as a school psychologist provided that the certificate required at least two graduate years.

5. Minutes of the Board of Professional Affairs meeting, Washington, D.C., March 8-9, 1974.

6. This definition is less restrictive than Recommendation 4 of the APA (1967) policy statement setting forth model state legislation affecting the practice of psychology (hereinafter referred to as State Guidelines), proposing one level for state license or certificate and "requiring the doctoral degree from an accredited university or college in a program that is primarily psychological, and no less than 2 years of supervised experience, one of which is subsequent to the granting of the doctoral degree. This level should be designated by the title of 'psychologist' " (p. 1099).

The 1972 APA "Guidelines for Conditions of Employment of Psychologists" (hereinafter referred to as CEP Guidelines) introduces slightly different shadings of meaning in its section on "Standards for Entry into the Profession" as follows:

> Persons are properly identified as psychologists when they have completed the training and experience recognized as necessary to perform functions consistent with one of the several levels in a career in psychology. This training includes possession of a degree earned in a program primarily psychological in content. In the case of psychological practice, in involves services for a fee, appropriate registration, certification, or licensing as provided by laws of the state in which the practices will apply. (APA 1972, p. 331)

In some situations, specialty designations and standards may be relevant. The National Register of Health Service Providers in Psychology, which based its criteria on this standard, identifies qualified psychologists in the health services field.

7. As noted in the opening section of these Standards, functions and activities of psychologists relating to the teaching of

psychology, the writing or editing of scholarly or scientific manuscripts, and the conduct of scientific research do not fall within the purview of these Standards.

8. These definitions should be compared to the State Guidelines, which include definitions of "psychologist" and the "practice of psychology" as follows:

A person represents himself to be a psychologist when he holds himself out to the public by any title or description of services incorporating the words "psychology," "psychological," "psychologist," and/or offers to render services as defined below to individuals, groups, organizations, or the public for a fee, monetary or otherwise.

The practice of psychology within the meaning of this act is defined as rendering to individuals, groups or organizations, or the public any psychological service involving the application of principles, methods, and procedures of understanding, predicting, and influencing behavior, such as the principles pertaining to learning, perception, motivation, thinking, emotions, and interpersonal relationships; the methods and procedures of interviewing, counseling, and psychotherapy, of constructing, administering, and interpreting tests of mental abilities, aptitudes, interests, attitudes, personality characteristics, emotion, and motivation; and of assessing public opinion.

The application of said principles and methods includes but is not restricted to: diagnosis, prevention, and amelioration of adjustment problems and emotional and mental disorders of individuals and groups; hypnosis; educational and vocational counseling; personnel selection and management; the evaluation and planning for effective work and learning situations; advertising and market research; and the resolution of interpersonal and social conflicts.

Psychotherapy within the meaning of this act means the use of learning, conditioning methods, and emotional reactions, in a professional relationship, to assist a person or persons to modify feelings, attitudes, and behavior which are intellectually, socially, or emotionally maladjustive or ineffectual.

The practice of psychology shall be as defined above, any existing statute in the state of _____ to the contrary notwithstanding. (APA 1967, pp. 1098-1099)

9. The relation of a psychological service unit to a larger facility or institution is also addressed indirectly in the CEP Guidelines, which emphasize the roles, responsibilities, and prerogatives of the psychologist when he or she is employed by or provides services for another agency, institution, or business.

10. This Standard replaces earlier recommendations in the 1967 State Guidelines concerning exemption of psychologists from licensure. Recommendations 8 and 9 of those Guidelines read as follows:

> 8. Persons employed as psychologists by accredited academic institutions, governmental agencies, research laboratories, and business corporations should be exempted, provided such employees are performing those duties for which they are employed by such organizations, and within the confines of such organizations.
>
> 9. Persons employed as psychologists by accredited academic institutions, governmental agencies, research laboratories, and business corporations consulting or offering their research findings or providing scientific information to like organizations for a fee should be exempted. (APA 1967, p. 1100)

On the other hand, the 1967 State Guidelines specifically denied exemptions under certain conditions, as noted in Recommendations 10 and 11:

> 10. Persons employed as psychologists who offer or provide psychological services to the public for a fee, over and above the salary that they receive for the performance of their regular duties, should not be exempted.
>
> 11. Persons employed as psychologists by organizations that sell psychological services to the public should not be exempted. (APA 1967, pp. 1100-1101)

The present APA policy, as reflected in this Standard, establishes a single code of practice for psychologists providing covered services to users in any setting. The present minimum requirement is that a psychologist providing any covered service must meet local statutory requirements for licensure or certification. See the section Principles and Implications of the Standards for an elaboration of this position.

11. A closely related principle is found in the APA (1972) CEP Guidelines:

> It is the policy of APA that psychology as an independent profession is entitled to parity with other health

and human service professions in institutional practices and before the law.  Psychologists in interdisciplinary settings such as colleges and universities, medical schools, clinics, private practice groups,
and other agencies expect parity with other professions
in such matters as academic rank, board status, salaries, fringe benefits, fees, participation in administrative decisions, and all other conditions of employment, private contractual arrangements, and status
before the law and legal institutions.  (APA 1972,
p. 333)

12.  See CEP Guidelines (section entitled "Career Development") for a closely related statement:

Psychologists are expected to encourage institutions
and agencies which employ them to sponsor or conduct
career development programs.  The purpose of these
programs would be to enable psychologists to engage
in study for professional advancement and to keep
abreast of developments in their field.  (APA 1972,
p. 332)

13.  This Standard follows closely the statement regarding
"Policy on Training for Psychologists Wishing to Change Their
Specialty" adopted by the APA Council of Representatives in January 1976.  Included therein was the implementing provision that
"this policy statement shall be incorporated in the guidelines of the
Committee on Accreditation so that appropriate sanctions can be
brought to bear on university and internship training programs
which violate [it]. "

14.  See also APA's (1977) Ethical Standards of Psychologists,
especially Principles 5 (Confidentiality), 6 (Welfare of the Consumer),
and 9 (Pursuit of Research Activities); and see Ethical Principles in
the Conduct of Research with Human Participants (APA 1973a).

15.  Support for this position is found in the section in Psychology as a Profession on relations with other professions:

Professional persons have an obligation to know and
take into account the traditions and practices of other
professional groups with whom they work and to cooperate fully with members of such groups with whom
research, service, and other functions are shared.
(APA 1968, p. 5)

16.  One example of a specific application of this principle is
found in Guideline 2 in APA's (1973b) "Guidelines for Psychologists
Conducting Growth Groups":

The following information should be made available <u>in writing</u> [emphasis added] to all prospective participants:

(a) An explicit statement of the purpose of the group;

(b) Types of techniques that may be employed;

(c) The education, training, and experience of the leader or leaders;

(d) The fee and any additional expense that may be incurred;

(e) A statement as to whether or not a follow-up service is included in the fee;

(f) Goals of the group experience and techniques to be used;

(g) Amounts and kinds of responsibility to be assumed by the leader and by the participants. For example, (i) the degree to which a participant is free not to follow suggestions and prescriptions of the group leader and other group members; (ii) any restrictions on a participant's freedom to leave the group at any time; and,

(h) Issues of confidentiality. (p. 933)

17. See again Principle 5 (Confidentiality) in <u>Ethical Standards of Psychologists</u> (APA 1977).

18. Support for the principle of privileged communication is found in at least two policy statements of the Association:

In the interest of both the public and the client and in accordance with the requirements of good professional practice, the profession of psychology seeks recognition of the privileged nature of confidential communications with clients, preferably through statutory enactment or by administrative policy where more appropriate. (APA 1968, p. 8)

25. Wherever possible, a clause protecting the privileged nature of the psychologist-client relationship be included.

26. When appropriate, psychologists assist in obtaining general "across the board" legislation for such privileged communications. (APA 1967, p. 1103)

19. This paragraph is drawn directly from the CEP Guidelines (APA 1972, p. 333).

20. "It is recognized that under certain circumstances, the interests and goals of a particular community or segment of interest in the population may be in conflict with the general welfare. Under

such circumstances, the psychologist's professional activity must be primarily guided by the principle of promoting human welfare" (APA 1972, p. 334).

21. Support for the principle of the independence of psychology as a profession is found in the following:

> As a member of an autonomous profession, a psychologist rejects limitations upon his freedom of thought and action other than those imposed by his moral, legal, and social responsibilities. The Association is always prepared to provide appropriate assistance to any responsible member who becomes subjected to unreasonable limitations upon his opportunity to function as a practitioner, teacher, researcher, administrator, or consultant. The Association is always prepared to cooperate with any responsible professional organization in opposing any unreasonable limitations on the professional functions of the members of that organization.
>
> This insistence upon professional autonomy has been upheld over the years by the affirmative actions of the courts and other public and private bodies in support of the right of the psychologist—and other professionals—to pursue those functions for which he is trained and qualified to perform. (APA 1968, p. 9)

> Organized psychology has the responsibility to define and develop its own profession, consistent with the general canons of science and with the public welfare.
>
> Psychologists recognize that other professions and other groups will, from time to time, seek to define the roles and responsibilities of psychologists. The APA opposes such developments on the same principles that it is opposed to the psychological profession taking positions which would define the work and scope of responsibility of other duly recognized professions.
> . . . (APA 1972, p. 333)

22. APA support for peer review is detailed in the following excerpt from the APA (1971) statement entitled "Psychology and National Health Care":

> All professions participating in a national health plan should be directed to establish review mechanisms (or performance evaluations) that include not only peer review but active participation by persons representing the consumer. In situations where there are fiscal agents, they should also have representation when appropriate. (p. 1026)

23.  This Standard on program evaluation is based directly on the following excerpts of two APA position papers:

> The quality and availability of health services should be evaluated continuously by both consumers and health professionals.  Research into the efficiency and effectiveness of the system should be conducted both internally and under independent auspices.  (APA 1971, p. 1025)

> The comprehensive community mental health center should devote an explicit portion of its budget to program evaluation.  All centers should inculcate in their staff attention to and respect for research findings; the larger centers have an obligation to set a high priority on basic research and to give formal recognition to research as a legitimate part of the duties of staff members.
>
> . . . Only through explicit appraisal of program effects can worthy approaches be rtained and refined, ineffective ones dropped.  Evaluative monitoring of program achievements may vary, of course, from the relatively informal to the systematic and quantitative, depending on the importance of the issue, the availability of resources, and the willingness of those responsible to take the risks of substituting informed judgment for evidence.  (Smith and Hobbs 1966, pp. 21-22)

24.  See also the CEP Guidelines for the following statement: "A psychologist recognizes that . . . he alone is accountable for the consequences and effects of his services, whether as teacher, researcher, or practitioner.  This responsibility cannot be shared, delegated, or reduced" (APA 1972, p. 334).

REFERENCES

Accreditation Council for Facilities for the Mentally Retarded. 1971.  Standards for residential facilities for the mentally retarded.  Chicago, Ill. : Joint Commission on Accreditation of Hospitals.

American Psychological Association. 1968.  Psychology as a profession.  Washington, D.C.: APA.

_____. 1971. Psychology and national health care. American Psychologist, 26: 1025–1026.

_____. 1972. Guidelines for conditions of employment of psychologists. American Psychologist, 27: 331–334.

_____. 1973a. Ethical principles in the conduct of research with human participants. Washington, D.C.: APA.

_____. 1973b. Guidelines for psychologists conducting growth groups. American Psychologist, 28: 933.

_____. 1974. Standards for educational and psychological tests. Washington, D.C.: APA.

_____. 1977. Ethical standards of psychologists. Rev. ed. Washington, D.C.: APA.

American Psychological Association, Committee on Legislation. 1967. A model for state legislation affecting the practice of psychology 1967. American Psychologist, 22: 1095–1103.

Joint Commission on Accreditation of Hospitals. 1972. Accreditation manual for psychiatric facilities 1972. Chicago, Ill.: JCAH.

Smith, M. B., and N. Hobbs. 1966. The community and the community mental health center. Washington, D.C.: APA.

# APPENDIX B
# ETHICAL PRINCIPLES
# OF PSYCHOLOGISTS

PREAMBLE

Psychologists respect the dignity and worth of the individual and strive for the preservation and protection of fundamental human rights. They are committed to increasing knowledge of human behavior and of people's understanding of themselves and others and to the utilization of such knowledge for the promotion of human welfare. While pursuing these objectives, they make every effort to protect the welfare of those who seek their services and of the

---

This version of the Ethical Principles of Psychologists (formerly entitled Ethical Standards of Psychologists) was adopted by the American Psychological Association's Council of Representatives on January 24, 1981. The revised Ethical Principles contain both substantive and grammatical changes in each of the nine ethical principles constituting the Ethical Standards of Psychologists previously adopted by the Council of Representatives in 1979, plus a new tenth principle entitled Care and Use of Animals. Inquiries concerning the Ethical Principles of Psychologists should be addressed to the Administrative Officer for Ethics, American Psychological Association, 1200 Seventeenth Street, N.W., Washington, D.C. 20036.

These revised Ethical Principles apply to psychologists, to students of psychology, and to others who do work of a psychological nature under the supervision of a psychologist. They are also intended for the guidance of nonmembers of the Association who are engaged in psychological research or practice.

Any complaints of unethical conduct filed after January 24, 1981, shall be governed by this 1981 revision. However, conduct (a) complained about after January 24, 1981, but which occurred prior to that date, and (b) not considered unethical under prior versions of the principles but considered unethical under the 1981 revision, shall not be deemed a violation of ethical principles. Any complaints pending as of January 24, 1981, shall be governed either by the 1979 or by the 1981 version of the Ethical Principles, at the sound discretion of the Committee on Scientific and Professional Ethics and Conduct.

research participants that may be the object of study. They use their skills only for purposes consistent with these values and do not knowingly permit their misuse by others. While demanding for themselves freedom of inquiry and communication, psychologists accept the responsibility this freedom requires: competence, objectivity in the application of skills, and concern for the best interests of clients, colleagues, students, research participants, and society. In the pursuit of these ideals, psychologists subscribe to principles in the following areas: 1. Responsibility, 2. Competence, 3. Moral and Legal Standards, 4. Public Statements, 5. Confidentiality, 6. Welfare of the Consumer, 7. Professional Relationships, 8. Assessment Techniques, 9. Research With Human Participants, and 10. Care and Use of Animals.

Acceptance of membership in the American Psychological Association commits the member to adherence to these principles.

Psychologists cooperate with duly constituted committees of the American Psychological Association, in particular, the Committee on Scientific and Professional Ethics and Conduct, by responding to inquiries promptly and completely. Members also respond promptly and completely to inquiries from duly constituted state association ethics committees and professional standards review committees.

Principle 1
RESPONSIBILITY

In providing services, psychologists maintain the highest standards of their profession. They accept responsibility for the consequences of their acts and make every effort to ensure that their services are used appropriately.

a. As scientists, psychologists accept responsibility for the selection of their research topics and the methods used in investigation, analysis, and reporting. They plan their research in ways to minimize the possibility that their findings will be misleading. They provide thorough discussion of the limitations of their data, especially where their work touches on social policy or might be construed to the detriment of persons in specific age, sex, ethnic, socioeconomic, or other social groups. In publishing reports of their work, they never suppress disconfirming data, and they acknowledge the existence of alternative hypotheses and explanations of their findings. Psychologists take credit only for work they have actually done.

b. Psychologists clarify in advance with all appropriate persons and agencies the expectations for sharing and utilizing research data. They avoid relationships that may limit their objectivity or create a conflict of interest. Interference with the milieu in which data are collected is kept to a minimum.

    c. Psychologists have the responsibility to attempt to prevent distortion, misuse, or suppression of psychological findings by the institution or agency of which they are employees.

    d. As members of governmental or other organizational bodies, psychologists remain accountable as individuals to the highest standards of their profession.

    e. As teachers, psychologists recognize their primary obligation to help others acquire knowledge and skill. They maintain high standards of scholarship by presenting psychological information objectively, fully, and accurately.

    f. As practitioners, psychologists know that they bear a heavy social responsibility because their recommendations and professional actions may alter the lives of others. They are alert to personal, social, organizational, financial, or political situations and pressures that might lead to misuse of their influence.


Principle 2
COMPETENCE

The maintenance of high standards of competence is a responsibility shared by all psychologists in the interest of the public and the profession as a whole. Psychologists recognize the boundaries of their competence and the limitations of their techniques. They only provide services and only use techniques for which they are qualified by training and experience. In those areas in which recognized standards do not yet exist, psychologists take whatever precautions are necessary to protect the welfare of their clients. They maintain knowledge of current scientific and professional information related to the services they render.

    a. Psychologists accurately represent their competence, education, training, and experience. They claim as evidence of educational qualifications only those degrees obtained from institutions acceptable under the Bylaws and Rules of Council of the American Psychological Association.

    b. As teachers, psychologists perform their duties on the basis of careful preparation so that their instruction is accurate, current, and scholarly.

    c. Psychologists recognize the need for continuing education and are open to new procedures and changes in expectations and values over time.

d. Psychologists recognize differences among people, such
as those that may be associated with age, sex, socioeconomic, and
ethnic backgrounds. When necessary, they obtain training, experience, or counsel to assure competent service or research relating
to such persons.

e. Psychologists responsible for decisions involving individuals or policies based on test results have an understanding of
psychological or educational measurement, validation problems,
and test research.

f. Psychologists recognize that personal problems and conflicts may interfere with professional effectiveness. Accordingly,
they refrain from undertaking any activity in which their personal
problems are likely to lead to inadequate performance or harm to
a client, colleague, student, or research participant. If engaged
in such activity when they become aware of their personal problems,
they seek competent professional assistance to determine whether
they should suspend, terminate, or limit the scope of their professional and/or scientific activities.


Principle 3
MORAL AND LEGAL STANDARDS

Psychologists' moral and ethical standards of behavior are a personal matter to the same degree as they are for any other citizen,
except as these may compromise the fulfillment of their professional responsibilities or reduce the public trust in psychology and
psychologists. Regarding their own behavior, psychologists are
sensitive to prevailing community standards and to the possible impact that conformity to or deviation from these standards may have
upon the quality of their performance as psychologists. Psychologists are also aware of the possible impact of their public behavior
upon the ability of colleagues to perform their professional duties.

a. As teachers, psychologists are aware of the fact that their
personal values may affect the selection and presentation of instructional materials. When dealing with topics that may give offense,
they recognize and respect the diverse attitudes that students may
have toward such materials.

b. As employees or employers, psychologists do not engage
in or condone practices that are inhumane or that result in illegal
or unjustifiable actions. Such practices include, but are not limited to, those based on considerations of race, handicap, age, gender, sexual preference, religion, or national origin in hiring, promotion, or training.

c. In their professional roles, psychologists avoid any action that will violate or diminish the legal and civil rights of clients or of others who may be affected by their actions.

d. As practioners and researchers, psychologists act in accord with Association standards and guidelines related to practice and to the conduct of research with human beings and animals. In the ordinary course of events, psychologists adhere to relevant governmental laws and institutional regulations. When federal, state, provincial, organizational, or institutional laws, regulations, or practices are in conflict with Association standards and guidelines, psychologists make known their commitment to Association standards and guidelines and, wherever possible, work toward a resolution of the conflict. Both practitioners and researchers are concerned with the development of such legal and quasi-legal regulations as best serve the public interest, and they work toward changing existing regulations that are not beneficial to the public interest.

Principle 4
PUBLIC STATEMENTS

Public statements, announcements of services, advertising, and promotional activities of psychologists serve the purpose of helping the public make informed judgments and choices. Psychologists represent accurately and objectively their professional qualifications, affiliations, and functions, as well as those of the institutions or organizations with which they or the statements may be associated. In public statements providing psychological information or professional opinions or providing information about the availability of psychological products, publications, and services, psychologists base their statements on scientifically acceptable psychological findings and techniques with full recognition of the limits and uncertainties of such evidence.

a. When announcing or advertising professional services, psychologists may list the following information to describe the provider and services provided: name, highest relevant academic degree earned from a regionally accredited institution, date, type, and level of certification or licensure, diplomate status, APA membership status, address, telephone number, office hours, a brief listing of the type of psychological services offered, an appropriate presentation of fee information, foreign languages spoken, and policy with regard to third-party payments. Additional relevant or important consumer information may be included if not prohibited by other sections of these Ethical Principles.

b. In announcing or advertising the availability of psychological products, publications, or services, psychologists do not present their affiliation with any organization in a manner that falsely implied sponsorship or certification by that organization. In particular and for example, psychologists do not state APA membership or fellow status in a way to suggest that such status implies specialized professional competence or qualifications. Public statements include, but are not limited to, communication by means of periodical, book, list, directory, television, radio, or motion picture. They do not contain (i) a false, fraudulent, misleading, deceptive, or unfair statement; (ii) a misinterpretation of fact or a statement likely to mislead or deceive because in context it makes only a partial disclosure of relevant facts; (iii) a testimonial from a patient regarding the quality of a psychologist's services or products; (iv) a statement intended or likely to create false or unjustified expectations of favorable results; (v) a statement implying unusual, unique, or one-of-a-kind abilities; (vi) a statement intended or likely to appeal to a client's fears, anxieties, or emotions concerning the possible results of failure to obtain the offered services; (vii) a statement concerning the comparative desirability of offered services; (viii) a statement of direct solicitation of individual clients.

c. Psychologists do not compensate or give anything of value to a representative of the press, radio, television, or other communication medium in anticipation of or in return for professional publicity in a news item. A paid advertisement must be identified as such, unless it is apparent from the context that it is a paid advertisement. If communicated to the public by use of radio or television, an advertisement is prerecorded and approved for broadcast by the psychologist, and a recording of the actual transmission is retained by the psychologist.

d. Announcements or advertisements of "personal growth groups," clinics, and agencies give a clear statement of purpose and a clear description of the experiences to be provided. The education, training, and experience of the staff members are appropriately specified.

e. Psychologists associated with the development or promotion of psychological devices, books, or other products offered for commercial sale make reasonable efforts to ensure that announcements and advertisements are presented in a professional, scientifically acceptable, and factually informative manner.

f. Psychologists do not participate for personal gain in commercial announcements or advertisements recommending to the public the purchase or use of proprietary or single-source products or services when that participation is based solely upon their identification as psychologists.

g.  Psychologists present the science of psychology and offer their services, products, and publications fairly and accurately, avoiding misrepresentation through sensationalism, exaggeration, or superficiality.  Psychologists are guided by the primary obligation to aid the public in developing informed judgments, opinions, and choices.

h.  As teachers, psychologists ensure that statements in catalogs and course outlines are accurate and not misleading, particularly in terms of subject matter to be covered, bases for evaluating progress, and the nature of course experiences.  Announcements, brochures, or advertisements describing workshops, seminars, or other educational programs accurately describe the audience for which the program is intended as well as eligibility requirements, educational objectives, and nature of the materials to be covered.  These announcements also accurately represent the education, training, and experience of the psychologists presenting the programs and any fees involved.

i.  Public announcements or advertisements soliciting research participants in which clinical services or other professional services are offered as an inducement make clear the nature of the services as well as the costs and other obligations to be accepted by participants in the research.

j.  A psychologist accepts the obligation to correct others who represent the psychologist's professional qualifications, or associations with products or services, in a manner incompatible with these guidelines.

k.  Individual diagnostic and therapeutic services are provided only in the context of a professional psychological relationship.  When personal advice is given by means of public lectures or demonstrations, newspaper or magazine articles, radio or television programs, mail, or similar media, the psychologist utilizes the most current relevant data and exercises the highest level of professional judgment.

l.  Products that are described or presented by means of public lectures or demonstrations, newspaper or magazine articles, radio or television programs, or similar media meet the same recognized standards as exist for products used in the context of a professional relationship.

Principle 5
CONFIDENTIALITY

Psychologists have a primary obligation to respect the confidentiality of information obtained from persons in the course of their work as psychologists. They reveal such information to others only with the consent of the person or the person's legal representative, except in those unusual circumstances in which not to do so would result in clear danger to the person or to others. Where appropriate, psychologists inform their clients of the legal limits of confidentiality.

a. Information obtained in clinical or consulting relationships, or evaluative data concerning children, students, employees, and others, is discussed only for professional purposes and only with persons clearly concerned with the case. Written and oral reports present only data germane to the purposes of the evaluation, and every effort is made to avoid undue invasion of privacy.

b. Psychologists who present personal information obtained during the course of professional work in writings, lectures, or other public forums either obtain adequate prior consent to do so or adequately disguise all identifying information.

c. Psychologists make provisions for maintaining confidentiality in the storage and disposal of records.

d. When working with minors or other persons who are unable to give voluntary, informed consent, psychologists take special care to protect these persons' best interests.

Principle 6
WELFARE OF THE CONSUMER

Psychologists respect the integrity and protect the welfare of the people and groups with whom they work. When conflicts of interest arise between clients and psychologists' employing institutions, psychologists clarify the nature and direction of their loyalties and responsibilities and keep all parties informed of their commitments. Psychologists fully inform consumers as to the purpose and nature of an evaluative, treatment, educational, or training procedure, and they freely acknowledge that clients, students, or participants in research have freedom of choice with regard to participation.

a. Psychologists are continually cognizant of their own needs and of their potentially influential position vis-à-vis persons such as clients, students, and subordinates. They avoid exploiting the trust and dependency of such persons. Psychologists make every effort to avoid dual relationships that could impair their professional judgment or increase the risk of exploitation. Examples of such dual relationships include, but are not limited to, research with and treatment of employees, students, supervisees, close friends, or relatives. Sexual intimacies with clients are unethical.

b. When a psychologist agrees to provide services to a client at the request of a third party, the psychologist assumes the responsibility of clarifying the nature of the relationships to all parties concerned.

c. Where the demands of an organization require psychologists to violate these Ethical Principles, psychologists clarify the nature of the conflict between the demands and these principles. They inform all parties of psychologists' ethical responsibilities and take appropriate action.

d. Psychologists make advance financial arrangements that safeguard the best interests of and are clearly understood by their clients. They neither give nor receive any remuneration for referring clients for professional services. They contribute a portion of their services to work for which they receive little or no financial return.

e. Psychologists terminate a clinical or consulting relationship when it is reasonably clear that the consumer is not benefiting from it. They offer to help the consumer locate alternative sources of assistance.


Principle 7
PROFESSIONAL RELATIONSHIPS

Psychologists act with due regard for the needs, special competencies, and obligations of their colleagues in psychology and other professions. They respect the prerogatives and obligations of the institutions or organizations with which these other colleagues are associated.

a. Psychologists understand the areas of competence of related professions. They make full use of all the professional, technical, and administrative resources that serve the best interests of consumers. The absence of formal relationships with other professional workers does not relieve psychologists of the responsibility of securing for their clients the best possible professional service, nor does it relieve them of the obligation to exercise foresight, diligence, and tact in obtaining the complementary or alternative assistance needed by clients.

b. Psychologists know and take into account the traditions and practices of other professional groups with whom they work and cooperate fully with such groups. If a person is receiving similar services from another professional, psychologists do not offer their own services directly to such a person. If a psychologist is contacted by a person who is already receiving similar services from another professional, the psychologist carefully considers that professional relationship and proceeds with caution and sensitivity to the therapeutic issues as well as the client's welfare. The psychologist discusses these issues with the client so as to minimize the risk of confusion and conflict.

    c. Psychologists who employ or supervise other professionals or professionals in training accept the obligation to facilitate the further professional development of these individuals. They provide appropriate working conditions, timely evaluations, constructive consultation, and experience opportunities.

    d. Psychologists do not exploit their professional relationships with clients, supervisees, students, employees, or research participants sexually or otherwise. Psychologists do not condone or engage in sexual harassment. Sexual harassment is defined as deliberate or repeated comments, gestures, or physical contacts of a sexual nature that are unwanted by the recipient.

    e. In conducting research in institutions or organizations, psychologists secure appropriate authorization to conduct such research. They are aware of their obligations to future research workers and ensure that host institutions receive adequate information about the research and proper acknowledgment of their contributions.

    f. Publication credit is assigned to those who have contributed to a publication in proportion to their professional contributions. Major contributions of a professional character made by several persons to a common project are recognized by joint authorship, with the individual who made the principal contribution listed first. Minor contributions of a professional character and extensive clerical or similar nonprofessional assistance may be acknowledged in footnotes or in an introductory statement. Acknowledgment through specific citations is made for unpublished as well as published material that has directly influenced the research or writing. Psychologists who compile and edit material of others for publication publish the material in the name of the originating group, if appropriate, with their own name appearing as chairperson or editor. All contributors are to be acknowledged and named.

    g. When psychologists know of an ethical violation by another psychologist, and it seems appropriate, they informally attempt to resolve the issue by bringing the behavior to the attention of the psychologist. If the misconduct is of a minor nature and/or appears to be due to lack of sensitivity, knowledge, or experience, such an informal solution is usually appropriate. Such informal corrective efforts are made with sensitivity to any rights to confidentiality involved. If the violation does not seem amenable to an informal solution, or is of a more serious nature, psychologists bring it to the attention of the appropriate local, state, and/or national committee on professional ethics and conduct.

Principle 8
ASSESSMENT TECHNIQUES

In the development, publication, and utilization of psychological assessment techniques, psychologists make every effort to promote the welfare and best interests of the client. They guard against the misuse of assessment results. They respect the client's right to know the results, the interpretations made, and the bases for their conclusions and recommendations. Psychologists make every effort to maintain the security of tests and other assessment techniques within limits of legal mandates. They strive to ensure the appropriate use of assessment techniques by others.

    a. In using assessment techniques, psychologists respect the right of clients to have full explanations of the nature and purpose of the techniques in language the clients can understand, unless an explicit exception to this right has been agreed upon in advance. When the explanations are to be provided by others, psychologists establish procedures for ensuring the adequacy of these explanations.

    b. Psychologists responsible for the development and standardization of psychological tests and other assessment techniques utilize established scientific procedures and observe the relevant APA standards.

    c. In reporting assessment results, psychologists indicate any reservations that exist regarding validity or reliability because of the circumstances of the assessment or the inappropriateness of the norms for the person tested. Psychologists strive to ensure that the results of assessments and their interpretations are not misused by others.

    d. Psychologists recognize that assessment results may become obsolete. They make every effort to avoid and prevent the misuse of obsolete measures.

    e. Psychologists offering scoring and interpretation services are able to produce appropriate evidence for the validity of the programs and procedures used in arriving at interpretations. The public offering of an automated interpretation service is considered a professional-to-professional consultation. Psychologists make every effort to avoid misuse of assessment reports.

    f. Psychologists do not encourage or promote the use of psychological assessment techniques by inappropriately trained or otherwise unqualified persons through teaching, sponsorship, or supervision.

## Principle 9
## RESEARCH WITH HUMAN PARTICIPANTS

The decision to undertake research rests upon a considered judgment by the individual psychologist about how best to contribute to psychological science and human welfare. Having made the decision to conduct research, the psychologist considers alternative directions in which research energies and resources might be invested. On the basis of this consideration, the psychologist carries out the investigation with respect and concern for the dignity and welfare of the people who participate and with cognizance of federal and state regulations and professional standards governing the conduct of research with human participants.

a. In planning a study, the investigator has the responsibility to make a careful evaluation of its ethical acceptability. To the extent that the weighing of scientific and human values suggests a compromise of any principle, the investigator incurs a correspondingly serious obligation to seek ethical advice and to observe stringent safeguards to protect the rights of human participants.

b. Considering whether a participant in a planned study will be a "subject at risk" or a "subject at minimal risk," according to recognized standards, is of primary ethical concern to the investigator.

c. The investigator always retains the responsibility for ensuring ethical practice in research. The investigator is also responsible for the ethical treatment of research participants by collaborators, assistants, students, and employees, all of whom, however, incur similar obligations.

d. Except in minimal-risk research, the investigator establishes a clear and fair agreement with research participants, prior to their participation, that clarifies the obligations and responsibilities of each. The investigator has the obligation to honor all promises and commitments included in that agreement. The investigator informs the participants of all aspects of the research that might reasonably be expected to influence willingness to participate and explains all other aspects of the research about which the participants inquire. Failure to make full disclosure prior to obtaining informed consent requires additional safeguards to protect the welfare and dignity of the research participants. Research with children or with participants who have impairments that would limit understanding and/or communication requires special safeguarding procedures.

e. Methodological requirements of a study may make the use of concealment or deception necessary. Before conducting such a study, the investigator has a special responsibility to (i) determine whether the use of such techniques is justified by the study's prospective scientific, educational, or applied value; (ii) determine whether alternative procedures are available that do not use concealment or deception; and (iii) ensure that the participants are provided with sufficient explanation as soon as possible.

f. The investigator respects the individual's freedom to decline to participate in or to withdraw from the research at any time. The obligation to protect this freedom requires careful thought and consideration when the investigator is in a position of authority or influence over the participant. Such positions of authority include, but are not limited to, situations in which research participation is required as part of employment or in which the participant is a student, client, or employee of the investigator.

g. The investigator protects the participant from physical and mental discomfort, harm, and danger that may arise from research procedures. If risks of such consequences exist, the investigator informs the participant of that fact. Research procedures likely to cause serious or lasting harm to a participant are not used unless the failure to use these procedures might expose the participant to risk of greater harm, or unless the research has great potential benefit and fully informed and voluntary consent is obtained from each participant. The participant should be informed of procedures for contacting the investigator within a reasonable time period following participation should stress, potential harm, or related questions or concerns arise.

h. After the data are collected, the investigator provides the participant with information about the nature of the study and attempts to remove any misconceptions that may have arisen. Where scientific or humane values justify delaying or withholding this information, the investigator incurs a special responsibility to monitor the research and to ensure that there are no damaging consequences for the participant.

i. Where research procedures result in undesirable consequences for the individual participant, the investigator has the responsibility to detect and remove or correct these consequences, including long-term effects.

j. Information obtained about a research participant during the course of an investigation is confidential unless otherwise agreed upon in advance. When the possibility exists that others may obtain access to such information, this possibility, together with the plans for protecting confidentiality, is explained to the participant as part of the procedure for obtaining informed consent.

Principle 10
CARE AND USE OF ANIMALS

An investigator of animal behavior strives to advance understanding of basic behavioral principles and/or to contribute to the improvement of human health and welfare. In seeking these ends, the investigator ensures the welfare of animals and treats them humanely. Laws and regulations notwithstanding, an animal's immediate protection depends upon the scientist's own conscience.

a. The acquisition, care, use, and disposal of all animals are in compliance with current federal, state or provincial, and local laws and regulations.

b. A psychologist trained in research methods and experienced in the care of laboratory animals closely supervises all procedures involving animals and is responsible for ensuring appropriate consideration of their comfort, health, and humane treatment.

c. Psychologists ensure that all individuals using animals under their supervision have received explicit instruction in experimental methods and in the care, maintenance, and handling of the species being used. Responsibilities and activities of individuals participating in a research project are consistent with their respective competencies.

d. Psychologists make every effort to minimize discomfort, illness, and pain of animals. A procedure subjecting animals to pain, stress, or privation is used only when an alternative procedure is unavailable and the goal is justified by its prospective scientific, educational, or applied value. Surgical procedures are performed under appropriate anesthesia; techniques to avoid infection and minimize pain are followed during and after surgery.

e. When it is appropriate that the animal's life be terminated, it is done rapidly and painlessly.

# APPENDIX C
# SPECIALTY GUIDELINES FOR
# THE DELIVERY OF SERVICES

In September 1976, the APA Council of Representatives reviewed and commented on the draft revisions of the <u>Standards for Providers of Psychological Services</u> prepared by the Committee on Standards for Providers of Psychological Services. During that discussion, the Council acknowledged the need for standards in certain specialty areas in addition to the generic <u>Standards</u> covered by the draft revision. The Council authorized the committee to hold additional meetings to develop multiple standards in all specialty areas of psychology.

Following the adoption of the revised generic <u>Standards</u> in January 1977, the committee, working with psychologists in the four recognized specialty areas of psychology, spent the next three years revising the generic <u>Standards</u> to meet the needs of clinical, counseling, industrial/organizational, and school psychologists. The four documents produced by the committee went through extensive revisions. Convention programs discussing these developments were held every year. Comments were solicited from all major constituencies in psychology and from thousands of individuals. The comments received and reviewed by the committee also numbered in the thousands.

In January 1980, following this extensive process, the Council of Representatives adopted the four documents (Specialty Guidelines for the Delivery of Services by Clinical [Counseling, Industrial/ Organizational, School] Psychologists) as APA policy after making several modifications. As adopted by the Council of Representatives, the intent of these Specialty Guidelines is "to educate the public, the profession, and other interested parties regarding specialty professional practices . . . and to facilitate the continued systematic development of the profession."

At the same meeting, the Council also approved a reorganization of the Board of Professional Affairs' committee structure, which included the establishment of the Committee on Professional Standards* to succeed the Committee on Standards for Providers of

---

*The current members of the Committee on Professional Standards are Murphy Thomas (Chair), Juanita Braddock, Lorraine

Psychological Services. As directed by the Council at that meeting, the Committee on Professional Standards is requesting comments on these Specialty Guidelines. It is the responsibility of this committee to review all feedback received as it considers each set of Guidelines for revisions.

---

Eyde, Morris Goodman, Judy Hall, John H. Jackson, and Milton Schwebel. APA staff liaisons are Sharon A. Shueman and Pam Arnold.

The following persons also served on the committee during the time the Specialty Guidelines were being revised: Gilfred Tanabe (1980 Chair), Dave Mills (partial 1981 Chair), Nadine Lambert, and Joy Burke (APA staff liaison).

SPECIALTY GUIDELINES FOR THE DELIVERY
OF SERVICES BY CLINICAL PSYCHOLOGISTS

The Specialty Guidelines that follow are based on the generic
Standards for Providers of Psychological Services originally adopted
by the American Psychological Association (APA) in September 1974
and revised in January 1977 (APA 1974b; 1977b). Together with the
generic Standards, these Specialty Guidelines state the official policy of the Association regarding delivery of services by clinical
psychologists. Admission to the practice of psychology is regulated by state statute. It is the position of the Association that licensing be based on generic, and not on specialty, qualifications.
Specialty guidelines serve the additional purpose of providing potential users and other interested groups with essential information
about particular services available from the several specialties in
professional psychology.

Professional psychology specialties have evolved from generic practice in psychology and are supported by university training programs. There are now at least four recognized professional
specialties—clinical, counseling, school, and industrial/organiza-
tional psychology.

The knowledge base in each of these specialty areas has increased, refining the state of the art to the point that a set of uniform specialty guidelines is now possible and desirable. The present Guidelines are intended to educate the public, the profession,
and other interested parties regarding specialty professional practices. They are also intended to facilitate the continued systematic
development of the profession.

The content of each Specialty Guideline reflects a consensus
of university faculty and public and private practitioners regarding
the knowledge base, services provided, problems addressed, and
clients served.

Traditionally, all learned disciplines have treated the designation of specialty practice as a reflection of preparation in greater

---

These Specialty Guidelines were prepared through the cooperative efforts of the APA Committee on Standards for Providers
of Psychological Services (COSPOPS) and many professional clinical psychologists from the divisions of APA, including those involved in education and training programs and in public and private
practice. Jules Barron, succeeded by Morris Goodman, served
as the clinical psychology representative on COSPOPS. The committee was chaired by Durand F. Jacobs; the Central Office liaisons
were Arthur Centor and Richard Kilburg.

depth in a particular subject matter, together with a voluntary limiting of focus to a more restricted area of practice by the professional. Lack of specialty designation does not preclude general providers of psychological services from using the methods or dealing with the populations of any specialty, except insofar as psychologists voluntarily refrain from providing services they are not trained to render. It is the intent of these Guidelines, however, that after the grandparenting period, psychologists not put themselves forward as specialists in a given area of practice unless they meet the qualifications noted in the Guidelines (see Definitions). Therefore, these Guidelines are meant to apply only to those psychologists who voluntarily wish to be designated as clinical psychologists. They do not apply to other psychologists.

These Guidelines represent the profession's best judgment of the conditions, credentials, and experience that contribute to competent professional practice. The APA strongly encourages, and plans to participate in, efforts to identify professional practitioner behaviors and job functions and to validate the relation between these and desired client outcomes. Thus, future revisions of these Guidelines will increasingly reflect the results of such efforts.

These Guidelines follow the format and, wherever applicable, the wording of the generic Standards.[1] (Note: Notes appear at the end of the Specialty Guidelines.) The intent of these Guidelines is to improve the quality, effectiveness, and accessibility of psychological services. They are meant to provide guidance to providers, users, and sanctioners regarding the best judgment of the profession on these matters. Although the Specialty Guidelines have been derived from and are consistent with the generic Standards, they may be used as separate documents. However, Standards for Providers of Psychological Services (APA 1977b) shall remain the basic policy statement and shall take precedence where there are questions of interpretation.

Professional psychology in general and clinical psychology as a specialty have labored long and diligently to codify a uniform set of guidelines for the delivery of services by clinical psychologists that would serve the respective needs of users, providers, third-party purchasers, and sanctioners of psychological services.

The Committee on Professional Standards, established by the APA in January 1980, is charged with keeping the generic Standards and the Specialty Guidelines responsive to the needs of the public and the profession. It is also charged with continually reviewing, modifying, and extending them progressively as the profession and the science of psychology develop new knowledge, improved methods, and additional modes of psychological services.

The Specialty Guidelines for the Delivery of Services by Clinical Psychologists that follow have been established by the APA as a means of self-regulation to protect the public interest. They guide the specialty practice of clinical psychology by specifying important areas of quality assurance and performance that contribute to the goal of facilitating more effective human functioning.

Principles and Implications of
the Specialty Guidelines

These Specialty Guidelines have emerged from and reaffirm the same basic principles that guided the development of the generic Standards for Providers of Psychological Services (APA 1977b):

1. These Guidelines recognize that admission to the practice of psychology is regulated by state statute.

2. It is the intention of the APA that the generic Standards provide appropriate guidelines for statutory licensing of psychologists. In addition, although it is the position of the APA that licensing be generic and not in specialty areas, these Specialty Guidelines in clinical psychology provide an authoritative reference for use in credentialing specialty providers of clinical psychological services by such groups as divisions of the APA and state associations and by boards and agencies that find such criteria useful for quality assurance.

3. A uniform set of Specialty Guidelines governs the quality of services to all users of clinical psychological services in both the private and the public sectors. Those receiving clinical psychological services are protected by the same kinds of safeguards, irrespective of sector; these include constitutional guarantees, statutory regulation, peer review, consultation, record review, and supervision.

4. A uniform set of Specialty Guidelines governs clinical psychological service functions offered by clinical psychologists, regardless of setting or form of remuneration. All clinical psychologists in professional practice recognize and are responsive to a uniform set of Specialty Guidelines, just as they are guided by a common code of ethics.

5. Clinical psychology Guidelines establish clearly articulated levels of quality for covered clinical psychological service functions, regardless of the nature of the users, purchasers, or sanctioners of such covered services.

6. All persons providing clinical psychological services meet specified levels of training and experience that are consistent with,

and appropriate to, the functions they perform. Clinical psychological services provided by persons who do not meet the APA qualifications for a professional clinical psychologist (see Definitions) are supervised by a professional clinical psychologist. Final responsibility and accountability for services provided rest with professional clinical psychologists.

7. When providing any of the covered clinical psychological service functions at any time and in any setting, whether public or private, profit or nonprofit, clinical psychologists observe these Guidelines in order to promote the best interests and welfare of the users of such services. The extent to which clinical psychologists observe these Guidelines is judged by peers.

8. These Guidelines, while assuring the user of the clinical psychologist's accountability for the nature and quality of services specified in this document, do not preclude the clinical psychologist from using new methods or developing innovative procedures in the delivery of clinical services.

These Specialty Guidelines have broad implications both for users of clinical psychological services and for providers of such services:

1. Guidelines for clinical psychological services provide a foundation for mutual understanding between provider and user and facilitate more effective evaluation of services provided and outcomes achieved.

2. Guidelines for clinical psychologists are essential for uniformity in specialty credentialing of clinical psychologists.

3. Guidelines give specific content to the profession's concept of ethical practice as it applies to the functions of clinical psychologists.

4. Guidelines for clinical psychological services may have significant impact on tomorrow's education and training models for both professional and support personnel in clinical psychology.

5. Guidelines for the provision of clinical psychological services in human service facilities influence the determination of acceptable structure, budgeting, and staffing patterns in these facilities.

6. Guidelines for clinical psychological services require continual review and revision.

The Specialty Guidelines here presented are intended to improve the quality and delivery of clinical psychological services by specifying criteria for key aspects of the practice setting. Some settings may require additional and/or more stringent criteria for specific areas of service delivery.

Systematically applied, these Guidelines serve to establish a more effective and consistent basis for evaluating the performance of individual service providers as well as to guide the organization of clinical psychological service units in human service settings.

Definitions

"Providers of clinical psychological services" refers to two categories of persons who provide clinical psychological services:

A. Professional clinical psychologists.[2] Professional clinical psychologists have a doctoral degree from a regionally accredited university or professional school providing an organized, sequential clinical psychology program in a department of psychology in a university or college, or in an appropriate department or unit of a professional school. Clinical psychology programs that are accredited by the American Psychological Association are recognized as meeting the definition of a clinical psychology program. Clinical psychology programs that are not accredited by the American Psychological Association meet the definition of a clinical psychology program if they satisfy the following criteria:
1. The program is primarily psychological in nature and stands as a recognizable, coherent organizational entity within the institution.
2. The program provides an integrated, organized sequence of study.
3. The program has an identifiable body of students who are matriculated in that program for a degree.
4. There is a clear authority with primary responsibility for the core and specialty areas, whether or not the program cuts across administrative lines.
5. There is an identifiable psychology faculty, and a psychologist is responsible for the program.
In addition to a doctoral education, clinical psychologists acquire doctoral and postdoctoral training. Patterns of education and training in clinical psychology[3] are consistent with the functions to be performed and the services to be provided, in accordance with the ages, populations, and problems encountered in various settings.
B. All other persons who are not professional clinical psychologists and who participate in the delivery of clinical psychological services under the supervision of a professional clinical psychologist. Although there may be variations in the titles of such persons, they are not referred to as clinical psychologists. Their functions may be indicated by use of the adjective "psychological"

preceding the noun, for example, "psychological associate," "psychological assistant," "psychological technician," or "psychological aide." Their services are rendered under the supervision of a professional clinical psychologist, who is responsible for the designation given them and for quality control. To be assigned such a designation, a person has the background, training, or experience that is appropriate to the functions performed.

"Clinical psychological services" refers to the application of principles, methods, and procedures for understanding, predicting, and alleviating intellectual, emotional, psychological, and behavioral disability and discomfort. Direct services are provided in a variety of health settings, and direct and supportive services are provided in the entire range of social, organizational, and academic institutions and agencies.[4] Clinical psychological services include the following:[5]

A. Assessment directed toward diagnosing the nature and causes, and predicting the effects, of subjective distress; of personal, social, and work dysfunction; and of the psychological and emotional factors involved in, and consequent to, physical disease and disability. Procedures may include, but are not limited to, interviewing, and administering and interpreting tests of intellectual abilities, attitudes, emotions, motivations, personality characteristics, psychoneurological status, and other aspects of human experience and behavior relevant to the disturbance.

B. Interventions directed at identifying and correcting the emotional conflicts, personality disturbances, and skill deficits underlying a person's distress and/or dysfunction. Interventions may reflect a variety of theoretical orientations, techniques, and modalities. These may include, but are not limited to, psychotherapy, psychoanalysis, behavior therapy, marital and family therapy, group psychotherapy, hypnotherapy, social-learning approaches, biofeedback techniques, and environmental consultation and design.

C. Professional consultation in relation to A and B above.

D. Program development services in the areas of A, B, and C above.

E. Supervision of clinical psychological services.

F. Evaluation of all services noted in A through E above.

A "clinical psychological service unit" is the functional unit through which clinical psychological services are provided; such a unit may be part of a larger psychological service organization comprising psychologists of more than one specialty and headed by a professional psychologist:

A. A clinical psychological service unit provides predominantly clinical psychological services and is composed of one or more professional clinical psychologists and supporting staff.

B. A clinical psychological service unit may operate as a professional service or as a functional or geographic component of a larger multipsychological service unit or of a governmental, educational, correctional, health, training, industrial, or commercial organizational unit.[6]

C. One or more clinical psychologists providing professional services in a multidisciplinary setting constitute a clinical psychological service unit.

D. A clinical psychological service unit may also be one or more clinical psychologists in a private practice or a psychological consulting firm.

"Users of clinical psychological services" include:

A. Direct users or recipients of clinical psychological services.

B. Public and private institutions, facilities, or organizations receiving clinical psychological services.

C. Third-party purchasers—those who pay for the delivery of services but who are not the recipients of services.

D. Sanctioners—those who have a legitimate concern with the accessibility, timeliness, efficacy, and standards of quality attending the provision of clinical psychological services. Sanctioners may include members of the user's family, the court, the probation officer, the school administrator, the employer, the union representative, the facility director, and so on. Sanctioners may also include various governmental, peer review, and accreditation bodies concerned with the assurance of quality.

Guideline 1
Providers

1.1 Each clinical psychological service unit offering psychological services has available at least one professional clinical psychologist and as many more professional clinical psychologists as are necessary to assure the adequacy and quality of services offered.

Interpretation: The intent of this Guideline is that one or more providers of psychological services in any clinical psychological service unit meet the levels of training and experience of the professional clinical psychologist as specified in the preceding definitions.[7]

When a facility offering clinical psychological services does not have a full-time professional clinical psychologist available, the facility retains the services of one or more professional clinical psychologists on a regular part-time basis. The clinical psychologist so retained directs and supervises the psychological services provided, participates sufficiently to be able to assess the need for services, reviews the content of services provided, and has the authority to assume professional responsibility and accountability for them.

The psychologist directing the service unit is responsible for determining and justifying appropriate ratios of psychologists to users and psychologists to support staff, in order to ensure proper scope, accessibility, and quality of services provided in that setting.

1.2 Providers of clinical psychological services who do not meet the requirements for the professional clinical psychologist are supervised directly by a professional clinical psychologist who assumes professional responsibility and accountability for the services provided. The level and extent of supervision may vary from task to task so long as the supervising psychologist retains a sufficiently close supervisory relationship to meet this Guideline. Special proficiency training or supervision may be provided by a professional psychologist of another specialty or by a professional from another discipline whose competence in the given area has been demonstrated by previous training and experience.

Interpretation: In each clinical psychological service unit there may be varying levels of responsibility with respect to the nature and quality of services provided. Support personnel are considered to be responsible for their functions and behavior when assisting in the provision of clinical psychological services and are accountable to the professional clinical psychologist. Ultimate professional responsibility and accountability for the services provided require that the supervisor review and approve reports and test protocols, review and approve intervention plans and strategies, and review outcomes. Therefore, the supervision of all clinical psychological services is provided directly by a professional clinical psychologist in individual and/or group face-to-face meetings.

In order to meet this Guideline, an appropriate number of hours per week are devoted to direct face-to-face supervision of each clinical psychological service unit staff member. In no event is such supervision less than 1 hour per week. The more comprehensive the psychological services are, the more supervision is needed. A plan or formula for relating increasing amounts of supervisory time to the complexity of professional responsibilities is to be developed. The amount and nature of supervision is made known to all parties concerned.

Such communications are in writing and describe and delineate the duties of the employee with respect to range and type of services to be provided. The limits of independent action and decision making are defined. The description of responsibility also specifies the means by which the employee will contact the professional clinical psychologist in the event of emergency or crisis situations.

1.3 Wherever a clinical psychological service unit exists, a professional clinical psychologist is responsible for planning, directing, and reviewing the provision of clinical psychological services. Whenever the clinical psychological service unit is part of a larger professional psychological service encompassing various psychological specialties, a professional psychologist is the administrative head of the service.

Interpretation: The clinical psychologist coordinates the activities of the clinical psychological service unit with other professional, administrative, and technical groups, both within and outside the facility. This clinical psychologist, who may be the director, chief, or coordinator of the clinical psychological service unit, has related responsibilities including, but not limited to, recruiting qualified staff, directing training and research activities of the service, maintaining a high level of professional and ethical practice, and ensuring that staff members function only within the areas of their competency.

To facilitate the effectiveness of clinical services by raising the level of staff sensitivity and professional skills, the clinical psychologist designated as director is responsible for participating in the selection of staff and support personnel whose qualifications and skills (e.g., language, cultural and experiential background, race, sex, and age) are directly relevant to the needs and characteristics of the users served.

1.4 When functioning as part of an organizational setting, professional clinical psychologists bring their backgrounds and skills to bear on the goals of the organization, whenever appropriate, by participation in the planning and development of overall services.[8]

Interpretation: Professional clinical psychologists participate in the maintenance of high professional standards by representation on committees concerned with service delivery.

As appropriate to the setting, their activities may include active participation, as voting and as office-holding members, on the professional staffs of hospitals and other facilities and on other executive, planning, and evaluation boards and committees.

1.5 Clinical psychologists maintain current knowledge of scientific and professional developments to preserve and enhance their professional competence. [9]

Interpretation: Methods through which knowledge of scientific and professional developments may be gained include, but are not limited to, reading scientific and professional publications, attendance at workshops, participation in staff development programs, and other forms of continuing education. The clinical psychologist has ready access to reference material related to the provision of psychological services. Clinical psychologists are prepared to show evidence periodically that they are staying abreast of current knowledge and practices in the field of clinical psychology through continuing education.

1.6 Clinical psychologists limit their practice to their demonstrated areas of professional competence.

Interpretation: Clinical psychological services are offered in accordance with the providers' areas of competence as defined by verifiable training and experience. When extending services beyond the range of their usual practice, psychologists obtain pertinent training or appropriate professional supervision. Such training or supervision is consistent with the extension of functions performed and services provided. An extension of services may involve a change in the theoretical orientation of the clinical psychologist, a change in modality or technique, or a change in the type of client and/or the kinds of problems or disorders for which services are to be provided (e.g., children, elderly persons, mental retardation, neurological impairment).

1.7 Professional psychologists who wish to qualify as clinical psychologists meet the same requirements with respect to subject matter and professional skills that apply to doctoral and postdoctoral education and training in clinical psychology. [10]

Interpretation: Education of doctoral-level psychologists to qualify them for specialty practice in clinical psychology is under the auspices of a department in a regionally accredited university or of a professional school that offers the doctoral degree in clinical psychology. Such education is individualized, with due credit being given for relevant course work and other requirements that have previously been satisfied. In addition, doctoral-level training plus 1 year of postdoctoral experience supervised by a clinical psychologist is required. Merely taking an internship in clinical psychology or acquiring experience in a practicum setting is not adequate preparation for becoming a clinical psychologist when prior education has not been in that area. Fulfillment of such an individualized educational program is attested to by the awarding of a certificate by the supervising department or professional school that indicates the successful completion of preparation in clinical psychology.

1.8 Professional clinical psychologists are encouraged to develop innovative theories and procedures and to provide appropriate theoretical and/or empirical support for their innovations.

Interpretation: A specialty of a profession rooted in a science intends continually to explore and experiment with a view to developing and verifying new and improved methods of serving the public in ways that can be documented.

Guideline 2
Programs

2.1 Composition and organization of a clinical psychological service unit:

2.1.1 The composition and programs of a clinical psychological service unit are responsive to the needs of the persons or settings served.

Interpretation: A clinical psychological service unit is structured so as to facilitate effective and economical delivery of services. For example, a clinical psychological service unit serving predominantly a low-income, ethnic, or racial minority group has a staffing pattern and service programs that are adapted to the linguistic, experiential, and attitudinal characteristics of the users.

2.1.2 A description of the organization of the clinical psychological service unit and its lines of responsibility and accountability for the delivery of psychological services is available in written form to staff of the unit and to users and sanctioners upon request.

Interpretation: The description includes lines of responsibility, supervisory relationships, and the level and extent of accountability for each person who provides psychological services.

2.1.3 A clinical psychological service unit includes sufficient numbers of professional and support personnel to achieve its goals, objectives, and purposes.

Interpretation: The work load and diversity of psychological services required and the specific goals and objectives of the setting determine the numbers and qualifications of professional and support personnel in the clinical psychological service unit. Where shortages in personnel exist, so that psychological services cannot be rendered in a professional manner, the director of the clinical psychological service unit initiates action to remedy such shortages. When this fails, the director appropriately modifies the scope or work load of the unit to maintain the quality of the services rendered.

2.2 Policies:

2.2.1 When the clinical psychological service unit is composed of more than one person or is a component of a larger organization, a written statement of its objectives and scope of services is developed, maintained, and reviewed.

Interpretation: The clinical psychological service unit reviews its objectives and scope of services annually and revises them as necessary to ensure that the psychological services offered are consistent with staff competencies and current psychological knowledge and practice. This statement is discussed with staff, reviewed with the appropriate administrator, and distributed to users and sanctioners upon request, whenever appropriate.

2.2.2 All providers within a clinical psychological service unit support the legal and civil rights of the users. [11]

Interpretation: Providers of clinical psychological services safeguard the interests of the users with regard to personal, legal, and civil rights. They are continually sensitive to the issue of confidentiality of information, the short-term and long-term impacts of their decisions and recommendations, and other matters pertaining to individual, legal, and civil rights. Concerns regarding the safeguarding of individual rights of users include, but are not limited to, problems of self-incrimination in judicial proceedings, involuntary commitment to hospitals, protection of minors or legal incompetents, discriminatory practices in employment selection procedures, recommendation for special education provisions, information relative to adverse personnel actions in the armed services, and adjudication of domestic relations disputes in divorce and custodial proceedings. Providers of clinical psychological services take affirmative action by making themselves available to local committees, review boards, and similar advisory groups established to safeguard the human, civil, and legal rights of service users.

2.2.3 All providers within a clinical psychological service unit are familiar with and adhere to the American Psychological Association's Standards for Providers of Psychological Services,

Ethical Principles of Psychologists, Standards for Educational and Psychological Tests, Ethical Principles in the Conduct of Research With Human Participants, and other official policy statements relevant to standards for professional services issued by the Association.

Interpretation: Providers of clinical psychological services maintain up-to-date knowledge of the relevant standards of the American Psychological Association.

2.2.4 All providers within a clinical psychological service unit conform to relevant statutes established by federal, state, and local governments.

Interpretation: All providers of clinical psychological services are familiar with appropriate statutes regulating the practice of psychology. They observe agency regulations that have the force of law and that relate to the delivery of psychological services (e.g., evaluation for disability retirement and special education placements). In addition, all providers are cognizant that federal agencies such as the Veterans Administration, the Department of Education, and the Department of Health and Human Services have policy statements regarding psychological services, and where relevant, providers conform to them. Providers of clinical psychological services are also familiar with other statutes and regulations, including those addressed to the civil and legal rights of users (e.g., those promulgated by the federal Equal Employment Opportunity Commission), that are pertinent to their scope of practice.

It is the responsibility of the American Psychological Association to maintain current files of those federal policies, statutes, and regulations relating to this section and to assist its members in obtaining them. The state psychological associations and the state licensing boards periodically publish and distribute appropriate state statutes and regulations.

2.2.5 All providers within a clinical psychological service unit inform themselves about and use the network of human services in their communities in order to link users with relevant services and resources.

Interpretation: Clinical psychologists and support staff are sensitive to the broader context of human needs. In recognizing the matrix of personal and societal problems, providers make available to users information regarding human services such as legal aid societies, social services, employment agencies, health resources, and educational and recreational facilities. Providers of clinical psychological services refer to such community resources and, when indicated, actively intervene on behalf of the users.

Community resources include the private as well as the public sectors. Private resources include private agencies and centers and psychologists in independent private practice. Consultation is sought or referral made within the public or private network of services whenever required in the best interest of the users. Clinical psychologists, in either the private or the public setting, utilize other resources in the community whenever indicated because of limitations within the psychological service unit providing the services. Professional clinical psychologists in private practice are familiar with the types of services offered through local community mental health clinics and centers, including alternatives to hospitalization, and know the costs and eligibility requirements for those services.

2.2.6 In the delivery of clinical psychological services, the providers maintain a cooperative relationship with colleagues and co-workers in the best interest of the users. [12]

Interpretation: Clinical psychologists recognize the areas of special competence of other professional psychologists and of professionals in other fields for either consultation or referral purposes. Providers of clinical psychological services make appropriate use of other professional, research, technical, and administrative resources to serve the best interests of users and establish and maintain cooperative arrangements with such other resources as required to meet the needs of users.

2.3 Procedures:

2.3.1 Each clinical psychological service unit follows a set of procedural guidelines for the delivery of psychological services.

Interpretation: Providers are prepared to provide a statement of procedural guidelines, in either oral or written form, in terms that can be understood by users, including sanctioners and local administrators. This statement describes the current methods, forms, procedures, and techniques being used to achieve the objectives and goals for psychological services.

2.3.2 Providers of clinical psychological services develop plans appropriate to the providers' professional practices and to the problems presented by the users.

Interpretation: A clinical psychologist develops a plan that describes the psychological services, their objectives, and the manner in which they will be provided. [13,14] This plan is in written form; it serves as a basis for obtaining understanding and concurrence from the user and provides a mechanism for subsequent peer review. This plan is, of course, modified as new needs or information develops.

A clinical psychologist who provides services as one member of a collaborative effort participates in the development and implementation of the overall service plan and provides for its periodic review.

2.3.3 Accurate, current, and pertinent documentation of essential clinical psychological services provided is maintained.

Interpretation: Records kept of clinical psychological services may include, but are not limited to, identifying data, dates of services, types of services, significant actions taken, and outcome at termination. Providers of clinical psychological services ensure that essential information concerning services rendered is recorded within a reasonable time following their completion.

2.3.4 Each clinical psychological service unit follows an established record retention and disposition policy.

Interpretation: The policy on record retention and disposition conforms to federal or state statutes or administrative regulations where such are applicable. In the absence of such regulations, the policy is (a) that the full record be retained intact for 3 years after the completion of planned services or after the date of last contact with the user, whichever is later; (b) that a full record or summary of the record be maintained for an additional 12 years; and (c) that the record may be disposed of no sooner than 15 years after the completion of planned services or after the date of the last contact, whichever is later. These temporal guides are consistent with procedures currently in use by federal record centers.

In the event of the death or incapacity of a clinical psychologist in independent practice, special procedures are necessary to ensure the continuity of active services to users and the proper safeguarding of inactive records being retained to meet this Guideline. Following approval by the affected user, it is appropriate for another clinical psychologist, acting under the auspices of the local professional standards review committee (PSRC), to review the records with the user and recommend a course of action for continuing professional service, if needed. Depending on local circumstances, the reviewing psychologist may also recommend appropriate arrangements for the balance of the record retention and disposition period.

This Guideline has been designed to meet a variety of circumstances that may arise, often years after a set of psychological services has been completed. More and more records are being used in forensic matters, for peer review, and in response to requests from users, other professionals, or other legitimate parties requiring accurate information about the exact dates, nature, course, and outcome of a set of psychological services. These record retention procedures also provide valuable baseline data for the original psychologist-provider when a previous user returns for additional services.

2.3.5 Providers of clinical psychological services maintain a system to protect confidentiality of their records. [15]

Interpretation: Clinical psychologists are responsible for maintaining the confidentiality of information about users of services, from whatever source derived. All persons supervised by clinical psychologists, including nonprofessional personnel and students, who have access to records of psychological services are required to maintain this confidentiality as a condition of employment.

The clinical psychologist does not release confidential information, except with the written consent of the user directly involved or his or her legal representative. Even after consent for release has been obtained, the clinical psychologist clearly identifies such information as confidential to the recipient of the information. [16] If directed otherwise by statute or regulations with the force of law or by court order, the psychologist may seek a resolution to the conflict that is both ethically and legally feasible and appropriate.

Users are informed in advance of any limits in the setting for maintenance of confidentiality of psychological information. For instance, clinical psychologists in hospital, clinic, or agency settings inform their patients that psychological information in a patient's clinical record may be available without the patient's written consent to other members of the professional staff associated with the patient's treatment or rehabilitation. Similar limitations on confidentiality of psychological information may be present in certain school, industrial, military, or other institutional settings, or in instances in which the user has waived confidentiality for purposes of third-party payment.

Users have the right to obtain information from their psychological records. However, the records are the property of the psychologist or the facility in which the psychologist works and are, therefore, the responsibility of the psychologist and subject to his or her control.

When the user's intention to waive confidentiality is judged by the professional clinical psychologist to be contrary to the user's best interests or to be in conflict with the user's civil and legal rights, it is the responsibility of the clinical psychologist to discuss the implications of releasing psychological information and to assist the user in limiting disclosure only to information required by the present circumstance.

Raw psychological data (e. g. , questionnaire returns or test protocols) in which a user is identified are released only with the written consent of the user or his or her legal representative and released only to a person recognized by the clinical psychologist as qualified and competent to use the data.

Any use made of psychological reports, records, or data for research or training purposes is consistent with this Guideline. Additionally, providers of clinical psychological services comply with statutory confidentiality requirements and those embodied in the American Psychological Association's Ethical Principles of Psychologists (APA 1981b).

Providers of clinical psychological services remain sensitive to both the benefits and the possible misuse of information regarding individuals that is stored in large computerized data banks. Providers use their influence to ensure that such information is used in a socially responsible manner.

Guideline 3
Accountability

3.1 The clinical psychologist's professional activity is guided primarily by the principle of promoting human welfare.

Interpretation: Clinical psychologists provide services to users in a manner that is considerate, effective, economical, and humane. Clinical psychologists make their services readily accessible to users in a manner that facilitates the users' freedom of choice.

Clinical psychologists are mindful of their accountability to the sanctioners of clinical psychological services and to the general public, provided that appropriate steps are taken to protect the confidentiality of the service relationship. In the pursuit of their professional activities, they aid in the conservation of human, material, and financial resources.

The clinical psychological service unit does not withhold services to a potential client on the basis of that user's race, color, religion, gender, sexual orientation, age, or national origin. Recognition is given, however, to the following considerations: the professional right of clinical psychologists to limit their practice to a specific category of users (e. g. , children, adolescents, women); the right and responsibility of clinical psychologists to withhold an assessment procedure when not validly applicable; and the right and responsibility of clinical psychologists to withhold evaluative, psychotherapeutic, counseling, or other services in specific instances in which their own limitations or client characteristics might impair the effectiveness of the relationship.[17,18] Clinical psychologists seek to ameliorate through peer review, consultation, or other personal therapeutic procedures those factors that inhibit the provision of services to particular users. When indicated services are not available, clinical psychologists take whatever action is appropriate to inform responsible persons and agencies of the lack of such services.

Clinical psychologists who find that psychological services are being provided in a manner that is discriminatory or exploitative to users and/or contrary to these Guidelines or to state or federal statutes take appropriate corrective action, which may include the refusal to provide services. When conflicts of interest arise, the clinical psychologist is guided in the resolution of differences by the principles set forth in the American Psychological Association's Ethical Principles of Psychologists (APA 1981b) and "Guidelines for Conditions of Employment of Psychologists" (APA 1972).

3.2 Clinical psychologists pursue their activities as members of the independent, autonomous profession of psychology.[19]

Interpretation: Clinical psychologists, as members of an independent profession, are responsible both to the public and to their peers through established review mechanisms. Clinical psychologists are aware of the implications of their activities for the profession as a whole. They seek to eliminate discriminatory practices instituted for self-serving purposes that are not in the interest of the users (e.g., arbitrary requirements for referral and supervision by another profession). They are cognizant of their responsibilities for the development of the profession. They participate where possible in the training and career development of students and other providers, participate as appropriate in the training of paraprofessionals or other professionals, and integrate and supervise the implementation of their contributions within the structure established for delivering psychological services. Clinical psychologists facilitate the development of, and participate in, professional standards review mechanisms.[20]

Clinical psychologists seek to work with other professionals in a cooperative manner for the good of the users and the benefit of the general public. Clinical psychologists associated with multidisciplinary settings support the principle that members of each participating profession have equal rights and opportunities to share all privileges and responsibilities of full membership in hospital facilities or other human service facilities and to administer service programs in their respective areas of competence.

3.3 There are periodic, systematic, and effective evaluations of clinical psychological services.[21]

Interpretation: When the clinical psychological service unit is a component of a larger organization, regular evaluation of progress in achieving goals is provided for in the service delivery plan, including consideration of the effectiveness of clinical psychological services relative to costs in terms of use of time and money and the availability of professional and support personnel.

Evaluation of the clinical psychological service delivery system is conducted internally and, when possible, under independent auspices as well. This evaluation includes an assessment of effectiveness (to determine what the service unit accomplished), efficiency (to determine the total costs of providing the services), continuity (to ensure that the services are appropriately linked to other human services), availability (to determine appropriate levels and distribution of services and personnel), accessibility (to ensure that the services are barrier free to users), and adequacy (to determine whether the services meet the identified needs for such services).

There is a periodic reexamination of review mechanisms to ensure that these attempts at public safeguards are effective and cost efficient and do not place unnecessary encumbrances on the providers or impose unnecessary additional expenses on users or sanctioners for services rendered.

3.4 Clinical psychologists are accountable for all aspects of the services they provide and are responsive to those concerned with these services.[22]

Interpretation: In recognizing their responsibilities to users, and where appropriate and consistent with the users' legal rights and privileged communications, clinical psychologists make available information about, and provide opportunity to participate in, decisions concerning such issues as initiation, termination, continuation, modification, and evaluation of clinical psychological services.

Depending on the settings, accurate and full information is made available to prospective individual or organizational users regarding the qualifications of providers, the nature and extent of services offered, and where appropriate, financial and social costs.

Where appropriate, clinical psychologists inform users of their payment policies and their willingness to assist in obtaining reimbursement. Those who accept reimbursement from a third party are acquainted with the appropriate statutes and regulations and assist their users in understanding procedures for submitting claims and limits on confidentiality of claims information, in accordance with pertinent statutes.

Guideline 4
Environment

4.1 Providers of clinical psychological services promote the development in the service setting of a physical, organizational, and social environment that facilitates optimal human functioning.

Interpretation: Federal, state, and local requirements for safety, health, and sanitation are observed.

As providers of services, clinical psychologists are concerned with the environment of their service unit, especially as it affects the quality of service, but also as it impinges on human functioning when the service unit is included in a larger context. Physical arrangements and organizational policies and procedures are conducive to the human dignity, self-respect, and optimal functioning of users and to the effective delivery of service. Attention is given to the comfort and the privacy of users. The atmosphere in which clinical psychological services are rendered is appropriate to the service and to the users, whether in an office, clinic, school, industrial organization, or other institutional setting.

NOTES

1. The notes appended to these Specialty Guidelines represent an attempt to provide a coherent context of other policy statements of the Association regarding professional practice. The Guidelines extend these previous policy statements where necessary to reflect current concerns of the public and the profession.

2. The following two categories of professional psychologists who met the criteria indicated below on or before the adoption of these Specialty Guidelines on January 31, 1980, are also considered clinical psychologists: Category 1—persons who completed (a) a doctoral degree program primarily psychological in content at a regionally accredited university or professional school and (b) 3 postdoctoral years of appropriate education, training, and experience in providing clinical psychological services as defined herein, including a minimum of 1 year in a clinical setting; Category 2—persons who on or before September 4, 1974 (a) completed a master's degree from a program primarily psychological in content at a regionally accredited university or professional school and (b) held a license or certificate in the state in which they practiced, conferred by a state board of psychological examiners, or the endorsement of the state psychological association through voluntary certification, and who, in addition, prior to January 31, 1980,

(c) obtained 5 postmaster's years of appropriate education, training, and experience in providing clinical psychological services as
defined herein, including a minimum of 2 years in a clinical setting.

After January 31, 1980, professional psychologists who wish
to be recognized as professional clinical psychologists are referred
to Guideline 1.7.

The definition of the professional clinical psychologist in these
Guidelines does not contradict or supersede in any way the broader
definition accorded the term "clinical psychologist" in the Federal
Employees Health Benefits Program (see Access to Psychologists
and Optometrists Under Federal Health Benefits Program, U.S.
Senate Report no. 93-961, June 25, 1974).

3. The areas of knowledge and training that are a part of the
educational program for all professional psychologists have been
presented in two APA documents, Education and Credentialing in
Psychology II (APA 1977a) and Criteria for Accreditation of Doctoral Training Programs and Internships in Professional Psychology
(APA 1979). There is consistency in the presentation of core areas
in the education and training of all professional psychologists. The
description of education and training in these Guidelines is based
primarily on the document Education and Credentialing in Psychology II. It is intended to indicate broad areas of required curriculum,
with the expectation that training programs will undoubtedly want to
interpret the specific content of these areas in different ways depending on the nature, philosophy, and intent of the programs.

4. Functions and activities of psychologists relating to the
teaching of psychology, the writing or editing of scholarly or scientific manuscripts, and the conduct of scientific research do not fall
within the purview of these Guidelines.

5. The definitions should be compared with the APA (1967)
guidelines for state legislation (hereinafter referred to as state
guidelines), which define "psychologist" and the "practice of psychology" as follows:

A person represents himself [or herself] to be a psychologist when he [or she] holds himself [or herself]
out to the public by any title or description of services
incorporating the words "psychology," "psychological,"
"psychologist," and/or offers to render or renders
services as defined below to individuals, groups, organizations, or the public for a fee, monetary or
otherwise.

The practice of psychology within the meaning
of this act is defined as rendering to individuals,
groups, organizations, or the public any psychological service involving the application of principles,

methods, and procedures of understanding, predicting, and influencing behavior, such as the principles pertaining to learning, perception, motivation, thinking, emotions, and interpersonal relationships; the methods and procedures of interviewing, counseling, and psychotherapy; of constructing, administering, and interpreting tests of mental abilities, aptitudes, interests, attitudes, personality characteristics, emotion, and motivation; and of assessing public opinion.

The application of said principles and methods includes, but is not restricted to: diagnosis, prevention, and amelioration of adjustment problems and emotional and mental disorders of individuals and groups; hypnosis; educational and vocational counseling; personnel selection and management; the evaluation and planning for effective work and learning situations; advertising and market research; and the resolution of interpersonal and social conflicts.

Psychotherapy within the meaning of this act means the use of learning, conditioning methods, and emotional reactions, in a professional relationship, to assist a person or persons to modify feelings, attitudes, and behavior which are intellectually, socially, or emotionally maladjustive or ineffectual.

The practice of psychology shall be as defined above, any existing statute in the state of _____ to the contrary notwithstanding. (APA 1967, pp. 1098–1099)

6. The relation of a psychological service unit to a larger facility or institution is also addressed indirectly in the APA (1972) "Guidelines for Conditions of Employment of Psychologists" (hereinafter referred to as CEP Guidelines), which emphasizes the roles, responsibilities, and prerogatives of the psychologist when he or she is employed by or provides services for another agency, institution, or business.

7. This Guideline replaces earlier recommendations in the 1967 state guidelines concerning exemption of psychologists from licensure. Recommendations 8 and 9 of those guidelines read as follows:

Persons employed as psychologists by accredited academic institutions, governmental agencies, research laboratories, and business corporations should be exempted, provided such employees are performing those duties for which they are employed by such organizations, and within the confines of such organizations.

Persons employed as psychologists by accredited academic institutions, governmental agencies, research laboratories, and business corporations consulting or offering their research findings or providing scientific information to like organizations for a fee should be exempted. (APA 1967, p. 1100)

On the other hand, the 1967 state guidelines specifically denied exemptions under certain conditions, as noted in Recommendations 10 and 11:

Persons employed as psychologists who offer or provide psychological services to the public for a fee, over and above the salary that they receive for the performance of their regular duties, should not be exempted.

Persons employed as psychologists by organizations that sell psychological services to the public should not be exempted. (APA 1967, pp. 1100-1101)

The present APA policy, as reflected in this Guideline, establishes a single code of practice for psychologists providing covered services to users in any setting. The present position is that a psychologist providing any covered service meets local statutory requirements for licensure or certification. See the section entitled Principles and Implications of the Specialty Guidelines for an elaboration of this position.

8. A closely related principle is found in the APA (1972) CEP Guidelines:

It is the policy of APA that psychology as an independent profession is entitled to parity with other health and human service professions in institutional practices and before the law. Psychologists in interdisciplinary settings such as colleges and universities, medical schools, clinics, private practice groups, and other agencies expect parity with other professions in such matters as academic rank, board status, salaries, fringe benefits, fees, participation in administrative decisions, and all other conditions of employment, private contractual arrangements, and status before the law and legal institutions. (APA 1972, p. 333)

9. See CEP Guidelines (section entitled Career Development) for a closely related statement:

Psychologists are expected to encourage institutions
and agencies which employ them to sponsor or conduct
career development programs. The purpose to these
programs would be to enable psychologists to engage
in study for professional advancement and to keep
abreast of developments in their field. (APA 1972,
p. 332)

10. This Guideline follows closely the statement regarding
"Policy on Training for Psychologists Wishing to Change Their
Specialty" adopted by the APA Council of Representatives in January 1976. Included therein was the implementing provision that
"this policy statement shall be incorporated in the guidelines of the
Committee on Accreditation so that appropriate sanctions can be
brought to bear on university and internship training programs that
violate [it]" (Conger 1976, p. 424).

11. See also APA's (1981b) Ethical Principles of Psychologists, especially Principles 5 (Confidentiality), 6 (Welfare of the
Consumer), and 9 (Research with Human Participants); and see
Ethical Principles in the Conduct of Research With Human Participants (APA 1973a). Also, in 1978 Division 17 approved in principle
a statement on "Principles for Counseling and Psychotherapy With
Women, " which was designed to protect the interests of female
users of clinical psychological services.

12. Support for this position is found in Psychology as a Profession in the section on relations with other professions:

Professional persons have an obligation to know and take
into account the traditions and practices of other professional groups with whom they work and to cooperate
fully with members of such groups with whom research,
service, and other functions are shared. (APA 1968,
p. 5)

13. One example of a specific application of this principle is
found in Guideline 2 in APA's (1973b) "Guidelines for Psychologists
Conducting Growth Groups":

The following information should be made available in
writing [emphasis added] to all prospective participants:
    (a) An explicit statement of the purpose of the group.
    (b) Types of techniques that may be employed;
    (c) The education, training, and experience of the
leader or leaders;
    (d) The fee and any additional expense that may
be incurred;

(e) A statement as to whether or not a follow-up service is included in the fee;

(f) Goals of the group experience and techniques to be used;

(g) Amounts and kinds of responsibility to be assumed by the leader and by the participants. For example, (i) the degree to which a participant is free not to follow suggestions and prescriptions of the group leader and other group members; (ii) any restrictions on a participant's freedom to leave the group at any time; and

(h) Issues of confidentiality. (p. 933)

14. See APA's (1981a) APA/CHAMPUS Outpatient Psychological Provider Manual.

15. See Principle 5 (Confidentiality) in Ethical Principles of Psychologists (APA 1981b).

16. Support for the principle of privileged communication is found in at least two policy statements of the Association:

In the interest of both the public and the client and in accordance with the requirements of good professional practice, the profession of psychology seeks recognition of the privileged nature of confidential communications with clients, preferably through statutory enactment or by administrative policy where more appropriate. (APA 1968, p. 8)

Wherever possible, a clause protecting the privileged nature of the psychologist-client relationship be included.

When appropriate, psychologists assist in obtaining general "across the board" legislation for such privileged communications. (APA 1967, p. 1103)

17. This paragraph is directly adapted from the CEP Guidelines (APA 1972, p. 333).

18. The CEP Guidelines also include the following:

It is recognized that under certain circumstances, the interests and goals of a particular community or segment of interest in the population may be in conflict with the general welfare. Under such circumstances, the psychologist's professional activity must be primarily guided by the principle of "promoting human welfare." (APA 1972, p. 334)

19. Support for the principle of the independence of psychology as a profession is found in the following:

> As a member of an autonomous profession, a psychologist rejects limitations upon his [or her] freedom of thought and action other than those imposed by his [or her] moral, legal, and social responsibilities. The Association is always prepared to provide appropriate assistance to any responsible member who becomes subjected to unreasonable limitations upon his [or her] opportunity to function as a practitioner, teacher, researcher, administrator, or consultant. The Association is always prepared to cooperate with any responsible professional organization in opposing any unreasonable limitations on the professional functions of the members of that organization.
>
> This insistence upon professional autonomy has been upheld over the years by the affirmative actions of the courts and other public and private bodies in support of the right of the psychologist—and other professionals—to pursue those functions for which he [or she] is trained and qualified to perform. (APA 1968, p. 9)

> Organized psychology has the responsibility to define and develop its own profession, consistent with the general canons of science and with the public welfare.
>
> Psychologists recognize that other professions and other groups will, from time to time, seek to define the roles and responsibilities of psychologists. The APA opposes such developments on the same principle that it is opposed to the psychological profession taking positions which would define the work and scope of responsibility of other duly recognized professions. (APA 1972, p. 333)

20. APA support for peer review is detailed in the following excerpt from the APA (1971) statement entitled "Psychology and National Health Care":

> All professions participating in a national health plan should be directed to establish review mechanisms (or performance evaluations) that include not only peer review but active participation by persons representing the consumer. In situations where there are fiscal agents, they should also have representation when appropriate. (p. 1026)

21. This Guideline on program evaluation is based directly on the following excerpts from two APA position papers:

> The quality and availability of health services should be evaluated continuously by both consumers and health professionals. Research into the efficiency and effectiveness of the system should be conducted both internally and under independent auspices. (APA 1971, p. 1025)

> The comprehensive community mental health center should devote an explicit portion of its budget to program evaluation. All centers should inculcate in their staff attention to and respect for research findings; the larger centers have an obligation to set a high priority on basic research and to give formal recognition to research as a legitimate part of the duties of staff members.
>     . . . Only through explicit appraisal of program effects can worthy approaches be retained and refined, ineffective ones dropped. Evaluative monitoring of program achievements may vary, of course, from the relatively informal to the systematic and quantitative, depending on the importance of the issue, the availability of resources, and the willingness of those responsible to take risks of substituting informed judgment for evidence. (Smith and Hobbs 1966, pp. 21-22)

22. See also the CEP Guidelines for the following statement: "A psychologist recognizes that . . . he [or she] alone is accountable for the consequences and effects of his [or her] services, whether as teacher, researcher, or practitioner. This responsibility cannot be shared, delegated, or reduced" (APA 1972, p. 334).

REFERENCES

American Psychological Association. 1968. Psychology as a profession. Washington, D.C.: APA.

_____. 1971. Psychology and national health care. American Psychologist, 26: 1025-1026.

_____. 1972. Guidelines for conditions of employment of psychologists. American Psychologist, 27: 331-334.

_____. 1973a. Ethical principles in the conduct of research with human participants. Washington, D.C.: APA.

_____. 1973b. Guidelines for psychologists conducting growth groups. American Psychologist, 28: 933.

_____. 1974a. Standards for educational and psychological tests. Washington, D.C.: APA.

_____. 1974b. Standards for providers of psychological services. Washington, D.C.: APA.

_____. 1977a. Education and credentialing in psychology II. Report of a meeting, June 4-5, 1977. Washington, D.C.: APA.

_____. 1977b. Standards for providers of psychological services. Rev. ed. Washington, D.C.: APA.

_____. 1979. Criteria for accreditation of doctoral training programs and internships in professional psychology. Washington, D.C.: APA. (Amended 1980.)

_____. 1981a. APA/CHAMPUS outpatient psychological provider manual. Rev. ed. Washington, D.C.: APA.

_____. 1981b. Ethical principles of psychologists. Rev. ed. Washington, D.C.: APA.

American Psychological Association, Committee on Legislation. 1967. A model for state legislation affecting the practice of psychology. American Psychologist, 22: 1095-1103.

Conger, J. J. 1976. Proceedings of the American Psychological Association, Incorporated, for the year 1975: Minutes of the annual meeting of the Council of Representatives. American Psychologist, 31: 406-434.

Smith, M. B., and N. Hobbs. 1966. The community and the community mental health center. Washington, D.C.: APA.

SPECIALTY GUIDELINES FOR THE DELIVERY
OF SERVICES BY COUNSELING PSYCHOLOGISTS

The Specialty Guidelines that follow are based on the generic Standards for Providers of Psychological Services originally adopted by the American Psychological Association (APA) in September 1974 and revised in January 1977 (APA 1974b; 1977b). Together with the generic Standards, these Specialty Guidelines state the official policy of the Association regarding delivery of services by counseling psychologists. Admission to the practice of psychology is regulated by state statute. It is the position of the Association that licensing be based on generic, and not on specialty, qualifications. Specialty guidelines serve the additional purpose of providing potential users and other interested groups with essential information about particular services available from the several specialties in professional psychology.

Professional psychology specialties have evolved from generic practice in psychology and are supported by university training programs. There are now at least four recognized professional specialties—clinical, counseling, school, and industrial/organizational psychology.

The knowledge base in each of these specialty areas has increased, refining the state of the art to the point that a set of uniform specialty guidelines is now possible and desirable. The present Guidelines are intended to educate the public, the profession, and other interested parties regarding specialty professional practices. They are also intended to facilitate the continued systematic development of the profession.

The content of each Specialty Guideline reflects a consensus of university faculty and public and private practitioners regarding the knowledge base, services provided, problems addressed, and clients served.

--------

These Specialty Guidelines were prepared by the APA Committee on Standards for Providers of Psychological Services (COSPOPS), chaired by Durand F. Jacobs, with the advice of the officers and committee chairpersons of the Division of Counseling Psychology (Division 17). Barbara A. Kirk and Milton Schwebel served successively as the counseling psychology representative of COSPOPS, and Arthur Centor and Richard Kilburg were the Central Office liaisons to the committee. Normal Kagan, Samuel H. Osipow, Carl E. Thoresen, and Allen E. Ivey served successively as Division 17 presidents.

Traditionally, all learned disciplines have treated the designation of specialty practice as a reflection of preparation in greater depty in a particular subject matter, together with a voluntary limiting of focus to a more restricted area of practice by the professional. Lack of specialty designation does not preclude general providers of psychological services from using the methods or dealing with the populations of any specialty, except insofar as psychologists voluntarily refrain from providing services they are not trained to render. It is the intent of these guidelines, however, that after the grandparenting period, psychologists not put themselves forward as specialists in a given area of practice unless they meet the qualifications noted in the Guidelines (see Definitions). Therefore, these Guidelines are meant to apply only to those psychologists who voluntarily wish to be designated as counseling psychologists. They do not apply to other psychologists.

These Guidelines represent the profession's best judgment of the conditions, credentials, and experience that contribute to competent professional practice. The APA strongly encourages, and plans to participate in, efforts to identify professional practitioner behaviors and job functions and to validate the relation between these and desired client outcomes. Thus, future revisions of these Guidelines will increasingly reflect the results of such efforts.

These Guidelines follow the format and, wherever applicable, the wording of the generic Standards. [1] (Note: Notes appear at the end of the Specialty Guidelines.) The intent of these Guidelines is to improve the quality, effectiveness, and accessibility of psychological services. They are meant to provide guidance to providers, users, and sanctioners regarding the best judgment of the profession on these matters. Although the Specialty Guidelines have been derived from and are consistent with the generic Standards, they may be used as separate documents. However, Standards for Providers of Psychological Services (APA 1977b) shall remain the basic policy statement and shall take precedence where there are questions of interpretation.

Professional psychology in general and counseling psychology as a specialty have labored long and diligently to codify a uniform set of guidelines for the delivery of services by counseling psychologists that would serve the respective needs of users, providers, third-party purchasers, and sanctioners of psychological services.

The Committee on Professional Standards, established by the APA in January 1980, is charged with keeping the generic Standards and the Specialty Guidelines responsive to the needs of the public and the profession. It is also charged with continually reviewing, modifying, and extending them progressively as the profession and the science of psychology develop new knowledge, improved methods, and additional modes of psychological services.

The Specialty Guidelines for the Delivery of Services by Counseling Psychologists that follow have been established by the APA as a means of self-regulation to protect the public interest. They guide the specialty practice of counseling psychology by specifying important areas of quality assurance and performance that contribute to the goal of facilitating more effective human functioning.

Principles and Implications of
the Specialty Guidelines

These Specialty Guidelines emerged from and reaffirm the same basic principles that guided the development of the generic <u>Standards for Providers of Psychological Services</u> (APA 1977b):

    1. These Guidelines recognize that admission to the practice of psychology is regulated by state statute.

    2. It is the intention of the APA that the generic <u>Standards</u> provide appropriate guidelines for statutory licensing of psychologists. In addition, although it is the position of the APA that licensing be generic and not in specialty areas, these Specialty Guidelines in counseling psychology provide an authoritative reference for use in credentialing specialty providers of counseling psychological services by such groups as divisions of the APA and state associations and by boards and agencies that find such criteria useful for quality assurance.

    3. A uniform set of Specialty Guidelines governs the quality of services to all users of counseling psychological services in both the private and the public sectors. Those receiving counseling psychological services are protected by the same kinds of safeguards, irrespective of sector; these include constitutional guarantees, statutory regulation, peer review, consultation, record review, and supervision.

    4. A uniform set of Specialty Guidelines governs counseling psychological service functions offered by counseling psychologists, regardless of setting or form of remuneration. All counseling psychologists in professional practice recognize and are responsive to a uniform set of Specialty Guidelines, just as they are guided by a common code of ethics.

    5. Counseling psychology Guidelines establish clear, minimally acceptable levels of quality for covered counseling psychological service functions, regardless of the nature of the users, purchasers, or sanctioners of such covered services.

    6. All persons providing counseling psychological services meet specified levels of training and experience that are consistent with, and appropriate to, the functions they perform. Counseling

psychological services provided by persons who do not meet the APA qualifications for a professional counseling psychologist (see Definitions) are supervised by a professional counseling psychologist. Final responsibility and accountability for services provided rest with professional counseling psychologists.

7. When providing any of the covered counseling psychological service functions at any time and in any setting, whether public or private, profit or nonprofit, counseling psychologists observe these Guidelines in order to promote the best interests and welfare of the users of such services. The extent to which counseling psychologists observe these Guidelines is judged by peers.

8. These Guidelines, while assuring the user of the counseling psychologist's accountability for the nature and quality of services specified in this document, do not preclude the counseling psychologist from using new methods or developing innovative procedures in the delivery of counseling services.

These Specialty Guidelines have broad implications both for users of counseling psychological services and for providers of such services:

1. Guidelines for counseling psychological services provide a foundation for mutual understanding between provider and user and facilitate more effective evaluation of services provided and outcomes achieved.

2. Guidelines for counseling psychologists are essential for uniformity in specialty credentialing of counseling psychologists.

3. Guidelines give specific content to the profession's concept of ethical practice as it applies to the functions of counseling psychologists.

4. Guidelines for counseling psychological services may have significant impact on tomorrow's education and training models for both professional and support personnel in counseling psychology.

5. Guidelines for the provision of counseling psychological services in human service facilities influence the determination of acceptable structure, budgeting, and staffing patterns in these facilities.

6. Guidelines for counseling psychological services require continual review and revision.

The Specialty Guidelines here presented are intended to improve the quality and delivery of counseling psychological services by specifying criteria for key aspects of the practice setting. Some settings may require additional and/or more stringent criteria for specific areas of service delivery.

Systematically applied, these Guidelines serve to establish a more effective and consistent basis for evaluating the performance of individual service providers as well as to guide the organization of counseling psychological service units in human service settings.

## Definitions

"Providers of counseling psychological services" refers to two categories of persons who provide counseling psychological services:

A. Professional counseling psychologists.[2] Professional counseling psychologists have a doctoral degree from a regionally accredited university or professional school providing an organized, sequential counseling psychology program in an appropriate academic department in a university or college, or in an appropriate department or unit of a professional school. Counseling psychology programs that are accredited by the American Psychological Association are recognized as meeting the definition of a counseling psychology program. Counseling psychology programs that are not accredited by the American Psychological Association meet the definition of a counseling psychology program if they satisfy the following criteria:

1. The program is primarily psychological in nature and stands as a recognizable, coherent organizational entity within the institution.

2. The program provides an integrated, organized sequence of study.

3. The program has an identifiable body of students who are matriculated in that program for a degree.

4. There is a clear authority with primary responsibility for the core and specialty areas, whether or not the program cuts across administrative lines.

5. There is an identifiable psychology faculty, and a psychologist is responsible for the program.

The professional counseling psychologist's doctoral education and training experience[3] is defined by the institution offering the program. Only counseling psychologists, that is, those who meet the appropriate education and training requirements, have the minimum professional qualifications to provide unsupervised counseling psychological services. A professional counseling psychologist and others providing counseling psychological services under supervision (described below) form an integral part of a multilevel counseling psychological service delivery system.

B.  All other persons who provide counseling psychological services under the supervision of a professional counseling psychologist.  Although there may be variations in the titles of such persons, they are not referred to as counseling psychologists. Their functions may be indicated by use of the adjective "psychological" preceding the noun, for example, "psychological associate," "psychological assistant," "psychological technician," or "psychological aide."

"Counseling psychological services" refers to services provided by counseling psychologists that apply principles, methods, and procedures for facilitating effective functioning during the lifespan developmental process. [4,5] In providing such services, counseling psychologists approach practice with a significant emphasis on positive aspects of growth and adjustment and with a developmental orientation.  These services are intended to help persons acquire or alter personal-social skills, improve adaptability to changing life demands, enhance environmental coping skills, and develop a variety of problem-solving and decision-making capabilities. Counseling psychological services are used by individuals, couples, and families of all age groups to cope with problems connected with education, career choice, work, sex, marriage, family, other social relations, health, aging, and handicaps of a social or physical nature.  The services are offered in such organizations as educational, rehabilitation, and health institutions and in a variety of other public and private agencies committed to service in one or more of the problem areas cited above.  Counseling psychological services include the following:

A.  Assessment, evaluation, and diagnosis.  Procedures may include, but are not limited to, behavioral observation, interviewing, and administering and interpreting instruments for the assessment of educational achievement, academic skills, aptitudes, interests, cognitive abilities, attitudes, emotions, motivations, psychoneurological status, personality characteristics, or any other aspect of human experience and behavior that may contribute to understanding and helping the user.

B.  Interventions with individuals and groups.  Procedures include individual and group psychological counseling (e.g., education, career, couples, and family counseling) and may use a therapeutic, group process, or social-learning approach, or any other deemed to be appropriate.  Interventions are used for purposes of prevention, remediation, and rehabilitation; they may incorporate a variety of psychological modalities, such as psychotherapy, behavior therapy, marital and family therapy, biofeedback techniques, and environmental design.

C. Professional consultation relating to A and B above, for example, in connection with developing in-service training for staff or assisting an educational institution or organization to design a plan to cope with persistent problems of its students.

D. Program development services in the areas of A, B, and C above, such as assisting a rehabilitation center to design a career-counseling program.

E. Supervision of all counseling psychological services, such as the review of assessment and intervention activities of staff.

F. Evaluation of all services noted in A through E above and research for the purpose of their improvement.

A "counseling psychological service unit" is the functional unit through which counseling psychological services are provided; such a unit may be part of a larger psychological service organization comprising psychologists of more than one specialty and headed by a professional psychologist:

A. A counseling psychological service unit provides predominantly counseling psychological services and is composed of one or more professional counseling psychologists and supporting staff.

B. A counseling psychological service unit may operate as a functional or geographic component of a larger multipsychological service unit or of a governmental, educational, correctional, health, training, industrial, or commercial organizational unit, or it may operate as an independent professional service.[6]

C. A counseling psychological service unit may take the form of one or more counseling psychologists providing professional services in a multidisciplinary setting.

D. A counseling psychological service unit may also take the form of a private practice, composed of one or more counseling psychologists serving individuals or groups, or the form of a psychological consulting firm serving organizations and institutions.

"Users of counseling psychological services" include:

A. Direct users or recipients of counseling psychological services.

B. Public and private institutions, facilities, or organizations receiving counseling psychological services.

C. Third-party purchasers—those who pay for the delivery of services but who are not the recipients of services.

D. Sanctioners—those who have a legitimate concern with the accessibility, timeliness, efficacy, and standards of quality attending the provision of counseling psychological services. Sanctioners may include members of the user's family, the court, the probation officer, the school administrator, the employer, the union representative, the facility director, and so on. Sanctioners may also include various governmental, peer review, and accreditation bodies concerned with the assurance of quality.

Guideline 1
Providers

1.1 Each counseling psychological service unit offering psychological services has available at least one professional counseling psychologist and as many more professional counseling psychologists as are necessary to assure the adequacy and quality of services offered.

Interpretation: The intent of this Guideline is that one or more providers of psychological services in any counseling psychological service unit meet the levels of training and experience of the professional counseling psychologist as specified in the preceding definitions.[7]

When a professional counseling psychologist is not available on a full-time basis, the facility retains the services of one or more professional counseling psychologists on a regular part-time basis. The counseling psychologist so retained directs the psychological services, including supervision of the support staff, has the authority and participates sufficiently to assess the need for services, reviews the content of services provided, and assumes professional responsibility and accountability for them.

The psychologist directing the service unit is responsible for determining and justifying appropriate ratios of psychologists to users and psychologists to support staff, in order to ensure proper scope, accessibility, and quality of services provided in that setting.

1.2 Providers of counseling psychological services who do not meet the requirements for the professional counseling psychologist are supervised directly by a professional counseling psychologist who assumes professional responsibility and accountability for the services provided. The level and extent of supervision may vary from task to task so long as the supervising psychologist retains a sufficiently close supervisory relationship to meet this Guideline. Special proficiency training or supervision may be provided by a professional psychologist of another specialty or by a professional from another discipline whose competence in the given area has been demonstrated by previous training and experience.

Interpretation: In each counseling psychological service unit there may be varying levels of responsibility with respect to the nature and quality of services provided. Support personnel are considered to be responsible for their functions and behavior when assisting in the provision of counseling psychological services and are account-able to the professional counseling psychologist. Ultimate profes-sional responsibility and accountability for the services provided require that the supervisor review reports and test protocols, and review and discuss intervention plans, strategies, and outcomes. Therefore, the supervision of all counseling psychological services is provided directly by a professional counseling psychologist in a face-to-face arrangement involving individual and/or group super-vision. The extent of supervision is determined by the needs of the providers, but in no event is it less than 1 hour per week for each support staff member providing counseling psychological services.

To facilitate the effectiveness of the psychological service unit, the nature of the supervisory relationship is communicated to support personnel in writing. Such communications delineate the duties of the employees, describing the range and type of services to be provided. The limits of independent action and decision mak-ing are defined. The description of responsibility specifies the means by which the employee will contact the professional counsel-ing psychologist in the event of emergency or crisis situations.

1.3 Wherever a counseling psychological service unit exists, a professional counseling psychologist is responsible for planning, directing, and reviewing the provision of counseling psychological services. Whenever the counseling psychological service unit is part of a larger professional psychological service encompassing various psychological specialties, a professional psychologist shall be the administrative head of the service.

Interpretation: The counseling psychologist who directs or coordi-nates the unit is expected to maintain an ongoing or periodic review of the adequacy of services and to formulate plans in accordance with the results of such evaluation. He or she coordinates the activi-ties of the counseling psychology unit with other professional, ad-ministrative, and technical groups, both within and outside the insti-tution or agency. The counseling psychologist has related responsi-bilities including, but not limited to, directing the training and re-search activities of the service, maintaining a high level of profes-sional and ethical practice, and ensuring that staff members func-tion only within the areas of their competency.

To facilitate the effectiveness of counseling services by rais-ing the level of staff sensitivity and professional skills, the counseling psychologist designated as director is responsible for participating in the selection of staff and support personnel whose qualifications and skills (e.g., language, cultural and experiential background, race, sex, and age) are relevant to the needs and characteristics of the users served.

1.4 When functioning as part of an organizational setting, professional counseling psychologists bring their backgrounds and skills to bear on the goals of the organization, whenever appropriate, by participation in the planning and development of overall services.[8]

Interpretation: Professional counseling psychologists participate in the maintenance of high professional standards by representation on committees concerned with service delivery.

As appropriate to the setting, their activities may include active participation, as voting and as office-holding members, on the facility's professional staff and on other executive, planning, and evaluation boards and committees.

1.5 Counseling psychologists maintain current knowledge of scientific and professional developments to preserve and enhance their professional competence.

Interpretation: Methods through which knowledge of scientific and professional developments may be gained include, but are not limited to, reading scientific and professional publications, attendance at professional workshops and meetings, participation in staff development programs, and other forms of continuing education.[9] The counseling psychologist has ready access to reference material related to the provision of psychological services. Counseling psychologists are prepared to show evidence periodically that they are staying abreast of current knowledge and practices in the field of counseling psychology through continuing education.

1.6 Counseling psychologists limit their practice to their demonstrated areas of professional competence.

Interpretation: Counseling psychological services are offered in accordance with the providers' areas of competence as defined by verifiable training and experience. When extending services beyond the range of their usual practice, counseling psychologists obtain pertinent training or appropriate professional supervision. Such training or supervision is consistent with the extension of functions performed and services provided. An extension of services may involve a change in the theoretical orientation of the counseling psychologist, in the modality or techniques used, in the type of client, or in the kinds of problems or disorders for which services are to be provided.

1.7 Professional psychologists who wish to qualify as counseling psychologists meet the same requirements with respect to subject matter and professional skills that apply to doctoral education and training in counseling psychology. [10]

Interpretation: Education of doctoral-level psychologists to qualify them for specialty practice in counseling psychology is under the auspices of a department in a regionally accredited university or of a professional school that offers the doctoral degree in counseling psychology. Such education is individualized, with due credit being given for relevant course work and other requirements that have previously been satisfied. In addition, doctoral-level training supervised by a counseling psychologist is required. Merely taking an internship in counseling psychology or acquiring experience in a practicum setting is not adequate preparation for becoming a counseling psychologist when prior education has not been in that area. Fulfillment of such an individualized educational program is attested to by the awarding of a certificate by the supervising department or professional school that indicates the successful completion of preparation in counseling psychology.

1.8 Professional counseling psychologists are encouraged to develop innovative theories and procedures and to provide appropriate theoretical and/or empirical support for their innovations.

Interpretation: A specialty of a profession rooted in a science intends continually to explore and experiment with a view to developing and verifying new and improved ways of serving the public and documents the innovations.

Guideline 2
Programs

2.1 Composition and organization of a counseling psychological service unit:

2.1.1 The composition and programs of a counseling psychological service unit are responsive to the needs of the persons or settings served.

Interpretation: A counseling psychological service unit is structured so as to facilitate effective and economical delivery of services. For example, a counseling psychological service unit serving predominantly a low-income, ethnic, or racial minority group has a staffing pattern and service programs that are adapted to the linguistic, experiential, and attitudinal characteristics of the users.

> 2.1.2 A description of the organization of the counseling psychological service unit and its lines of responsibility and accountability for the delivery of psychological services is available in written form to staff of the unit and to users and sanctioners upon request.

Interpretation: The description includes lines of responsibility, supervisory relationships, and the level and extent of accountability for each person who provides psychological services.

> 2.1.3 A counseling psychological service unit includes sufficient numbers of professional and support personnel to achieve its goals, objectives, and purposes.

Interpretation: The work load and diversity of psychological services required and the specific goals and objectives of the setting determine the numbers and qualifications of professional and support personnel in the counseling psychological service unit. Where shortages in personnel exist, so that psychological services cannot be rendered in a professional manner, the director of the counseling psychological service unit initiates action to remedy such shortages. When this fails, the director appropriately modifies the scope or work load of the unit to maintain the quality of the services rendered and, at the same time, makes continued efforts to devise alternative systems for delivery of services.

2.2 Policies:

> 2.2.1 When the counseling psychological service unit is composed of more than one person or is a component of a larger organization, a written statement of its objectives and scope of services is developed, maintained, and reviewed.

Interpretation: The counseling psychological service unit reviews its objectives and scope of services annually and revises them as necessary to ensure that the psychological services offered are consistent with staff competencies and current psychological knowledge and practice. This statement is discussed with staff, reviewed with the appropriate administrator, and distributed to users and sanctioners upon request, whenever appropriate.

> 2.2.2 All providers within a counseling psychological service unit support the legal and civil rights of the users.[11]

Interpretation: Providers of counseling psychological services safeguard the interests of the users with regard to personal, legal, and
civil rights. They are continually sensitive to the issue of confidentiality of information, the short-term and long-term impacts of
their decisions and recommendations, and other matters pertaining
to individual, legal, and civil rights. Concerns regarding the safeguarding of individual rights of users include, but are not limited
to, problems of access to professional records in educational institutions, self-incrimination in judicial proceedings, involuntary commitment to hospitals, protection of minors or legal incompetents,
discriminatory practices in employment selection procedures,
recommendation for special education provisions, information relative to adverse personnel actions in the armed services, and adjudication of domestic relations disputes in divorce and custodial proceedings. Providers of counseling psychological services take affirmative action by making themselves available to local committees, review boards, and similar advisory groups established to
safeguard the human, civil, and legal rights of service users.

    2.2.3 All providers within a counseling psychological service
unit are familiar with and adhere to the American Psychological
Association's Standards for Providers of Psychological Services,
Ethical Principles of Psychologists, Standards for Educational
and Psychological Tests, Ethical Principles in the Conduct of
Research With Human Participants, and other official policy
statements relevant to standards for professional services issued by the Association.

Interpretation: Providers of counseling psychological services
maintain current knowledge of relevant standards of the American
Psychological Association.

    2.2.4 All providers within a counseling psychological service
unit conform to relevant statutes established by federal, state,
and local governments.

Interpretation: All providers of counseling psychological services
are familiar with and conform to appropriate statutes regulating
the practice of psychology. They also observe agency regulations
that have the force of law and that relate to the delivery of psychological services (e.g., evaluation for disability retirement and
special education placements). In addition, all providers are cognizant that federal agencies such as the Veterans Administration,
the Department of Education, and the Department of Health and
Human Services have policy statements regarding psychological
services. Providers are familiar as well with other statutes and
regulations, including those addressed to the civil and legal rights

of users (e.g., those promulgated by the federal Equal Employment Opportunity Commission), that are pertinent to their scope of practice.

It is the responsibility of the American Psychological Association to maintain current files of those federal policies, statutes, and regulations relating to this section and to assist its members in obtaining them. The state psychological associations and the state licensing boards periodically publish and distribute appropriate state statutes and regulations, and these are on file in the counseling psychological service unit or the larger multipsychological service unit of which it is a part.

> 2.2.5 All providers within a counseling psychological service unit inform themselves about and use the network of human services in their communities in order to link users with relevant services and resources.

Interpretation: Counseling psychologists and support staff are sensitive to the broader context of human needs. In recognizing the matrix of personal and social problems, providers make available to clients information regarding human services such as legal aid societies, social services, employment agencies, health resources, and educational and recreational facilities. Providers of counseling psychological services refer to such community resources and, when indicated, actively intervene on behalf of the users.

Community resources include the private as well as the public sectors. Consultation is sought or referral made within the public or private network of services whenever required in the best interest of the users. Counseling psychologists, in either the private or the public setting, utilize other resources in the community whenever indicated because of limitations within the psychological service unit providing the services. Professional counseling psychologists in private practice know the types of services offered through local community mental health clinics and centers, through family-service, career, and placement agencies, and through reading and other educational improvement centers and know the costs and the eligibility requirements for those services.

> 2.2.6 In the delivery of counseling psychological services, the providers maintain a cooperative relationship with colleagues and co-workers in the best interest of the users. [12]

Interpretation: Counseling psychologists recognize the areas of special competence of other professional psychologists and of professionals in other fields for either consultation or referral purposes. Providers of counseling psychological services make appropriate use of other professional, research, technical, and administrative resources to serve the best interests of users and establish and maintain cooperative arrangements with such other resources as required to meet the needs of users.

2.3 Procedures:

2.3.1 Each counseling psychological service unit is guided by a set of procedural guidelines for the delivery of psychological services.

Interpretation: Providers are prepared to provide a statement of procedural guidelines, in either oral or written form, in terms that can be understood by users, including sanctioners and local administrators. This statement describes the current methods, forms, procedures, and techniques being used to achieve the objectives and goals for psychological services.

2.3.2 Providers of counseling psychological services develop plans appropriate to the providers' professional practices and to the problems presented by the users.

Interpretation: A counseling psychologist, after initial assessment, develops a plan describing the objectives of the psychological services and the manner in which they will be provided. [13] To illustrate, the agreement spells out the objective (e.g., a career decision), the method (e.g., short-term counseling), the roles (e.g., active participation by the user as well as the provider), and the cost. This plan is in written form. It serves as a basis for obtaining understanding and concurrence from the user and for establishing accountability and provides a mechanism for subsequent peer review. This plan is, of course, modified as changing needs dictate.

A counseling psychologist who provides services as one member of a collaborative effort participates in the development, modification (if needed), and implementation of the overall service plan and provides for its periodic review.

2.3.3 Accurate, current, and pertinent documentation of essential counseling psychological services provided is maintained.

Interpretation: Records kept of counseling psychological services include, but are not limited to, identifying data, dates of services, types of services, significant actions taken, and outcome at termination. Providers of counseling psychological services ensure that essential information concerning services rendered is recorded within a reasonable time following their completion.

2.3.4 Each counseling psychological service unit follows an established record retention and disposition policy.

Interpretation: The policy on record retention and disposition conforms to state statutes or federal regulations where such are applicable. In the absence of such regulations, the policy is (a) that the full record be maintained intact for at least 4 years after the completion of planned services or after the date of last contact with the user, whichever is later; (b) that if a full record is not retained, a summary of the record be maintained for an additional 3 years; and (c) that the record may be disposed of no sooner than 7 years after the completion of planned services or after the date of last contact, whichever is later.

In the event of the death or incapacity of a counseling psychologist in independent practice, special procedures are necessary to ensure the continuity of active service to users and the proper safeguarding of records in accordance with this Guideline. Following approval by the affected user, it is appropriate for another counseling psychologist, acting under the auspices of the professional standards review committee (PSRC) of the state, to review the record with the user and recommend a course of action for continuing professional service, if needed. Depending on local circumstances, appropriate arrangements for record retention and disposition may also be recommended by the reviewing psychologist.

This Guideline has been designed to meet a variety of circumstances that may arise, often years after a set of psychological services has been completed. Increasingly, psychological records are being used in forensic matters, for peer review, and in response to requests from users, other professionals, and other legitimate parties requiring accurate information about the exact dates, nature, course, and outcome of a set of psychological services. The 4-year period for retention of the full record covers the period of either undergraduate or graduate study of most students in postsecondary educational institutions, and the 7-year period for retention of at least a summary of the record covers the period during which a previous user is most likely to return for counseling psychological services in an educational institution or other organization or agency.

2.3.5 Providers of counseling psychological services maintain a system to protect confidentiality of their records.[14]

Interpretation: Counseling psychologists are responsible for maintaining the confidentiality of information about users of services, from whatever source derived. All persons supervised by counseling psychologists, including nonprofessional personnel and students, who have access to records of psychological services maintain this confidentiality as a condition of employment and/or supervision.

The counseling psychologist does not release confidential information, except with the written consent of the user directly involved or his or her legal representative. The only deviation from this rule is in the event of clear and imminent danger to, or involving, the user. Even after consent for release has been obtained, the counseling psychologist clearly identifies such information as confidential to the recipient of the information. [15] If directed otherwise by statute or regulations with the force of law or by court order, the psychologist seeks a resolution to the conflict that is both ethically and legally feasible and appropriate.

Users are informed in advance of any limits in the setting for maintenance of confidentiality of psychological information. For instance, counseling psychologists in agency, clinic, or hospital settings inform their clients that psychological information in a client's record may be available without the client's written consent to other members of the professional staff associated with service to the client. Similar limitations on confidentiality of psychological information may be present in certain educational, industrial, military, or other institutional settings, or in instances in which the user has waived confidentiality for purposes of third-party payment.

Users have the right to obtain information from their psychological records. However, the records are the property of the psychologist or the facility in which the psychologist works and are, therefore, the responsibility of the psychologist and subject to his or her control.

When the user's intention to waive confidentiality is judged by the professional counseling psychologist to be contrary to the user's best interests or to be in conflict with the user's civil and legal rights, it is the responsibility of the counseling psychologist to discuss the implications of releasing psychological information and to assist the user in limiting disclosure only to information required by the present circumstance.

Raw psychological data (e.g., questionnaire returns or test protocols) in which a user is identified are released only with the written consent of the user or his or her legal representative and released only to a person recognized by the counseling psychologist as qualified and competent to use the data.

Any use made of psychological reports, records, or data for research or training purposes is consistent with this Guideline. Additionally, providers of counseling psychological services comply with statutory confidentiality requirements and those embodied in the American Psychological Association's Ethical Principles of Psychologists (APA 1981b).

Providers of counseling psychological services who use information about individuals that is stored in large computerized data banks are aware of the possible misuse of such data as well as the benefits and take necessary measures to ensure that such information is used in a socially responsible manner.

Guideline 3
Accountability

3.1 The promotion of human welfare is the primary principle guiding the professional activity of the counseling psychologist and the counseling psychological service unit.

Interpretation: Counseling psychologists provide services to users in a manner that is considerate, effective, economical, and humane. Counseling psychologists are responsible for making their services readily accessible to users in a manner that facilitates the users' freedom of choice.

Counseling psychologists are mindful of their accountability to the sanctioners of counseling psychological services and to the general public, provided that appropriate steps are taken to protect the confidentiality of the service relationship. In the pursuit of their professional activities, they aid in the conservation of human, material, and financial resources.

The counseling psychological service unit does not withhold services to a potential client on the basis of that user's race, color, religion, gender, sexual orientation, age, or national origin; nor does it provide services in a discriminatory or exploitative fashion. Counseling psychologists who find that psychological services are being provided in a manner that is discriminatory or exploitative to users and/or contrary to these Guidelines or to state or federal statutes take appropriate corrective action, which may include the refusal to provide services. When conflicts of interest arise, the counseling psychologist is guided in the resolution of differences by the principles set forth in the American Psychological Association's Ethical Principles of Psychologists (APA 1981b) and "Guidelines for Conditions of Employment of Psychologists" (APA 1972). [16]

Recognition is given to the following considerations in regard to the withholding of service: (a) the professional right of counseling psychologists to limit their practice to a specific category of users with whom they have achieved demonstrated competence (e.g., adolescents or families); (b) the right and responsibility of counseling psychologists to withhold an assessment procedure when not validly applicable; (c) the right and responsibility of counseling psychologists to withhold services in specific instances in which their own limitations or client characteristics might impair the quality of the services; (d) the obligation of counseling psychologists to seek to ameliorate through peer review, consultation, or other personal therapeutic procedures those factors that inhibit the provision of services to particular individuals; and (e) the obligation of counseling psychologists who withhold services to assist clients in obtaining services from other sources. [17]

3.2 Counseling psychologists pursue their activities as members of the independent, autonomous profession of psychology.[18]

Interpretation: Counseling psychologists, as members of an independent profession, are responsible both to the public and to their peers through established review mechanisms. Counseling psychologists are aware of the implications of their activities for the profession as a whole. They seek to eliminate discriminatory practices instituted for self-serving purposes that are not in the interest of the users (e.g., arbitrary requirements for referral and supervision by another profession). They are cognizant of their responsibilities for the development of the profession, participate where possible in the training and career development of students and other providers, participate as appropriate in the training of paraprofessionals or other professionals, and integrate and supervise the implementation of their contributions within the structure established for delivering psychological services. Counseling psychologists facilitate the development of, and participate in, professional standards review mechanisms.[19]

Counseling psychologists seek to work with other professionals in a cooperative manner for the good of the users and the benefit of the general public. Counseling psychologists associated with multidisciplinary settings support the principle that members of each participating profession have equal rights and opportunities to share all privileges and responsibilities of full membership in human service facilities and to administer service programs in their respective areas of competence.

3.3 There are periodic, systematic, and effective evaluations of counseling psychological services.[20]

Interpretation: When the counseling psychological service unit is a component of a larger organization, regular evaluation of progress in achieving goals is provided for in the service delivery plan, including consideration of the effectiveness of counseling psychological services relative to costs in terms of use of time and money and the availability of professional and support personnel.

Evaluation of the counseling psychological service delivery system is conducted internally and, when possible, under independent auspices as well. This evaluation includes an assessment of effectiveness (to determine what the service unit accomplished), efficiency (to determine the total costs of providing the services), continuity (to ensure that the services are appropriately linked to other human services), availability (to determine appropriate levels and distribution of services and personnel), accessibility (to ensure that the services are barrier free to users), and adequacy (to determine whether the services meet the identified needs for such services).

There is a periodic reexamination of review mechanisms to ensure that these attempts at public safeguards are effective and cost efficient and do not place unnecessary encumbrances on the providers or impose unnecessary additional expenses on users or sanctioners for services rendered.

3.4 Counseling psychologists are accountable for all aspects of the services they provide and are responsive to those concerned with these services. [21]

Interpretation: In recognizing their responsibilities to users, sanctioners, third-party purchasers, and other providers, and where appropriate and consistent with the users' legal rights and privileged communications, counseling psychologists make available information about, and provide opportunity to participate in, decisions concerning such issues as initiation, termination, continuation, modification, and evaluation of counseling psychological services.

Depending on the settings, accurate and full information is made available to prospective individual or organizational users regarding the qualifications of providers, the nature and extent of services offered, and where appropriate, financial and social costs.

Where appropriate, counseling psychologists inform users of their payment policies and their willingness to assist in obtaining reimbursement. To assist their users, those who accept reimbursement from a third party are acquainted with the appropriate statutes and regulations, the procedures for submitting claims, and the limits on confidentiality of claims information, in accordance with pertinent statutes.

Guideline 4
Environment

4.1 Providers of counseling psychological services promote the development in the service setting of a physical, organizational, and social environment that facilitates optimal human functioning.

Interpretation: Federal, state, and local requirements for safety, health, and sanitation are observed.

As providers of services, counseling psychologists are concerned with the environment of their service unit, especially as it affects the quality of service, but also as it impinges on human functioning in the larger context. Physical arrangements and organizational policies and procedures are conducive to the human dignity, self-respect, and optimal functioning of users and to the effective delivery of service. Attention is given to the comfort and the privacy of providers and users. The atmosphere in which counseling psychological services are rendered is appropriate to the service and to the users, whether in an office, clinic, school, college, university, hospital, industrial organization, or other institutional setting.

NOTES

1. The notes appended to these Specialty Guidelines represent an attempt to provide a coherent context of other policy statements of the Association regarding professional practice. The Guidelines extend these previous policy statements where necessary to reflect current concerns of the public and the profession.

2. The following two categories of professional psychologists who met the criteria indicated below on or before the adoption of these Specialty Guidelines on January 31, 1980, are also considered counseling psychologists: Category 1—persons who completed (a) a doctoral degree program primarily psychological in content at a regionally accredited university or professional school and (b) 3 postdoctoral years of appropriate education, training, and experience in providing counseling psychological services as defined herein, including a minimum of 1 year in a counseling setting; Category 2—persons who on or before September 4, 1974, (a) completed a master's degree from a program primarily psychological in content at a regionally accredited university or professional school and (b) held a license or certificate in the state in which they practiced, conferred by a state board of psychological examiners, or the endorsement of the state psychological association through voluntary certification, and who, in addition, prior to January 31, 1980, (c) obtained 5 post-master's years of appropriate education, training, and experience in providing counseling psychological services as defined herein, including a minimum of 2 years in a counseling setting.

After January 31, 1980, professional psychologists who wish to be recognized as professional counseling psychologists are referred to Guideline 1.7.

3. The areas of knowledge and training that are a part of the educational program for all professional psychologists have been presented in two APA documents, Education and Credentialing in Psychology II (APA 1977a) and Criteria for Accreditation of Doctoral Training Programs and Internships in Professional Psychology (APA 1979). There is consistency in the presentation of core areas in the education and training of all professional psychologists. The

description of education and training in these Guidelines is based primarily on the document <u>Education and Credentialing in Psychology II</u>. It is intended to indicate broad areas of required curriculum, with the expectation that training programs will undoubtedly want to interpret the specific content of these areas in different ways depending on the nature, philosophy, and intent of the programs.

4. Functions and activities of counseling psychologists relating to the teaching of psychology, the writing or editing of scholarly or scientific manuscripts, and the conduct of scientific research do not fall within the purview of these Guidelines.

5. These definitions should be compared with the APA (1967) guidelines for state legislation (hereinafter referred to as state guidelines), which define "psychologist" (i.e., the generic professional psychologist, not the specialist counseling psychologist) and the "practice of psychology" as follows:

> A person represents himself [or herself] to be a psychologist when he [or she] holds himself [or herself] out to the public by any title or description of services incorporating the words "psychology," "psychological," "psychologist," and/or offers to render or renders services as defined below to individuals, groups, organizations, or the public for a fee, monetary or otherwise.
>
> The practice of psychology within the meaning of this act is defined as rendering to individuals, groups, organizations, or the public any psychological service involving the application of principles, methods, and procedures of understanding, predicting, and influencing behavior, such as the principles pertaining to learning, perception, motivation, thinking, emotions, and interpersonal relationships; the methods and procedures of interviewing, counseling, and psychotherapy; of constructing, administering, and interpreting tests of mental abilities, aptitudes, interests, attitudes, personality characteristics, emotion, and motivation; and of assessing public opinion.
>
> The application of said principles and methods includes, but is not restricted to: diagnosis, prevention, and amelioration of adjustment problems and emotional and mental disorders of individuals and groups; hypnosis; educational and vocational counseling; personnel selection and management; the evaluation and planning for effective work and learning

situations; advertising and market research; and the resolution of interpersonal and social conflicts.

Psychotherapy within the meaning of this act means the use of learning, conditioning methods, and emotional reactions, in a professional relationship, to assist a person or persons to modify feelings, attitudes, and behavior which are intellectually, socially, or emotionally maladjustive or ineffectual.

The practice of psychology shall be as defined above, any existing statute in the state of _____ to the contrary notwithstanding. (APA 1967, pp. 1098-1099)

6. The relation of a psychological service unit to a larger facility or institution is also addressed indirectly in the APA (1972) "Guidelines for Conditions of Employment of Psychologists" (hereinafter referred to as CEP Guidelines), which emphasize the roles, responsibilities, and prerogatives of the psychologist when he or she is employed by or provides services for another agency, institution, or business.

7. This Guideline replaces earlier recommendations in the 1967 state guidelines concerning exemption of psychologists from licensure. Recommendations 8 and 9 of those guidelines read as follows:

Persons employed as psychologists by accredited academic institutions, governmental agencies, research laboratories, and business corporations should be exempted, provided such employees are performing those duties for which they are employed by such organizations, and within the confines of such organizations.

Persons employed as psychologists by accredited academic institutions, governmental agencies, research laboratories, and business corporations consulting or offering their research findings or providing scientific information to like organizations for a fee should be exempted. (APA 1967, p. 1100)

On the other hand, the 1967 state guidelines specifically denied exemptions under certain conditions, as noted in Recommendations 10 and 11:

Persons employed as psychologists who offer or provide psychological services to the public for a fee, over and above the salary that they receive for the performance of their regular duties, should not be exempted.

> Persons employed as psychologists by organiza-
> tions that sell psychological services to the public
> should not be exempted. (APA 1967, pp. 1100–1101)

The present APA policy, as reflected in this Guideline, establishes a single code of practice for psychologists providing covered services to users in any setting. The present position is that
a psychologist providing any covered service meets local statutory
requirements for licensure or certification. See the section entitled Principles and Implications of the Specialty Guidelines for
further elaboration of this point.

8. A closely related principle is found in the APA (1972)
CEP Guidelines:

> It is the policy of APA that psychology as an indepen-
> dent profession is entitled to parity with other health
> and human service professions in institutional prac-
> tices and before the law. Psychologists in interdisci-
> plinary settings such as colleges and universities,
> medical schools, clinics, private practice groups, and
> other agencies expect parity with other professions in
> such matters as academic rank, board status, salaries,
> fringe benefits, fees, participation in administrative
> decisions, and all other conditions of employment, pri-
> vate contractual arrangements, and status before the
> law and legal institutions. (APA 1972, p. 333)

9. See CEP Guidelines (section entitled Career Development)
for a closely related statement:

> Psychologists are expected to encourage institutions
> and agencies which employ them to sponsor or conduct
> career development programs. The purpose of these
> programs would be to enable psychologists to engage
> in study for professional advancement and to keep
> abreast of developments in their field. (APA 1972,
> p. 332)

10. This Guideline follows closely the statement regarding
"Policy on Training for Psychologists Wishing to Change Their
Specialty" adopted by the APA Council of Representatives in January 1976. Included therein was the implementing provision that
"this policy statement shall be incorporated in the guidelines of the
Committee on Accreditation so that appropriate sanctions can be
brought to bear on university and internship training programs that
violate [it]" (Conger 1976, p. 424).

11. See also APA's (1981b) Ethical Principles of Psychologists, especially Principles 5 (Confidentiality), 6 (Welfare of the

Consumer), and 9 (Research With Human Participants); and see
Ethical Principles in the Conduct of Research With Human Participants (APA 1973a). Also, in 1978 Division 17 approved in principle
a statement on "Principles for Counseling and Psychotherapy With
Women," which was designed to protect the interests of female
users of counseling psychological services.

12. Support for this position is found in the section on relations with other professions in Psychology as a Profession:

> Professional persons have an obligation to know and take
> into account the traditions and practices of other profes-
> sional groups with whom they work and to cooperate
> fully with members of such groups with whom research,
> service, and other functions are shared. (APA 1968,
> p. 5)

13. One example of a specific application of this principle is
found in APA's (1981a) revised APA/CHAMPUS Outpatient Psychological Provider Manual. Another example, quoted below, is found
in Guideline 2 in APA's (1973b) "Guidelines for Psychologists Conducting Growth Groups":

> The following information should be made available in
> writing [emphasis added] to all prospective participants:
>
>   (a) An explicit statement of the purpose of the
> group;
>   (b) Types of techniques that may be employed;
>   (c) The education, training, and experience of
> the leader or leaders;
>   (d) The fee and any additional expense that may
> be incurred;
>   (e) A statement as to whether or not a follow-up
> service is included in the fee;
>   (f) Goals of the group experience and techniques
> to be used;
>   (g) Amounts and kinds of responsibility to be as-
> sumed by the leader and by the participants. For ex-
> ample, (i) the degree to which a participant is free not
> to follow suggestions and prescriptions of the group
> leader and other group members; (ii) any restrictions
> on a participant's freedom to leave the group at any
> time; and
>   (h) Issues of confidentiality. (p. 933)

14. See Principle 5 (Confidentiality) in Ethical Principles of
Psychologists (APA 1981b)

15. Support for the principles of privileged communication is found in at least two policy statements of the Association:

> In the interest of both the public and the client and in accordance with the requirements of good professional practice, the profession of psychology seeks recognition of the privileged nature of confidential communications with clients, preferably through statutory enactment or by administrative policy where more appropriate. (APA 1968, p. 8)

> Wherever possible, a clause protecting the privileged nature of the psychologist-client relationship be included.
> When appropriate, psychologists assist in obtaining general "across the board" legislation for such privileged communications. (APA 1967, p. 1103)

16. The CEP Guidelines include the following:

> It is recognized that under certain circumstances, the interests and goals of a particular community or segment of interest in the population may be in conflict with the general welfare. Under such circumstances, the psychologist's professional activity must be primarily guided by the principle of "promoting human welfare." (APA 1972, p. 334)

17. This paragraph is adapted in part from the CEP Guidelines (APA 1972, p. 333).

18. Support for the principle of the independence of psychology as a profession is found in the following:

> As a member of an autonomous profession, a psychologist rejects limitations upon his [or her] freedom of thought and action other than those imposed by his [or her] moral, legal, and social responsibilities. The Association is always prepared to provide appropriate assistance to any responsible member who becomes subjected to unreasonable limitations upon his [or her] opportunity to function as a practitioner, teacher, researcher, administrator, or consultant. The Association is always prepared to cooperate with any responsible professional organization in opposing any unreasonable limitations on the professional functions of the members of that organization.
> This insistence upon professional autonomy has been upheld over the years by the affirmative actions

of the courts and other public and private bodies in support of the right of the psychologist—and other professionals—to pursue those functions for which he [or she] is trained and qualified to perform. (APA 1968, p. 9)

Organized psychology has the responsibility to define and develop its own profession, consistent with the general canons of science and with the public welfare.

Psychologists recognize that other professions and other groups will, from time to time, seek to define the roles and responsibilities of psychologists. The APA opposes such developments on the same principle that it is opposed to the psychological profession taking positions which would define the work and scope of responsibility of other duly recognized professions. (APA 1972, p. 333)

19. APA support for peer review is detailed in the following excerpt from the APA (1971) statement entitled "Psychology and National Health Care":

All professions participating in a national health plan should be directed to establish review mechanisms (or performance evaluations) that include not only peer review but active participation by persons representing the consumer. In situations where there are fiscal agents, they should also have representation when appropriate. (p. 1026)

20. This Guideline on program evaluation is based directly on the following excerpts from two APA position papers:

The quality and availability of health services should be evaluated continuously by both consumers and health professionals. Research into the efficiency and effectiveness of the system should be conducted both internally and under independent auspices. (APA 1971, p. 1025)

The comprehensive community mental health center should devote an explicit portion of its budget to program evaluation. All centers should inculcate in their staff attention to and respect for research findings; the larger centers have an obligation to set a high priority on basic research and to give formal recognition to research as a legitimate part of the duties of staff members.

. . . Only through explicit appraisal of program effects can worthy approaches be retained and refined, ineffective ones dropped. Evaluative monitoring of program achievements may vary, of course, from the relatively informal to the systematic and quantitative, depending on the importance of the issue, the availability of resources, and the willingness of those responsible to take risks of substituting informed judgment for evidence. (Smith and Hobbs 1966, pp. 21-22)

21. See also the CEP Guidelines for the following statement: "A psychologist recognizes that . . . he [or she] alone is accountable for the consequences and effects of his [or her] services, whether as teacher, researcher, or practitioner. This responsibility cannot be shared, delegated, or reduced" (APA 1972, p. 334).

REFERENCES

American Psychological Association. 1968. Psychology as a profession. Washington, D.C.: APA.

_____. 1971. Psychology and national health care. American Psychologist, 26: 1025-1026.

_____. 1972. Guidelines for conditions of employment of psychologists. American Psychologist, 27: 331-334.

_____. 1973a. Ethical principles in the conduct of research with human participants. Washington, D.C.: APA.

_____. 1973b. Guidelines for psychologists conducting growth groups. American Psychologist, 28: 933.

_____. 1974a. Standards for educational and psychological tests. Washington, D.C.: APA

_____. 1974b. Standards for providers of psychological services. Washington, D.C.: APA.

_____. 1977a. Education and credentialing in psychology II. Report of a meeting, June 4-5, 1977. Washington, D.C.: APA.

_____. 1977b. Standards for providers of psychological services. Rev. ed. Washington, D.C.: APA.

_____. 1979. Criteria for accreditation of doctoral training programs and internships in professional psychology. Washington, D.C.: APA. (Amended 1980.)

_____. 1981a. APA/CHAMPUS outpatient psychological provider manual. Rev. ed. Washington, D.C.: APA.

_____. 1981b. Ethical principles of psychologists. Rev. ed. Washington, D.C.: APA.

American Psychological Association, Committee on Legislation. 1967. A model for state legislation affecting the practice of psychology. American Psychologist, 22: 1095-1103.

Conger, J. J. 1976. Proceedings of the American Psychological Association, Incorporated, for the year 1975: Minutes of the annual meeting of the Council of Representatives. American Psychologist, 31: 406-434.

Smith, M. B., and N. Hobbs. 1966. The community and the community mental health center. Washington, D.C.: American Psychological Association.

# AUTHOR INDEX

# SUBJECT INDEX

326 / COUNSELING IN HIGHER EDUCATION

# ABOUT THE EDITORS
# AND CONTRIBUTORS

PHILLIP J. GALLAGHER is a counselor-professor in the Counseling Center at California State University at Long Beach (CSULB). He joined the California state university system at San Jose State, transferred to Los Angeles, and then to Long Beach.

Dr. Gallagher, a licensed psychologist, is listed in the National Registry of Health Service Providers. He was coeditor of Counseling Center in Higher Education (1970) and has been actively counseling and teaching for over 20 years, as well as providing consultation services in clinical, assessment, and research psychology to private and governmental agencies.

Dr. Gallagher holds a B.A. and an M.A. from San Diego State College and a Ph.D. from the University of Denver.

GEORGE D. DEMOS is director of the Human Growth and Development Center in Long Beach, California, and holds the rank of professor at California State University at Long Beach. He has served as dean of students and associate dean of counseling and testing at CSULB and chief psychologist at the University of Southern California Veterans Guidance Center, and is a diplomate in clinical psychology. He has taught in a number of major universities and colleges throughout the country.

Dr. Demos has many publications in the area of psychology. His articles have appeared in Journal of Counseling Psychology and California Journal of Educational Research, as well as in other counseling, guidance, and education journals.

Dr. Demos holds a B.A. from Northern Illinois University, an M.S. from the University of Illinois, and a Ph.D. from the University of Southern California.

H. EDWARD BABBUSH is associate dean and director of career planning and placement at California State University at Long Beach. From 1958 through 1962 he served as the university's personnel director and budget officer, and in 1962-63 he was personnel analyst in the office of the chancellor of the California State University and Colleges.

Mr. Babbush's articles and reports have appeared in such publications as California Education Journal, College and University Business, Journal of College Student Personnel, Journal of Teacher Education, and Journal of College Placement.

STEPHEN E. BERK is an associate professor of history and has been affiliated with California State University, Long Beach, since 1970. A licensed marriage and family counselor, he is associated with the Living and Self-Management Center of Santa Ana, California.

Dr. Berk is a published scholar with a book, articles in such journals as The History Teacher, and media reviews to his credit.

EDMUND BOURNE's academic background was at the University of Chicago, where he completed a Ph.D. in personality psychology in 1976. Subsequent to his graduate studies he spent a year in clinical research under an NIMH postdoctoral fellowship at Michael Reese Center in Chicago. Recently he spent half-time teaching in the psychology department and half-time working at the University Counseling Center at California State University at Long Beach.

MARGARET E. GERLACH has done academic advising, career counseling, and research at California State University at Long Beach since 1970. She has been associate director of the Academic Advising Center since 1978.

Dr. Gerlach has given numerous workshops to adults changing careers or exploring alternatives. Her special field of interest is the relationship between liberal arts and the world of work, and her most recent study was a follow-up study of 9,000 liberal arts graduates of California State University, Long Beach.

STEVEN M. KATZ is coordinator for judicial affairs for California State University at Long Beach. He is also conducting a law practice with offices based in Huntington Beach.

Dr. Katz has earned an A.A. degree in business from Long Beach City College, a B.A. in psychology from the University of California, Los Angeles, and an M.S. in counseling in higher education from California State University at Long Beach, and his J.D. from Western State University College of Law.

DEE LEACH is a counselor-professor in the Counseling Center at California State University at Long Beach. In addition to counseling, she has taught psychology and human development in Florida and California since 1962.

Dr. Leach has been custodian of records at the CSULB Counseling Center for the past several years. She is also a licensed psychologist and is in private practice in Long Beach.

TRAVIS M. MEAD is a licensed marriage and family therapist and doctoral candidate at United States International University, San Diego. He holds national certification in biofeedback and state certification in hypnosis.

VINCE NOBLE is a professor of educational psychology and coordinator of pupil personnel programs at California State University at Long Beach.

Dr. Noble specializes in cross-cultural counseling and has published articles in professional journals, including Journal of Bilingual Resources. A licensed psychologist, he is professionally active in southern California.

LAWRENCE ONODA is a clinical psychologist-associate professor in the Counseling Center at California State University, Northridge. Previously he was a counseling psychologist at the University of California, Irvine.

Dr. Onoda is a licensed psychologist maintaining a private practice. He has published several articles on biofeedback, counseling, and psychotherapy. He is a diplomate of the American Board of Psychotherapy.

LOUIS A. PRESTON is a counselor and coordinator of vocational/career programs for the University Counseling Center at California State University at Long Beach.

Mr. Preston is a doctoral candidate at the University of San Francisco. He has taught in the Educational Psychology Department at CSULB since 1974, and is a licensed marriage and family counselor.

HENRY REYNA is a counselor in the Counseling Center at California State University at Long Beach.

Mr. Reyna is a doctoral candidate at the University of Southern California. He has been a counselor at CSULB since 1970, and is a licensed marriage and family counselor.

VAN ROUSSOS is test psychologist at California State University at Long Beach. He has served the CSULB Counseling Center as psychometrist and test psychologist for over two decades.

Dr. Roussos is a licensed psychologist and a marriage, family, and child counselor.

SPECIAL ASSISTANT

SALLY E. GRAETZ, M.S. is director of the Learning Center at Marymount Palos Verdes College in Rancho Palos Verdes, California. She has previously held positions at California State University, Long Beach and at several colleges in Taiwan.

Ms. Graetz has been involved actively in the following areas in higher education: learning assistance, international education, counseling, study skills, program development, academic advisement, cross-cultural education, staff development, and English as a Second Language.